JOHN U. MONRO

SOUTHERN BIOGRAPHY

Andrew Burstein, Series Editor

Toni-Lee Capossela

JOHN U. MONRO

UNCOMMON EDUCATOR

LOUISIANA STATE UNIVERSITY | BATON ROUGE

Published by Louisiana State University Press
Copyright © 2012 by Louisiana State University Press
All rights reserved
Manufactured in the United States of America
First printing

DESIGNER: Michelle A. Neustrom
TYPEFACES: Whitman, text; Franklin Gothic Itc D, display
PRINTER: McNaughton & Gunn, Inc.
BINDER: Acme Bookbinding

LIBRARY OF CONGRESS CATALOGING-IN-PUBLICATION DATA

Capossela, Toni-Lee.
  John U. Monro : uncommon educator / Toni-Lee Capossela.
    pages cm
  Includes bibliographical references and index.
  ISBN 978-0-8071-4556-2 (cloth : alk. paper) — ISBN 978-0-8071-4557-9 (pdf) (print) —
ISBN 978-0-8071-4558-6 (epub) (print) — ISBN 978-0-8071-4559-3 (mobi) (print) 1. Monro,
John U. (John Usher), 1912–2002. 2. Educators—United States—Biography. 3. Miles Col-
lege—Faculty—Biography. I. Title.
  LA2317.M55C37 2012
  370.92—dc23
  [B]
                                                                    2012006531

The paper in this book meets the guidelines for permanence and durability of the Committee
on Production Guidelines for Book Longevity of the Council on Library Resources. ∞

*This book is dedicated to the many students and teachers
who have enriched my life.*

True happiness comes from squandering ourselves for a purpose.
WILLIAM COWPER

Contents

Illustrations follow page 106

Acknowledgments

John Monro had a way of changing people's lives, and I am no exception. Reading his obituary in the *Boston Globe* triggered my decision to take early retirement, and writing his biography has provided me with a decade of inspiration, surprises, frustrations, and stimulation; put me in touch with fascinating people, many of whom deserve biographies of their own; forged a number of cherished friendships; and vastly expanded my understanding of the difference a committed individual can make.

To my good fortune Monro also had a way of bringing out the best in those he touched. By and large the people I contacted as I sought a greater understanding of Monro were delighted to learn that his story was being told, and they went out of their way to help, often far beyond the limits of what I had requested. Virtually every person who agreed to an interview, a phone call, or an e-mail exchange deserves acknowledgment, but because that is not feasible, I offer the bibliography as an extension of these acknowledgments, in addition to its traditional role as scholarly apparatus.

Several generous people got my research off to a promising start: Betsy Dean of Stonehill's McPhaidin Library shared my excitement about the project and conducted her own preliminary search for materials about Monro. Then Monro's daughter and son-in-law, Janet and Philip Dreyer, responded generously to my first inquiry and began putting me in touch with key people in Monro's life. They have since given me unfettered access to Monro's private papers as well as several day-long interviews, a guided tour of the South Freeport property, and prompt answers to a relentless blizzard of questions.

At the Harvard memorial service I met Monro's nephew Peter, who shared his impressive genealogical research, read most of the manuscript, and, with his wife, Jill Bock, put me up during my visit to the South Freeport cottage. Other gracious overnight hosts include Betty Bamberg, Judy Brook, Peggy Jolly, Anna Leon, and Don and Tommie Toner.

Faculty development funds and a summer grant from Stonehill College supported my first two years of research.

At the 2005 Conference on College Composition and Communication, Ken Autrey and Jeff Zorn joined me in presenting papers that explored Monro's work at Harvard, Miles, and Tougaloo.

Ken Autrey, Kurt Cerulli, Shane Crabtree, Phil Dreyer, Prill Ellis, Kerri English, Ruth Gove, George Hanford, Ruth and Ed LaMonte, Rose Parkman Davis Marshall, Mike Shinagel, and Kim Townsend, among others, provided supportive but rigorous feedback on early drafts.

Kevin Coachman, Tylvester Goss, Richard Hannon, Leslie Harmon, Keith Miller, Pamela Ralston Sanders, Lawrence Sledge, Pieter Teeuwissen, and Gloria McCrae Watson each provided a student's-eye view of Monro.

Family members—especially my mother, Jimmy Hagedorn; my sisters and brothers, Francette, Lynn, Mark, and Kurt; my sister-in-law, Mary McAvity; my sons, Dom, Mino, and Chris; their wives, Amanda, Maura, and Leigh; my nephew Tovar Cerulli and his wife, Catherine—and friends, especially Ann Hilferty, Sarah P. Morris, Martha Singer, and Ron Sudol, became cheerful if involuntary experts in all things Monro.

LSU Acquisitions Editor Rand Dotson and Southern Biography Series Editor Andrew Burstein helped me trim and focus the book. Copyeditor Elizabeth Gratch immeasurably improved its accuracy and readability, and LSU Press editor Neal Novak smoothly guided it through the publication process.

I gratefully acknowledge the help of the following and apologize to those I may have omitted. For details about Monro's family background, early years, and undergraduate career: Jim Batchelder of Andover High School; Joseph Boyd; Lewis Brown; Donald Carmichael; Karen and Ted English; Martha Ferede; Bill Foster; Augusta Noss Howe; Jean Kuropatkin, formerly of Cambridge High and Latin School; Jon Kuypers of Camp Abnaki; Mary Monro MacGregor; Barbara Ann McCahill of St. Paul's Episcopal Church, North Andover; Vicki Booth Demarest Monro; John Morison; Debbie Moskul of Christ Church Episcopalian, Andover; Ruth Hardie Scheidecker; Bob and Ditsie Scobie; James Scobie; Eben Sutton; Richard Sutton; Charles Tanenbaum; and Edward Tilton.

For information about the war years: James C. "Barney" Barnhill, editor of the *CV-6 Bulletin;* Arnold "Arne" Olson, public relations officer of the CV-6 Association; Rod Carlson; William Davis; John Dunbar; Robert Hehir; Dorothy Higgins; Jim Martin; Charlie Russert; Pedro Sandoval; CV-6 webmaster Joel Shepherd; Donald Speer; Mike Turnipseed; Kenneth Wyffels; and Norm Zafft.

For details about Monro's connections to Phillips Academy Andover: Sharon Britton, Barbara Landis Chase, John Cooper, Helen "Skip" Eccles, Fred and Susan Stott, Ted and Nancy Sizer, Tom Lyons, Robert and Susan Lloyd, Jack Richards, and Phebe Miner.

For their contributions about Monro's experiences as part of the Harvard administration, the College Board, and the Peace Corps: Mike Ansara; Heather Woodcock Ayres; Walter Bregman; Dustin "Dusty" Burke; Margot Chamberlain; Adam Clymer; Susan Collings, Phillips Brooks House fund-raising director; Craig Comstock; Stephen Cotton; Linda Cross; Matthew Davis; George Deptula; Ted Elliott; Norm Gary; John Giannetti; Fred Glimp; Sandra Grindlay of the Harvard Art Museums; Ann Hilferty; Hal Higginbotham of the College Board; Chester Higgins; Harry Hoehler; Martin Kilson; Susan King; Gary Knamiller; Ellen Lake; Andrew Leighton; Michael Lottman; Alan Margolis; Toby Marotta; David Mittell; Rex Moon; Geoffrey Movius; Paul Newman; Richard Oldenburg; Lois Rice; Robert Rombauer; Peter Rosenbaum; Jack Schuster; Lee Smith, Phillips Brooks House administrative assistant; Robert Ellis Smith; Graham Taylor; Andrew Tobias; and Dorothy Zinberg.

For details about Monro's time at Miles and Birmingham: Ed and Ruth LaMonte, in particular, as well as Rev. Rodney Franklin, June and J. Mason Davis, Corrine Moseley Coleman, and Helen M. Lewis, all of First Congregational Church Birmingham; Elaine Banderman, Robert Bauman, Delight Bethune, James Blacksher, Mary Brooks, Tippi Coley, Louis Dale, Charles "Doc" Dey, Rufus and Hazel Harrison Gilmore, Emma Henry, Keitha Hudson, Ronald Jackson, Jill Jensen, Rev. Larry Johnson, Peggy Jolly, Diana Knighton, Dean Hattie Lamar, Dr. Edward Logue, Bob Lowe, Stephanie Moore, Fred Noyes, Richard Parker, Kathy Palumbo, Bobby Piper, Libby Rich, Gale Goldberg Robinson, Mary Smith, and Emma Sloan.

For insights about Monro's experiences at Tougaloo: Rose Parkman Davis Marshall, in particular, as well as Gordon Ball; Elease Brown; James Brown; Peter Cassanello; Walter, Jelani, and Lumbe Davis; Eunice King Durgin; Kit Durgin; Linda Fuller; John Heyman; Dick Johnson and Margaret Wodetzki; Paul Krombholz; John E. Liebman; Bruce O'Hara; Eleanor Jackson Piel; Stephen Rozman; Regina Turner and Larry Barclay; Asoka Srinivasan; John Teeuwissen; and John Leo Wright Jr.

ACKNOWLEDGMENTS

For information about additional aspects of Monro's life: Julie Akert; Linda Blumberg; Stephen Coit; James G. Colbert Jr.; Richard W. Cowen of the *Allentown Morning Call*; Frank P. Davidson; Jan Devereux of Beaver Country Day School; Leslie Edwards of Cranbrook Academy of Art; Dick Freeman; Linda Hall of the Williams College Alumni Association; Judy Ingram Hatfield; Al King; Ilse Kramer of Central Congregational Church, Providence; Kelly Lachman of the *Brown Alumni Magazine*; Carol Maher of the Massachusetts Medical Society; Bill Minor; Jim Park; Jack Schuster; and Charles M. Sullivan of the Cambridge Historical Commission.

Finally, I want to acknowledge the invaluable assistance of archivists and librarians Karen Abramson of the Brandeis University Archives; Geraldine Bell of the Miles College Archives; Susan Boone of the Smith College Archives; Ginger Cain of the Emory University Archives; Rachael Dreyer and Jennifer Harold of Bentley Historical Library, University of Michigan; Shirley Epps of the Miles College Library; Michelle Gachette and Timothy Driscoll of the Harvard University Archives; Mary Gargan of the College Board Archives; Jay Gaidmore of the Brown University Archives; Bonnie Gurewitsch of the Museum of Jewish Heritage, New York City; Clarence Hunter of the Mississippi State Archives; Andrew Kaplan of the Francis W. Parker School Archives; Alana Lewis of the Paine College Archives; Keith Luf of the WGBH Archives; Denise Monbarren of the College of Wooster Libraries; Tim Pennycuff of the University of Alabama at Birmingham Archives; Ruth Quattlebaum of the Phillips Academy Archives; Katherine Ryner of St. Mary's College of Maryland Archives; Scott Sanders of the Antioch College Archives; Sarah Hartwell of Dartmouth College Library; Wilma Slaight of the Wellesley College Archives; B. J. Wahl of the Keene Public Library in New Hampshire; and Minnie Watson, Alma Fisher, and Tony Bounds of the Tougaloo College Archives.

Abbreviations

ACA	Amherst College Archives
BHLUM	Bentley Historical Library, University of Michigan
BTE	Brown-Tougaloo Exchange
BUA	Brown University Archives
DP	Dreyer Papers
FWPSA	Francis W. Parker School Archives
HC	*Harvard Crimson*
HUA	Harvard University Archives
MCA	Miles College Archives
MSA	Mississippi State Archives
NYT	*New York Times*
PAA	Phillips Academy Archives
PBHAA	Phillips Brooks House Association Archives
PCCCLA	Paine College Collins-Callaway Library Archives
SDCCWL	Department of Special Collections, College of Wooster Libraries
TCA	Tougaloo College Archives
UABA	UAB Archives, University of Alabama at Birmingham

JOHN U. MONRO

INTRODUCTION

Dateline New York City, 9 March 1967. Reporters from across the country are gathered at the New York Hilton. Facing them are two men, one black and one white. Both are tall, imposing, middle-aged figures, dressed in suits and ties. In spite of the formality of the occasion, they seem comfortable and relaxed in each other's presence. Finally the black man approaches the microphone. He is Lucius H. Pitts, the president of unaccredited, historically black Miles College, and he is about to drop a bombshell on the world of higher education.

Pencils poised and tape recorders cocked, the reporters learn that John U. Monro—the man at Pitts's side—is stepping down as dean of the college at Harvard to direct and teach in the Freshman Studies Program at Miles. The air is charged with unspoken questions. What could be prompting this fifty-four-year-old man, a lifelong New Englander, a graduate of Phillips Academy and Harvard, an administrator at his alma mater for more than two decades—in short, a member in good standing of the Ivy League old-boy network—to trade his cushy desk job for a grueling, poorly paid position at a hardscrabble college fighting for its very survival?

On the other hand, there is a lot of this kind of thing going around; it is the sixties, after all, and the reporters can be forgiven for assuming that Monro is just another privileged liberal going South for a brief time to exorcize his white guilt. But if they do jump to this conclusion, they will be mistaken. Monro knows exactly what he is getting into, having spent the previous three summers teaching at Miles, which stands in the shadow of the U.S. Steel mills and the pollution its smokestacks spew. He has worked with incoming students as they struggle to overcome the sobering academic deficiencies they bring with them from Birmingham's still-segregated public high schools.

He is all too familiar with the obstacles Miles faces. It is severely underfunded, and without accreditation it does not qualify for government grants. Its endowment is minuscule, and few of its graduates possess the discretionary income to make significant contributions to their alma mater. Faculty salaries are pitifully low. There is no sports center to speak of, and there are no dormitories at all. Local resistance to court-mandated desegregation is still very much alive, and white supremacists resent the college's tradition of civil rights engagement. Monro knows all this, but it makes him even more eager to get there and get started.

Another thing the reporters do not understand, even when Monro tries to explain it, is that for him going to Miles is not a sacrificial act. He considers himself lucky to be heading to the front lines, where a crucial revolution in higher education is taking place. This is no detour, no feel-good sabbatical. He intends the move to be permanent, and he will keep his word, spending the remaining three decades of his professional life on black college campuses, until he is diagnosed with Alzheimer's disease at the age of eighty-two.

Monro's life story is especially relevant now, as we scrutinize and interpret the sixties from the distance of a half-century. Not only did he embrace the idealism of that heady time, but he clung to it long after it had faded from the national consciousness. His quest was so enduring because it was buttressed by the virtues of the "Greatest Generation": loyalty, patriotism, a strong sense of personal responsibility, and a respect for tradition and hard work.

The forces in Monro's early life—even those, such as his ancestry, that preceded his birth—propelled him toward a search for social justice. The Clan Munro, from which he hailed, urged its members to help each other in times of need. His paternal grandfather, Hezekiah, was a stern Episcopalian clergyman who ministered to the needy and kept a sharp eye on family members lest they forget to do the same. His mother's family, wealthy mill owners, promoted the welfare of their workers through policies that were enlightened for the time. The YMCA camp he attended from an early age took as its motto "Help the Other Fellow," and the motto of Phillips Academy, from which he graduated, was "Non sibi," loosely translated as "Not for oneself alone."

But Monro's persistence in the pursuit of social justice, rather than merely reflecting early influences, was also shaped by his responses to the situations he encountered throughout his life. As an undergraduate, when he could easily have absorbed Harvard's near-endemic sense of entitlement, he used the school's newspaper, the *Crimson*, to campaign for a higher level of journalistic responsibility and a greater awareness of the world at large; hamstrung by resistance from other editors, he spearheaded the creation of a rival newspaper and for six weeks gave the *Crimson* a run for its money. His wartime service as damage control office aboard the USS *Enterprise,* rather than merely making him grateful that he had survived, left him with a profound sense of obligation to honor his fallen crewmates by doing something meaningful with his life.

As a Harvard administrator, he used each of his positions to render that quintessential gate-keeping institution more diverse and democratic. He smoothed the way for veterans coming to college through the GI Bill. He recruited applicants from areas other than New England and from high schools nobody had ever heard of. He developed a sophisticated financial aid formula that did a far better job than ever before of getting money to the students who needed it most. He encouraged Extension School students to follow their dreams and designed and taught a writing course to help them get there. When Harvard became one of the training sites for the fledgling Peace Corps, he headed the training program and defended the corps against its critics, hailing it as a golden opportunity for privileged students to discover firsthand what poverty looked like.

When he thought he had done as much as he could at Harvard, he moved to Miles, where he saw great potential to make a difference in the twin arenas of civil rights and equal opportunity in education. He began by spending a chunk of each summer teaching at Miles, then he agreed to help design a new freshman program. As he spent more time in the South, he became less patient with the issues that came across his desk at Harvard. They included the Timothy Leary drug flap (which the press translated into evidence of rampant drug use at Harvard), undergraduate demands for more relaxed parietal regulations (which the press translated into untrammeled sexual activity at Harvard), and the hostile treatment of Secretary of Defense Robert McNamara during a campus visit.

When the Freshman Studies Program was complete, Monro pulled up stakes and moved to Alabama with his supportive wife, Dottie. For three years he worked productively and happily with Pitts and academic dean Richard Arrington, using his contacts to bring fame and a modest amount of fortune to Miles. He spearheaded the creation of a satellite freshman program in hardscrabble Greene County, where classes were offered during the evening, when nontraditional students could more readily attend.

In 1970 Arrington left academe to begin a career in government, and the following year Pitts left Miles to become president of his alma mater, Paine College, in Augusta, Georgia. The change in administration was not kind to Monro and his program, which was eventually dismantled over his strenuous objections. Deciding that he could accomplish nothing more at Miles, in 1978 he joined the English Department at Tougaloo College, near Jackson, Mississippi, which boasted a freshman program similar to the one he had created at Miles.

Here he found a perfect niche in the Writing Center, where he worked with students in a collaborative relationship that suited his personality and teaching style. He helped design a literacy program, a senior research requirement, and a writing-across-the-curriculum program, and he spoke at conferences and commencements about the enduring value of black colleges. He sought out opportunities to work with faculty in other departments and had especially fruitful collaborations with teachers of mathematics and sociology. As chair of the committee that decided the fate of students on probation, he indefatigably analyzed their records, looking for ways to improve teaching methods and reduce the probation and dropout rates. His devotion to his work was a salvation when Dottie, his wife and childhood sweetheart, died in 1984.

When hearing and memory problems made classroom teaching impractical, Monro requested emeritus status and occupied the Writing Center full-time, helping a steady stream of students, one at a time, put their ideas into words. He struggled to overcome the symptoms of Alzheimer's until 1996 and even then retired with great reluctance. He spent the last few years of his life in an assisted living facility in California and died on 29 March 2002.

If success is measured by the heights one attains within an institutional hierarchy, then Monro was a failure, since his career resembles nothing more than a series of ignominious bumps down the academic ladder. Beginning as an Ivy League administrator, he became program director at an obscure historically black college, then "just" a teacher at another historically black college, and ended up a teacher without a classroom.

But measured against Monro's personal yardstick—the desire to make a difference—each step was indeed an improvement, allowing him to peel away extraneous concerns in order to concentrate more fully on what mattered to him most. Departing from Harvard, he discarded his involvement in undergraduate concerns with which he could no longer empathize. Leaving Miles, he shed administrative obligations so he could devote himself more fully to teaching. Finally, exiting the classroom, he distilled teaching to its essence: a series of collaborative encounters focused totally on the individual student's needs and aspirations.

Among the many roles he assumed in his lifelong commitment to social justice —war hero, crusading journalist, civil rights advocate, Peace Corps booster, financial aid pioneer, activist dean, master teacher—Monro found teaching the most meaningful. No wonder, then, that he called Tougaloo, where he was finally able to devote all his time to teaching, "my home in all the world."

The view from the top was magnificent, all the big Munros
in the neighborhood showing up clear and resplendent.

—*Scottish Mountaineering Club Journal*, 1903

1
FAMILY BACKGROUND AND CHILDHOOD
1912-1930

The Monro family name has been linked with challenge, adventure, and the dramatic contours of the Scottish landscape since 1891. That year Sir Hugh T. Munro finished identifying and charting the 279 mountain peaks in Scotland that are three thousand feet tall or higher, published his findings in the *Scottish Mountaineering Club Journal,* and dubbed the mountains "munros." In 1974 mountaineer and travel writer Hamish Brown, who spent nearly four months scaling all the munros and wrote a book about the experience, explained what had motivated him: "The lure of challenge and testing, the delight of achievement . . . the escape from a normal petty existence, the finding of values, of beauty, of vision. These are worth living for—and possibly dying for" (333). One can easily imagine John Monro using similar words to explain why, at the age of fifty-four, he was moving to the strife-torn South to begin a new life.

The recorded history of the Munro clan goes back to the eleventh century, when the king of Scotland gave property in Ross to Irish mercenaries as a reward for helping defeat the Viking invaders. The clan cast its lot with the throne and the Protestant Church during the Reformation and provided subsequent military support through the Highland Regiment. The original clan motto, "Dread God," has since been softened to "Reverence thou God" in deference to modern sensibilities, but clan members are still encouraged "to help the young of the clan and those in need" (Clan Munro). Patriotism, religious devotion, family loyalty, outreach to those in need—some of Monro's bedrock values were just waiting to be plucked from his tribal and ancestral history.

John was born into the tenth generation of the Lexington, Massachusetts, Munroes, who chose to drop the final *e* the name had acquired when Monro's forebears first arrived in America in 1657 (P. Monro 41). The first generation was represented by William Munroe, who was born near Inverness, Scotland, in 1625. Captured by Oliver Cromwell's forces, imprisoned, and banished to America in 1651, he took up farming and settled in Lexington. The official family record in the New World began with an act of civil disobedience, when William was cited for failing to put rings in his pigs' noses, as local regulation required. But he hewed scrupulously to the clan's code in attempting to keep his offspring near him. With fourteen children all living in close proximity, his house and its accretions eventually came to look more like a ropewalk than a dwelling, according to one of his great-granddaughters (Munroe 1).

Dr. Thomas Monro (1731–85), the descendant most relevant to our purposes, came close to tracing William's footsteps in reverse. Taken prisoner during the Revolutionary War, he was on his way back to Scotland on a prison ship when an officer's daughter became ill, and he used his skills as a surgeon's assistant to cure her; the grateful officer sent him back to New England loaded with gifts (Munroe 43–44). Thomas changed the *u* of his surname to *o* in honor of the Alexander Monros, father and son anatomists in Edinburgh whose work he admired (E. Monro).

His grandson, Thomas B. Monro (1794–1821), became a naval captain and died at sea, leaving his young widow, Clarissa Usher Sanford, with an infant and a toddler, born less than a year apart. Clarissa apprenticed her son, George Thomas, as a cabin boy when he was only nine years old, and by the time he was nineteen, he was commanding a ship of his own. Ten years later he married and, at his wife's request, ended his naval career. He studied and practiced medicine, taught navigation, and dabbled in painting but continued to consider himself a mariner at heart, describing himself as such in the 1860 census report (Munroe 209). The fourth of his ten children was Hezekiah Usher Monro (1854–1939), John's paternal grandfather.

GRANDFATHER HEZEKIAH

Hezekiah's life was fraught with loss. He suffered an early tragedy when he and his brother ignored their mother's command to go play outside. As they continued to roughhouse, they accidentally overturned an oil-burning lantern, which exploded and ignited a fire, causing their mother's death (P. Monro 3–4). Along with three of his siblings, he was raised by a first cousin on the family farm in

Bristol, Rhode Island; he eventually inherited the farm from his foster sister but almost immediately sold it. His first wife, Harriet Maria Barnes, gave birth to Hezekiah's only son, Claxton—John's father—and died three years later. His second wife, Edith Parker Jordan, died giving birth to their third daughter, Edith, on 22 December 1894, after having lost their infant daughter Phoebe just four months earlier. Five years later he married Edith's younger sister, Sarah Allen Jordan (Munroe 271). They had no children, and although the marriage was said to be an unhappy one, they remained together until her death twenty-five years later (P. Monro 4).

Hezekiah's professional life proceeded more smoothly than his domestic life. Ordained as an Episcopalian minister in 1882, he served at churches in Providence, East Boston, Newton Lower Falls, and finally, in 1902, at St. Paul's in North Andover, where he remained until he retired in 1919 ("Rev. H.").

Hezekiah was the third pastor of St. Paul's, which had been founded in 1880 as a mission extension of Grace Church in Lawrence. It was funded almost entirely by the local mill owners, and its location, halfway between their homes in the affluent Old Center section of North Andover and the millworkers' homes in Machine Shop Village, was unusually inclusive for the times. Another egalitarian gesture was the decision to make St. Paul's a free church, rather than having each family pay for its pew, the position of which was a highly visible status marker (McCahill, "St. Paul's" 498). The importance of the local mills to St. Paul's was physically embodied in the bishop's chair, with its left arm ending in a tall spindle staff.

A long-standing tradition of vigorous lay participation at St. Paul's meant that Reverend Monro collaborated with his flock rather than dictating to it (McCahill, "Note"). He had to obtain approval for disbursements from his private fund and permission to take his summer vacation (*Records* 41), and he was expected to take orders from members of the vestry: on one occasion, after voting to create a boys' and men's choir, they airily directed him to "take steps in that direction," a time-consuming job that required visiting other parishes, figuring out what physical changes were needed to make room for the group, and pricing lockers and vestments for the singers (*Records* 12–14).

When he was not dancing to the vestry's tune, Hezekiah initiated his own projects, which reflected his stern brand of religious fervor. He purged the Sunday school library of all works of fiction, had them packed up and sent to church missions, and replaced them with books of Bible stories and other religious topics (*Records* 44–45). Sarah barely appears in the parish records, aside from for-mulaic descriptions of her role as Hezekiah's helpmate and a single reference to a children's dance class she conducted in the parish hall (*Records* 84).

During their seventeen years at St. Paul's, Hezekiah and Sarah—and Clax-ton, when he was not at college—lived at 16 Elm Street, a dilapidated house that served as a makeshift rectory. They struggled constantly with plumbing, sewage, heating, and repair problems, and vestry minutes are filled with discussions of emergency repairs. By the time the vestry finally voted to build a real rectory, Hezekiah had requested permission to retire (*Records* 101).

Despite a reputation for sternness, Hezekiah seems to have won his parish-ioners' affection. They held a reception to celebrate his ten-year anniversary (*Records* 63), and when he retired, the vestry wrote a resolution praising his leadership, gave him emeritus status, and held another reception to bid him farewell (101)—none of these gestures had been extended to his predecessor. After boarding briefly in North Andover while he helped pick his successor, he moved with Sarah to North Scituate, fifty miles south, where they remained until her death.

Hezekiah embodied some of the values John U. Monro later claimed as his own.[1] The first was a keen sense of family pride: in addition to the Clan Munro Society, Hezekiah belonged to the John Howland Society, composed of descendants of one of the 102 English passengers who had come to America aboard the *Mayflower* in 1620 (John Howland Society). In a foreshadowing of John's proud naval service, Hezekiah was charged with creating a seaman's chapel while he was rector of St. John's Church, East Boston ("Rev. H."). He was also a model of civic engagement, serving as chaplain for his Lodge of Masons, supporting the Village Improvement Society of Andover, and founding the North Andover Boys' Club (Lawrence).

Although caring for the needy was part of Hezekiah's pastoral duties, his de-votion to social justice—a principle that determined virtually all of his grandson's major life choices—went beyond the requirements of his vocation. George B. Frost, a parishioner who accompanied Hezekiah on his charitable rounds, be-lieved that the pastor's reserved exterior concealed an empathetic core: "His heart went out towards the youth and his eye kindled as he told of his joy in col-lecting funds and building a clubhouse for them in North Andover. . . . He loved the sailor lads and established a home for them in East Boston. . . . He loved the men in the slums—'down and outers.' I have known him to share his clothing and blankets with them. . . . Mr. Monro loved the shut-ins and bed-ridden. His visits to them were frequent. At times I accompanied him and never did he leave them before offering prayer in their behalf."

Finally, as his grandson would do later, Hezekiah spurned life's amenities, and not just because his salary permitted little discretionary spending. A man with a taste for creature comforts would have objected when eighteen thousand dollars was allocated for a parish house while the rectory collapsed around his ears, but he presided over the parish house construction without complaint, and when a vestryman asked whether a new rectory and a raise might tempt him to reconsider his retirement, Hezekiah politely declined the offer (*Records* 102).[2]

CLAXTON MONRO

Hezekiah's many domestic tragedies demanded great flexibility from his only son and eldest child, Claxton, whose mother died when he was two, his half-sister when he was eight, and his stepmother when he was nine. In addition, he and his half-sisters, Dorothy and Edith, were the church equivalent of army brats, frequently pulling up stakes, leaving friends, and switching schools to accommodate Hezekiah's postings. Claxton was three when the family moved from Providence and five when they moved to Newton Lower Falls. There they stayed for twelve years, giving him time to prove himself academically and win admission to Boston Latin School, the prestigious public exam school, where he completed the demanding program so rapidly that he graduated too young to go directly to college. After a year at Worcester Academy, he enrolled at Harvard in 1902, the same year that the family moved to North Andover. In 1906 he graduated cum laude with a degree in chemistry (Munroe 334–35). His first job was with the Lawrence Dye Works, where he established a chemical laboratory (*Class of 1906: Second Report*). In the fall of 1909 he joined the chemical department of the American Woolen Company (AWC) and went to work at its Washington Mill in Lawrence. He remained on the AWC payroll for the rest of his life ("Former Official").

Claiming to be "the greatest name in woolens," AWC was a national trendsetter (Dreyer n.p.). In an industry that was inherently conservative because its raw material was expensive and easily damaged, AWC founder William M. Wood challenged the widely held assumption that each mill should handle the entire process of turning uncleaned wool into finished cloth. The two AWC mills in Lawrence used what was then a revolutionary model: one mill scoured and carded the clumps of wool, and the other mill produced finished worsted cloth

(21). Joining the AWC put Claxton on the cutting edge of the textile industry and marked him as a young man with promise. That promise was enough to encourage him to woo Frances Sutton.

THE SUTTONS

The Suttons and the Monros met in church, although it was the ancestors who met, rather than the two young people who would eventually become John's parents. In fact, church was just about the only place that the two families could conceivably have intersected, given that the social and economic prominence of the Suttons dwarfed that of the Monros. Today the Sutton reputation survives in North Andover's landscape, preserved in place names such as Sutton Pond, Sutton Hill Road, Sutton Street, and Sutton Mills.

A Richard Sutton lived briefly in Andover in the seventeenth century, barely eking out a living as a weaver, but the Sutton textile dynasty did not truly begin until 1826, when William Sutton, president of the Danvers bank and a wealthy woolen merchant, acquired a struggling North Andover mill from Samuel Ayer through foreclosure. Although the mill was a convenient spot for local sheep farmers to process their fleeces, none of the previous owners had been able to turn a profit (Bailey 586).

Sutton quickly reversed the fortunes of the mill, installing power looms to increase efficiency. At his death on 26 February 1832, he left a thriving business to his two sons, William and Eben. By the time Eben died, on 11 December 1864, the fortune he left his son, William, had ballooned so impressively that his obituary called it "a princely fortune" and estimated it was one of the largest in the state (qtd. in Bailey 587). Less than a year later William handed the mill over to his son Eben, better known as "the General" for the rank at which he retired from the Massachusetts militia after thirty years of service.

When he took possession of the mill, the General moved his family to North Andover from New York, where he had made another fortune as the founder of Sutton, Smith, and Company and as an agent for several mills besides his own. In 1867 he became an incorporator of the North Andover Mills, along with his brother, William, and the area's other leading textile baron, T. Stevens (Fuess 3:154). Under the General's management the mills thrived, and by 1880, the year that John's mother, Frances, was born, they were employing 230 people and processing 750,000 pounds of wool a year (Bailey 587–89).

The most impressive mark the Suttons made on the local landscape was Hill Crest, a two hundred–acre estate overlooking the Merrimack River Valley, the town of North Andover, and the mills. The mansion itself dominated the complex and was seven stories tall in places, but even the outbuildings were impressive: the carriage house had room for ten carriages, and a bowling alley existed in solitary splendor in its own building (P. Monro 7).

The General was doing so well that he could easily afford to do good, and he became a key figure in the founding of St. Paul's Episcopal Church in 1888, donating the land on which the church was built and making the largest single contribution toward its construction (*Parish Record* 45). Drawing on the fiscal prudence that had helped him amass his fortune, he insisted that the building fund reach its four thousand–dollar goal before ground breaking took place (Mc-Cahill, "St. Paul's" 498). Then he loosened his purse strings again and donated five Tiffany-style chancel windows commemorating assorted family members—a gift so munificent that the insurance company immediately doubled its estimate of the building's value (McCahill, "Report").

Despite his wealth, the General expected his family to honor the egalitarian philosophy embodied in the church constitution: granddaughter Anna Howe recalls that she and the other Sutton girls were not allowed to wear new bonnets to church on Easter because, they were told, the mill children could not afford luxuries such as new bonnets (Barbara McCahill, personal interview, 8 Aug. 2006). When the General died at Hill Crest on 4 January 1890, his widow moved back to New York, and his two sons sold their interest in the mills, which passed to a corporation. Although a nephew, William, and another son, Harry, remained engaged in the mills, John Hasbrouck—John's maternal grandfather—and his branch of the family did not, and from 1890 on, they essentially lived off the family fortune.

In spite of Hezekiah's leadership of the church the Suttons had helped establish, they vehemently opposed Frances Sutton's courtship with Claxton Monro. Egalitarianism was all well and good in its place, but the gap between the dilapidated, makeshift rectory and the lavish estate on the hill was too dramatic to ignore.

SCANDAL AND PRIVILEGE IN NORTH ANDOVER

Frances, born in Peabody on 2 March 1886, was the eldest daughter of John Hasbrouck Sutton and Mary (Jacobs) Sutton, the second of six children, and the favorite of her childless aunt, Frances Lefavour. When Joseph Lefavour died in 1995, the family's shoe manufacturing business left his widow very well-off, and she enjoyed pampering her young niece, who spent so much time with her in nearby Beverly Farms that the family took to teasing Frances that she was being raised by her aunt ("More than $22,000").

The Beverly Farms home was an especially welcome retreat during the summer, when the Sutton contingent from New York City more than doubled the population at Hill Crest. Another of Frances's aunts, Lila Sutton, had married John Hasbrouck Scoville, a wealthy stockbroker and director of both the Detroit, Toledo & Ironton Railway Company and the Superior Coal Company. When they decamped from the city, they brought along not only their daughter—another Frances—but their retinue of servants and Mary H. Sutton, the middle-aged widow of Eben "the General" Sutton. The New York Summer Social Register dutifully recorded their change of address every year, as befitted their position in polite society ("Took Stafford").

The summer of 1906, as Claxton graduated from Harvard, Hill Crest became part of a decidedly impolite scandal. It was just as well that Frances was tucked away in Beverly Farms. Shortly after midnight on 10 June 1906, Mary Sutton's twenty-five-year-old chauffeur, Reginald Stafford, was shot and killed inside the mansion by her first butler, Edward Ruby. Ruby claimed that he had heard a noise, left his ground-floor bedroom to investigate, seen a figure hiding under the drawing room sofa, and assumed it was a burglar. He said he had fired in self-defense, believing that the intruder had a gun. Since Stafford was living in a nearby house and had no duties inside the mansion, there was no obvious reason for his presence in the drawing room at such a late hour or for his hiding under the sofa in his stocking feet—investigators found his shoes, along with a raincoat, a bundle of laundry, and a bundle of fruit, on the veranda.

According to the *Boston Globe*'s account of the shooting, Mary Sutton had regarded Stafford as "a faithful and efficient employe [*sic*]" ("Took Stafford" 8). But for some time the family—particularly Scoville, who took a proprietary interest in the family fortune—had suspected a closer relationship between the two, and their unease had recently been fueled by Mary's plans to sail for Europe along with Stafford, whom she said she needed to drive the new car she planned to buy in France. True, Mary was also bringing Mary, her sixteen-year-old granddaughter and Frances's younger sister. But in spite of the veneer of respectability the young woman's presence might add, the trip looked suspiciously like a romantic idyll.[3]

The Suttons and Scovilles feared that Mary, who had been a widow for sixteen years, was making a fool of herself over Stafford and might even remarry or otherwise compromise the estate. According to family lore, one evening Scoville announced at dinner—and within earshot of Ruby and the other servants—that "it would be worth $5,000 to him to 'see something happen'" to Stafford (P. Monro, e-mail, 28 May 2010).

At a court hearing the day after the shooting, Justice Newton P. Frye ruled the incident a justifiable homicide and released Ruby, thus preventing the case from going to trial ("Ruby Justified"). The public record of the shooting ends there, but there is an unofficial epilogue. One Sunday morning, years after the incident, Hezekiah encountered Judge Frye leaving church and complimented him on the fine watch he was wearing. To Hezekiah's astonishment, Frye removed the watch and handed it over, saying, "Well, why don't you have it, then. It has always weighed on my conscience." Hezekiah passed the watch and its story along to Claxton, who took them as proof that Frye had been bribed to let Ruby off (P. Monro, e-mail).

Scandal notwithstanding, between the Suttons and Scovilles at Hill Crest and Aunt Frances in Beverly Farms, Frances grew up with the best of everything, and it was taken for granted that she would marry well, given the family's prominence and her vivacious personality. But precisely because of her personality and privileged lifestyle, Frances was used to getting what she wanted, and what she wanted once she had met Claxton was to be with this quiet, intelligent, diligent chemist. It did not matter to her—or perhaps it made Claxton even more attractive—that he worked in the kind of mill that paid for her expensive clothes and fashionable social life. According to Frances, she was packed off to Europe and enrolled in a French convent school in an attempt to cool her ardor, but she indulged in a forbidden correspondence with Claxton, returned home early, and continued to insist that they would marry (P. Monro 7).

Frances and Claxton were a classic case of opposites attracting. She was gregarious and extroverted, whereas he was self-contained, even solemn—some acquaintances described him as cold. In photographs he invariably wore a dark suit and presented himself formally, both to the camera and in everyday life. But Frances did not find Claxton distant or cold, and in spite of her family's continued displeasure, they were married on 16 June 1911. Reading between the lines, it is clear that what the *Andover Townsman* referred to as "a very pretty June wedding" at the Lefavour home—rather than at St. Paul's or at Hill Crest, the obvious choice for a society wedding—was designed to keep the event as low profile as possible ("North Andover").

The modest wedding may have been the only nonextravagant moment in John Hasbrouck's entire life, for in stark contrast to Grandfather Hezekiah's disciplined, measured habits, "Grandpa Johnny" favored excess of all kinds. His Christmas dinners, for which he was both chef and impresario, were legendary, and it was said that the preparations alone required a minimum of a week: "The dinner itself took all afternoon and featured about a dozen courses, starting with raw oysters and going on through turkey, ham, assorted game birds, and ending with a fantastic dessert," and the holiday invariably ended with the children climbing onto Grandpa Johnny's massive stomach after he had fallen into a postprandial stupor (Philip Dreyer, qtd. in P. Monro 8).

It did not take John Hasbrouck and his large family long to run through their share of the General's fortune. Grandpa Johnny eventually went back to the mills, not as an owner or supervisor but as a steamroller operator, and to his credit he enjoyed life just as much in straitened circumstances as he had when lord of the manor (P. Monro 8). After years of living beyond their means, John Hasbrouck's children—including Frances Sutton Monro—faced the prospect of making their own way in the world.

NEWLYWEDS

As newlyweds, Claxton and Frances set up housekeeping at 43 Pearl Street in Lawrence, which was convenient to Claxton's job at Washington Mills. But North Andover was right across the Merrimack River, and John's birth at Hill Crest on 23 December 1912 suggests that the Suttons were becoming reconciled to the match—or at least that they wanted to be part of their grandson's life. The year that ended with John's birth had opened with the violent "Bread and Roses" mill strike, which lasted more than two months. Claxton, who had to cross the picket line every day, carried a lead-weighted billy club for protection (P. Dreyer 30). For the first time, strikers formed marching picket lines, a strategy so unnerving that the mayor called in the state militia (Watson 124). Eventually, the workers got what they asked for: wages were adjusted, sometimes by as little as thirty cents a week, so that the state-mandated reduction in the workweek, from fifty-six to fifty-four hours, no longer resulted in a pay cut (206).

Gradually the raw emotions generated by the strike subsided, just as the Suttons' initial hostility to Claxton was further eroded by the birth of Claxton Jr. on 7 May 1914. A month later Claxton Sr. was transferred to the AWC mill in Winooski, Vermont, and the little family moved to nearby Burlington. While Claxton familiarized himself with his new workplace, Frances struggled to care for two young children in a town where she did not know a soul—a far cry from her cocooned upbringing surrounded by relatives (*Class of 1906: Third Report*).

They stayed for ten years and grew to love the area. Burlington was beautifully situated, clinging to the eastern edge of Lake Champlain, with Mt. Mansfield a brief drive away. The University of Vermont and St. Michael's College provided intellectual and cultural stimulation, and the mill where Claxton worked was just across the Winooski River. Frances and Claxton's youngest son, Sutton, was born in their home at 124 Prospect Street on 15 November 1919. He developed an especially deep bond with his birthplace, but the entire family was drawn back repeatedly, to hike, see friends and relatives, and revisit the place where they had lived long enough to forge a family identity of their own. John and Claxton attended the public elementary schools in Burlington. When he was nine or ten, John developed rheumatic fever and missed almost an entire year of school; treatment at the time involved bed rest, quiet, and little physical activity. Housebound, he read for days on end, an experience that created a lifelong love of reading (Philip and Janet Dreyer, personal interview, 9 Feb. 2005).

CAMP ABNAKI

One of John's earliest formative influences was Camp Abnaki, located on the southernmost tip of North Hero Island in Lake Champlain. It had been founded in 1901 and became one of the largest YMCA camps in New England. Its motto, "Help the other fellow," reinforced Clan Munro values as well as Hezekiah's commitment to caring for those in need.

John attended the camp for seven summers, beginning in 1922. At the time it was still being run by its founder, Byron Clark, fondly known as "Doc" or "Dad." An avid scoutmaster, he had served as a noncombatant during World War I, organizing camps and supervising hospitals throughout Europe ("Camp Abnaki" 1–6). Abnaki was Doc's crowning achievement, and he stamped it with his strong personality. During his peripatetic career he had become an early proponent of diversity, and he amassed a huge collection of flags from around the world, many solicited through personal correspondence to heads of state. In that isolated location the flags hanging from the rafters reminded campers of the larger, more complicated world awaiting them at the end of the summer.

There was more than a whiff of barracks mentality at Abnaki, and John's life-long pride in his navy career may well have begun during the summers he spent in this quasi-military community. The day began with reveille and flag raising and ended with flag lowering and taps. Tents were arranged in two rows, like a military encampment, and there was a clear chain of command, both within each tent and across the camp. An individual camper joined the chain when he became officer of the day and was responsible for the camp's logistics (*Seventy-Five Years*). The most impressive man-made object on the grounds is the Great Stone Seat, a monument to camp members who had died in World War I. Ample enough to embrace one hundred campers for group photographs, the seat was built by the campers out of locally gathered stones; in the center is a row of stones from the battlefields on which campers died (Snow).

Dress Rehearsal for Adulthood

Abnaki gave John his first taste of journalism. The *Abnaki Herald,* which began life in 1911 as a typed sheet posted on the bulletin board, eventually became a mimeographed newsletter that was read aloud during the Monday campfire meeting. It contained descriptions of the week's activities at camp as well as reports on the outside world, radios still being a rarity in the upper reaches of Vermont (Snow). Each fall the newsletters were bound into a volume and used for promotion, publicity, and fund-raising, and editorial positions were highly coveted by the campers.

The fate of one of John's articles introduced him at the tender age of fifteen to the frustrations that are part and parcel of the journalist's life. In 1927 he wrote a lively account of "An Overnight Hike to the Blockhouse." The night before the newsletter was scheduled to be printed, a fire broke out in the block of buildings containing the YMCA offices, and all the copy was destroyed. John's article never saw the light of day.

While still a camper, John made an impressive debut as an after-dinner speaker, a role in which he became highly skilled as an adult. Accompanied by some of his fellow campers, he spoke at a local meeting of the Men's Fraternal League. After thanking his hosts for the invitation, he explored the topic of intergenerational understanding and equality, which he would return to many

times in his administrative career. Asserting that young men were in fact equal
to the older men gathered there, he appealed to their sense of a shared world and
future:

> We boys have an equal interest in all the great and wise things you men do.
> Take the matter of the schools. We appreciate what you have done in the matter of
> giving us schools. We couldn't build school houses for ourselves and we certainly
> couldn't pay the teachers' salaries. Some boys wouldn't even try.
>
> But we boys are just as vitally interested in the schools as you are. For we have
> to go to the schools you organize, and we have to recite to the teachers you hire.
>
> We have an equal interest in town government. We can't vote, but we have to
> walk on the sidewalks you build and drink the water you put in the reservoir, and
> see the movies you let come to town.
>
> The same thing is true of the whole world of tomorrow. Yours is the heavy
> responsibility of making the world of tomorrow, but ours is the equally heavy risk
> of having to live in it.
>
> And yet, of course, we know in many ways we are not your equals. We address
> you rather as our superiors, begging you to try harder to understand us and to see
> life from our point of view. Play games with us more. That may help you too, more
> than you think. I know it would help us.
>
> Sympathize with us more in the trying task of making a start in life. There
> are so many obstacles in the way. Before some of them we feel like the little fel-
> low who was helping his father clean out the garden in the fall. He had hold of
> a cornstalk and was tugging away at it for a long time. Finally he did pull it up.
> "My aren't you strong" said his father who had been watching him. "Well I guess
> I am," said the little fellow. "The whole world had hold of the other end." ("Men's
> Fraternal League Speech").

By turns funny and earnest, modest and assertive, entertaining and supplicatory,
the speech is a remarkable achievement for a teenager, demonstrating a germ of
the keen audience awareness that would mark John's mature public addresses.

NEW ADDRESSES, NEW SCHOOLS

Camp Abnaki provided much-needed continuity at a time when the family was
constantly uprooted and the boys had to switch schools. In 1923 Claxton was
transferred to the AWC's Assabet Mill, and the family moved to Maynard, Mas-

sachusetts (*Class of 1906: 20th* 197). Frances and Claxton were convinced that Concord had a better school system than Maynard, so John commuted to Concord High School (Pupil Transfer Card, 24 Nov. 1926).

In late 1926 Claxton was transferred to the AWC mills in Lawrence, the family moved to Andover, and John enrolled at Punchard, the town's public high school. For a year they rented half of a duplex at 53 Bartlet Street, which was conveniently located across the street from the school. Its motto, "Scalas aedificamus quibis ascendimas" (We build the ladder by which we rise), reinforced the gospel of self-reliance and personal responsibility John was already absorbing from other sources.

The following year Frances and Claxton finally felt financially secure enough to buy their own home, a three-story white clapboard house at 105 Chestnut Street, with a generous front porch and a small yard. It was close to the town center and to Christ Church Andover, where they now worshipped, and except for one brief interval, it would serve as the family home for almost three decades.

Hezekiah had joined the household in 1925, when he was widowed for a third time. Just as Hezekiah's relatives had taken him in when his parents died, Claxton and Frances accepted their responsibility to care for him in his widowhood. Such an arrangement was an act of Christian charity in keeping with the creed of the Munro Clan as well as part of the social fabric of the time, prefiguring the multigenerational households that World War II would soon spawn. But that did not make it easy to live in a three-generation household—for any of the generations. Hezekiah was seventy-three and had just buried his wife; he had no obligations to give order to his life and nothing but informal ties to his former parish. Frances was grieving over her father's death, Claxton was adjusting to yet another new job, and the two adolescent boys—John was thirteen, Claxton Jr. was eleven, and Sutton was seven—were at just the right age to test the limits of parental authority. The family dynamics were complex, to say the least.

There was already a good deal of sibling rivalry in the house, particularly between John and Claxton. With less than two years between them, tension was inevitable, and John, who was older, faster, a better athlete, an excellent student, and a hit with the girls, seized every opportunity to tease Clax, calling him "Old lady, mop lady," and berating him as a nuisance (P. Monro 20). Perhaps as a defense mechanism, Clax developed a habit of talking at length and in a slightly superior tone, which earned him the nickname "Windy" (Scheidecker). As the youngest child, Sutton was universally cosseted and petted, but he also suffered from the youngest child's sense of being left behind and left out.

Phillips Academy

In the spring of 1927 John applied for admission to Phillips Academy, the venerable prep school he could practically glimpse from his bedroom window. Transferring would mean repeating his sophomore year, but there was simply no comparison between its rigorous curriculum and the public school offerings. Known as "Andover" when it might be confused with Phillips Exeter, as "Phillips" when it might be confused with the town of Andover, and as "PA" by insiders, the school had been founded in 1778 and was a feeder school for the Ivy League colleges, especially Yale (Allis 43).

Phillips labored to instill in its students a character-building work ethic and to preserve traditional values against the onslaught of passing educational fads (Allis 43, 53). Its motto was "Non sibi" (Not for oneself alone), and in theory it was democratic, pledging to "be ever equally open to Youth, of requisite qualification, from every quarter" (57). In practice the phrase *of requisite qualification* was sometimes invoked to reject students deemed undesirable for one reason or another, and founder Samuel Phillips originally had doubts about the wisdom of accepting "charity scholars" who could not pay their own way. It was a foregone conclusion that even though John had been awarded a scholarship, he would enroll as a day student, living at home and working part-time. As a further cost-cutting measure, Clax remained at Punchard.

On his first day at Phillips, John promptly revealed himself as an outsider by showing up for his early-morning Latin class wearing a sweater instead of the mandatory jacket and tie (P. Monro 21). Even after he learned the dress rules, he found the class itself so traumatic that it remained for him the quintessential rite of passage: "It was a rough way to start the day, but it had the immediate advantage of making the rest of every day seem easy. And it had the happily unforeseen long-run advantage of making a depression and war seem easy too. The subject matter was Latin but that was subordinate to the main thing, which was simply ordeal," he recalled many years later (qtd. in Allis 413–14).

His favorite class by far was English, taught by Claude "Jack" Fuess, whom he captured in a vivid, affectionate thumbnail sketch that already revealed a journalist's keen eye for physical detail: "His manner was to stand straight before us on the low platform, hands cocked on hips, heels together, a knee twitching, now and then the flat of a hand brushing back nervously over the bald head; his smile was broad and confident, his voice quick and firm; here was a friendly, lively, interested man, keen to have you share with him the fun, the work, and the importance of clear, expressive, disciplined writing" (qtd. in Allis 457).[4]

John adjusted quickly to Phillips, and at the close of his junior year he received the Smith Lewis Multer Jr. Scholarship, named after a 1923 graduate who had died of scarlet fever during his freshman year at Yale. Given his off-campus job, he fit in a surprising number of extracurricular activities: at various times he was assistant football manager, played goalie for club soccer and then varsity soccer, and served on the executive board society of inquiry, senior prom committee, senior council, police force, class day committee, and spring cheerleading squad (*Phillips Andover Yearbook* 49).

In 1930 he graduated cum laude and walked away with a fistful of prizes, including subject prizes in American history, math, and Greek; the Andrew Potter Prize for one of the two best original essays delivered by a senior at commencement; and an outside award, the Brooks-Bright Prize, for his essay on Anglo-American relations (Ruth Quattlebaum, e-mail, 4 Jan. 2005). He narrowly missed, by five-hundredths of a point, winning the Faculty Prize for High Scholarship, which went to Amory Hall Bradford. "Pretty close work," John noted in his journal, adding, in a fit of good sportsmanship, "Good old Brady. Mighty fine chap."

THE GIRL NEXT DOOR—ALMOST

John's senior portrait in the Andover yearbook depicts a serious young man, neatly attired and apparently relaxed in the now-familiar suit and tie. He was strikingly handsome, with dramatic eyebrows; deep-set, piercing eyes; abundant dark hair; and a dazzling smile. But the girls who found him attractive were out of luck, for he already had a sweetheart. She was Dorothy "Dottie" Stevens Foster, a former classmate from Punchard, whose home at 71 Chestnut Street made her almost literally the girl next door.

William Harnden Foster, Dottie's father, was a successful, hardworking sportsman, artist, editor, and writer. Dottie's mother, Marion Dorothy Lowd, had graduated from Punchard and Bridgewater Normal School, then taught in the Andover and Swansea schools (Barry). The relationship between the Foster siblings was almost identical to that of the Monro brothers: Dottie was the oldest, followed two years later by William Harnden Foster II, who was called Bill. Then, after a six-year gap, came Helen, the youngest and very much the baby, like Sutton.

The "cute-meet" version of John and Dottie's first encounter is that they collided while ice-skating, Dottie went sprawling, and John helped her back up to her feet. For a brief time Clax was also attracted to Dottie—and there is even a family story that he and John came to blows over her—but soon John and Dottie were considered a couple by everyone who knew them. He squired her to Punchard social events, and when the 1930 Punchard yearbook predicted that a classmate would become housekeeper to Mr. and Mrs. John Monro, everyone knew who "Mrs. Monro" would be (*Punchard* 23).

Dottie was petite, quiet, and pretty, and people who knew her as Mrs. John Monro unfailingly commented on her sweetness and supportiveness. But her high school yearbook adds some welcome spice to the cloying image; she was elected the snobbiest girl in her class, and the "I Wonder If . . . " feature, which speculated about the future, mused, "I wonder if Dot Foster will ever lose her sharp tongue" (49). She was jokes editor for the school publication, *Punch Harder,* and the quote she chose to accompany her photograph was, "Laugh and the world laughs with you" (15).

After Phillips commencement John stayed in Andover for Dottie's graduation then drove with the Fosters to their vacation home in South Freeport, Maine, where they regularly spent the summers. Dottie's father had designed the cottage and done a good deal of the construction as well, after stumbling on the site in 1908 and being drawn to the breathtaking view across island-strewn Casco Bay (P. Dreyer, personal interview, 3 Aug. 2005). Throughout John and Dottie's life together, the cottage was a reassuring fixed point, impervious to whatever social, geographic, or academic upheaval they faced elsewhere, and they returned faithfully almost every summer.

The sporadic journal that John kept in June and July 1930 paints an attractive picture of the Fosters' summer lifestyle. It was casual but not lazy, and recreation was simple: swimming, visiting, boating, playing cards, riding around, buying and setting off illicit fireworks, looking at the stars, and canoodling on the porch. During his visit John gingerly carved out a place for himself in the family's interpersonal dynamics. He enjoyed his time with Bill and found Helen's childishness amusing. He took responsibility for teaching her to swim, patiently encouraging her and then rejoicing in her progress: "Helen coming along fine with her swimming. Getting more and more courage all the time" (9 July).

That brief vacation in South Freeport was all the more delicious because of its rarity. At an early age John had become aware that his parents worried about money, so he filled his spare time with gainful employment, eager to put something in the family till. From his first year at Camp Abnaki he had worked in the office (Clark, Byron), then he angled for a more lucrative job as a camp counselor even though he was underage. While he was still at Punchard, he got a part-time job at a local grocery store, which he kept after he transferred to Andover, where he also worked in the library (Kemper). During his senior year he earned $150 as a history tutor, and when listing his graduation honors in his journal, he carefully recorded their cash value as well as the academic achievement they reflected (3–4 July 1930). As he headed to Harvard, he was determined to exploit all the opportunities it offered and to make sure he got his—and his parents'—money's worth.

So much does the college differ from the cold, wide world.

—CLAXTON MONRO

2
UNDERGRADUATE YEARS
1930-1934

Monro began undergraduate life in Smith Hall, where he shared a top-floor dormer suite with Arthur T. Hamlin and George W. "Cat" Caturani (Hamlin 1). Fortunately for posterity, Hamlin was so fascinated by Monro that he wrote an informal memoir-sketch of their years together, filling it with vivid descriptions of his suite mate's behavior and appearance. Monro struck him as obsessively focused on his academic goals: "He was at Harvard to study, to get A's in fact, and really for no other purpose. . . . He would be a good guy, and he would give us a little of his time for sociability, but only a little" (3).

According to Hamlin, in addition to "killing himself" to get an A in history, Monro lavished hours on his intensive German course: "He sat there at his desk, chair tilted back, expounding in German by the hour. He was never one to whisper, and I was glad of a thick door to my room" (8). Once the suite mates acquired a radio, the German recitations were accompanied by an endless stream of jazz, with Monro beating out the tempo, then re-creating it on the Common Room piano (5). He also flirted briefly with communism, attending seminars on Marxism but ultimately deciding against party membership: "Any time you disagreed to any item of dogma, they'd try to bulldoze you out of the way instead of arguing with you," he later recalled. "I was never a very good theorist, but I did and still do believe in historical materialism—that whoever owns the means of production governs our lives in this country. But I decided that I could profit from knowing that without joining the party" (qtd. in Greenhouse 57).

No matter how busy he got, his mother expected "Johnnie"—as Frances called him all her life—to write frequently during the week and come home on weekends. She scrutinized his daily life to the extent that she could from a distance, suggesting that he and his roommates put up curtains (22 Sept. 1930), inviting them all home for Thanksgiving (23 Oct. 1930), reminding him to get enough sleep (15 Jan. 1931), making doctor's appointments for him (31 Oct. 1930), and lecturing him on the importance of keeping up with his laundry (29 Jan. 1931). When John skipped a weekend at home, she made her disappointment clear: "We all kind of sat around waiting for you in the afternoon" (8 Oct. 1930). Frances was so emotionally invested in him that his father, who rarely criticized, felt compelled to chide John on a major oversight: "You forgot your mother's birthday . . . and should write her—she missed your greeting" (5 Mar. 1931).[1]

Dottie, majoring in home economics at Framingham Teachers College, expected John to write to her too, even though they saw each other most weekends in Andover. She seldom came to Harvard, but she staked her claim to Monro out of all proportion to her physical presence, and Hamlin marveled at "the fierce possessiveness of this very attractive, very quiet young lady" (4).

Claxton Sr. also wrote regularly to John, but his letters differed dramatically in both tone and content from those of his wife. Given the fact that he was often described as distant and emotionally inaccessible, the letters are surprisingly affectionate and positive, written man-to-man and emphasizing shared experiences. Fiercely proud of his Harvard degree, he saw his own undergraduate years through rose-colored glasses and was delighted that his eldest son was following in his footsteps. He praised John for picking good courses and getting off to a strong start: "I think you are handling things splendidly. . . . Your instructors will be aware, in that rather uncanny way that Harvard instructors have, of your previous work in their subject, and you will find ready help and encouragement to meet your earnest effort—so much does the college differ from the cold wide world!" (21 Sept. 1930).

Claxton liked to linger in John's rooms at Harvard after driving him back from weekends at home, and during these visits Hamlin was impressed by the closeness between father and son, whose mutual love and respect were obvious. When John talked about his father, Hamlin noticed, "his voice took on a slightly different timbre" than when he was discussing more pedestrian matters, and Hamlin suspected that although John boasted of Claxton's professional accomplishments, "had his father only dug ditches, John would have been just as proud" (7).

John's pride in his father's success was justified: that October Claxton had been made chief chemist of the American Woolen Company—quite a coup, given that AWC was the first textile company to create its own in-house chemical department (Dreyer 31). Because the woolen industry had developed along the lines of a craft, it was heavily dependent on individuals with a thorough understanding of the part of the process they supervised. The head chemist was one of those individuals: he "kept all dye formulas and secrets of his trade to himself or in his 'Blackbook.' . . . Without [these experts] and their special knowledge, the entire production of a specific fabric might halt and the whole mill would be crippled" (47). Working with the dye formulas was especially tricky because they had to be adjusted seasonally in response to the changing speed and chemical makeup of the river water (Judy Brook, personal interview, 16 May 2005).

Even more important than the prestige of Claxton's promotion was its promise of financial security, which remained a major family concern. Claxton Jr. was still at Punchard but hoped to transfer to Phillips, and Sutton was rapidly approaching prep school age. In a letter relaying the good news of his promotion, Claxton's relief was palpable: "It means a lot to all of us especially you boys—a chance to salt away something—we are comfortably housed and fed at least. And if we can go along as is for awhile we shall get ahead and feel more solid comfort for future needs. . . . My greatest satisfaction is that at last I am within reach of the means to at least back you and the other boys more surely in your advancement" (17 Oct. 1930).

Claxton's workload soon began to take a toll on his health. His back bothered him, and he postponed dental work until it reached crisis proportions and he had to have six teeth extracted (15 Jan 1931). He remained upbeat in his letters, congratulating John on his good grades and the continuation of his scholarship and praising his plan to look for tutoring work at Phillips during the summer. But an ominous note thrummed beneath all the good news: "You are on the track that leads to the status where you will not need to fear the cutting off of your course, if anything should happen to me—for the college, if met by your earnest efforts, would find some way for a high scholar to 'finish clean': and I think that the insurance would see you on your feet if you are pulled together" (5 Mar. 1931). Unable to find work at Phillips, John worked at the mills during the summer, and by the fall there was enough money for Claxton Jr., with some financial assistance from the school, to transfer to Phillips for his senior year.

EMBARKING ON A LIFE OF "CRIME"

As a sophomore, Monro and Hamlin moved to Lowell House, one of the first two buildings to be completed in Harvard's shift to the house system. Each house was a self-contained social, residential, and academic unit with its own tutors, dining hall, and commons room, and from the beginning Lowell House was identified with elegance and the social graces. High Table dinners were held every Monday evening, "lady guests" were permitted to attend lunch on weekends, and it soon boasted a fine library, a music society, a piano room, a music listening room, and a publication, the *House Chronicle* (*Class Album: 1934* 131).

But in spite of its gregarious image, Monro made few friends at Lowell House, becoming immersed instead in Harvard's prestigious student-run daily newspaper, the *Crimson*. The editorial board was not open to freshman, but he applied at the earliest opportunity and won a spot on the board during spring of his sophomore year.

Dating back to 1873, the "Crime," as the paper has long been called, has attracted the likes of Franklin Delano Roosevelt, who postponed his graduation so that he could serve as its president; Cleveland Amory, Daniel J. Boorstin, James Bryant Conant, Susan Faludi, David Halberstam, Hendrik Hertzberg, John F. Kennedy, Anthony J. Lukas, David Riesman, and Casper Weinberger. Its home at 14 Plympton Street was and is a small but elegant brick building built in 1915 and occupied by the Crimson Printing Company and the *Alumni Bulletin* offices. The tenants' rent created a much-needed financial buffer for the *Crimson* in the post-Depression economy (*Harvard Crimson* 34–35). The top floor, dubbed the "Sanctum," was restricted to members of the editorial board, who bunked there when the newspaper was put to bed late—which happened a lot. Its most notable piece of furniture is the president's chair, its back bristling with plaques, one for each of the newspaper's presidents (55).

Monro's involvement with the newspaper would dominate—and extend—the remainder of his undergraduate career at Harvard. With more than a hint of jealousy, Hamlin noted that Monro's universe was shrinking to the dimensions of the newspaper: "Almost immediately the Crimson became his absorbing interest and the Crimson associates his only friends" (10–11). Monro stayed out late to get the paper to press, overslept, skipped classes, and missed deadlines. But somehow he kept his grades high enough to receive one of ninety-three Harvard College scholarships, awarded on the basis of both class rank and financial need ("Award Honorary Scholarships").

Midway through his junior year Monro was elected editorial chair and put in charge of all editorial material appearing in the *Crimson*. Because bylines were scarce, it is difficult to determine which editorials he actually wrote, but because he had to approve them all, their subjects reflect his ideas about what was within the purview of a college newspaper. He clearly believed that local, national, and international issues should be addressed, since almost every issue published on his watch included at least one editorial on such a topic.

Many editorials grappled with issues that would engage him throughout his life. Two editorials (21 Dec. 1932 and 14 April 1933) about the Scottsboro boys—black men convicted of raping a white woman, in what was generally acknowledged to be a mistrial—pointed toward his commitment to eliminating racism. He also devoted considerable editorial space to the plight of underfunded students. On 3 March 1933 "Good Collateral" encouraged a more generous student loan policy, especially for students who were struggling financially and not making the Dean's List. Monro would champion this same population in the 1950s, proposing a sophisticated formula for needs-based financial aid. On 22 March "Student Employment" lauded the one-year extension of an experimental student employment plan and suggested that it be made permanent, arguing that it served "to combat the current belief that Harvard is a rich man's college." As director of the Financial Aid Office, Monro would greatly expand student employment opportunities and create a program for student entrepreneurs as well.

During his senior year Monro was elected literary editor and put in charge of the newspaper's many theater, book, and music reviews. When his term expired, he did not run for another office, hoping to free up more time to write articles of his own. At that point, with graduation looming, he might have been expected to relax, coast a bit, and perhaps begin job hunting. But he rarely did what was expected, especially when it smacked of complacency or ease or when a daunting challenge was afoot. What happened next almost cost him his Harvard degree.

THE *HARVARD JOURNAL*

Monro was one of a small cadre of active editors on the *Crimson* who hoped to become journalists and treated the newspaper as their training ground. They were heavily outnumbered by a group of editors in name only, who basked in the newspaper's cachet but contributed little or nothing to its production. Monro and his career-oriented colleagues were constantly prodding the *Crimson* toward greater professionalism; they wanted writing that was crisper as well as a paper that served the entire university and covered local, national, and international news.

But expanded coverage required a larger newspaper than the four pages that had been the norm since the Depression. To make a six-page paper economically feasible, Joseph Boyd '35, the enterprising managing editor, talked the printer into charging only six dollars more for six pages than for four pages. Even at this attractive rate, business manager Thomas Dammann '35 and managing editor John H. Morison '35 opposed the increase as fiscally risky, but over their objections the editorial board approved a six-page format in February 1934.

Just before spring break, the *Crimson* staff met to debate the page number controversy and elect new officers. Usually the candidates backed by the aspiring journalist cadre were elected out of sheer inertia, but this time Morison, Dammann, and other fiscal conservatives hustled the nonparticipants out to vote for Morison. At the end of the three-hour meeting, over which Monro presided, Morison was elected president by a vote of forty-four to thirty-two ("*Harvard Crimson* Faces").

The day after the meeting, the college emptied out for spring break, but Monro and others who had lost the election were angry enough to stick around and argue about what to do next. If they could not support the direction the *Crimson* was taking, they decided, they would start their own newspaper and show the world—or at least the college—how it should be done. Monro was elected president, Thomas B. O'Connor '37, managing editor, and Boyd business manager.

Although Monro was not a *Crimson* officer at the time, he immediately assumed a leadership position in the splinter group, first shaping and then aggressively pursuing its goal. One source of his authority was his reputation for fairness; he was chosen to run the election meeting because he was considered "an elder statesman" and because "everyone respected and deferred to him," according to Joseph Iseman '37 (letter, 23 Sept. 2002).

Another of Monro's leadership credentials was, literally, seniority: he was a member of the class of '34 and boasted three years of newspaper experience, two of them as an officer. Outgoing president Joseph Thorndike Jr. '34, the only *Crimson* officer from the senior class to defect to the *Journal*, left before graduation, having lined up an assistant editorship at *Time Magazine*. So Monro was the most experienced *Crimson* editor willing to throw himself into a grueling crusade in the final months of his senior year.

Finally, it did not hurt that he looked the part. In the yearbook's group portrait of the *Crimson*, Monro virtually leaps off the page. He sits in the front row, formally dressed, his hands folded in his lap, his face half in shadow. The slicked-down hair of his fellow editors makes his abundant thatch even more impressive, and compared to their sober expressions, his broad smile appears even more animated; he looks like he is harboring a delightful secret. Physical descriptions of him at the time rely heavily on the Hollywood image of the crusading journalist. Iseman described him as "very tall, somewhat lugubrious . . . dark and sallow-skinned, cigarette drooping from mouth, clad in a filthy gray overcoat and permanently behatted (all of us wore fedoras, indoors and out, in those days)" (letter). Boyd reduced Monro's appearance to a vivid tagline: "He was the Clark Gable of the *Crimson*" (telephone interview, 16 Sept. 2003). He even typed like a journalist, becoming so proficient in the two-fingered "hunt and peck" style that his rapid-fire performance sounded like a machine gun (J. Martin).

It was decided that the new publication would be called the *Harvard Journal*, and for maximum effect the first issue had to be waiting for students when they returned from spring break. Monro and his crew had less than a week to drum up an office, a printer, and funding—not to mention enough news, features, and editorials to fill the pages of a newspaper that was still just a gleam in their collective eye.

Frank Sweetser '36, who had worked for the *Harvard Advocate* at one time, wheedled the literary quarterly into lending the *Journal* its building at 69 Mt. Auburn Street, rent free, for three months. Iseman, who was a freshman during the coup, described the ramshackle quarters: "Packing boxes were used as desks, and old benches were sat on. Its exterior was a dirty gray of extremely ugly New England architecture, its interior of old fashioned crushed and torn wallpaper" (Iseman, *Journal*). The weekly *Cambridge Tribune* agreed to let the upstart journalists use its printing presses for the time being. Because it was too late in the semester to solicit advertising, the business staff patched together start-up funds from a variety of sources, mostly friends and relatives. Boyd, using the powers of persuasion that had earlier won a deep discount from the printer, extracted five hundred dollars from Iseman's father (Iseman, *Journal*).

Miraculously, the slapdash arrangements succeeded. The debut issue of the *Harvard Journal* appeared on Monday, 9 April 1934, the day that the college reopened after spring break. It was eight pages long, and with very few exceptions, it stayed that size until its final issue. Its officers and twenty-nine editors included the *Crimson*'s former president, business manager, editorial chair, literary editor, and most of its active staff members. One aspiring career journalist remained with the *Crimson:* Osborn "Ozzie" Ingram '35, who took over as issue editor for 9 April and became managing editor for the rest of the school year (*Harvard Crimson* 76–77).

Based on their comparative assets and pedigrees, the *Crimson* and the *Journal* looked as mismatched as David and Goliath, but Ingram and his largely untrained crew saw the *Journal* as a serious threat. "The most active and capable people had left," Ingram recalls, "so we had to work like demons. It was a real struggle. . . . We were really hard up, shaken up, and worked around the clock. We realized we had to be more like a newspaper than a club sheet" (personal interview, 15 Feb. 2005).

Day after day both papers appeared. To all outward appearances the *Journal* was thriving. The 21 April issue announced that free copies would no longer be available, and paid circulation was reported to be just under fifteen hundred, a decent figure for such a new enterprise. But the shoestring nature of the operation quickly took its toll on both manpower and the bottom line. Monro stepped down as president on 13 May, but it was too late to save his coursework. Summoned by dean of the college A. Chester Hanford, he reluctantly agreed to take a leave of absence, a move that would salvage his grade point average but postpone his graduation by a year.[2] The *Journal*'s death blow was dealt by Dammann, who shrewdly persuaded local *Crimson* advertisers to renew their contracts, in advance, for the following school year, thus decimating future revenue for the *Journal*. After almost two months of continuous publication, the final issue of the *Journal* appeared on 6 June.

Given his sensitivity to family finances, Monro might have hesitated to cast his lot with the *Journal* if he had known in advance that the adventure would delay his graduation and require another semester of tuition. But in all other ways the move was consistent with his love of challenge. Indeed, the *Journal* was an especially alluring challenge because it allowed him to test his still-evolving ideas about the power of writing and the role of journalism in shaping an informed citizenry.

Professionalism and Inclusiveness

Monro was strongly drawn to the prospect of putting out a college newspaper that met professional journalistic standards. As he and the rest of his staff knew from personal experience, the *Crimson* fell far short of professionalism: there was a lot of dead wood on its staff and a lot of inflated prose on its pages. Journalistic mediocrity was fostered by the paper's application procedure, which had the advantage of significantly lightening the editors' workload. During their eight-week candidacy *Crimson* aspirants had to crank out, with little or no supervision, at least one article or editorial per issue. Flooding the newspaper with articles by unsupervised, inexperienced candidates was a recipe for disaster, as Ingram confirmed in his comment book excoriation of the final issue before spring break: "The [articles written by] the candidates were lousy" (11).

The *Journal's* tryout procedure was designed to avoid the pitfalls the editors had experienced at the *Crimson*, as Monro's front-page article made clear. Tryouts would run for a maximum of three weeks, but even more important, "in contrast to previous custom, candidates obviously unfitted for the work will be dropped as soon as their incapacity has become evident." Instead of providing unpaid labor for the editors, applicants would enjoy a productive, instructive apprenticeship: "If [a candidate] shows interest in the ins and outs of journalism but is slow to get the knack of bringing in a good story, he will enjoy the cooperation of the editors who will show him how" (Monro, "Journal to Open").

In addition to professionalism, the *Journal* also aspired to inclusiveness, in terms of audience, staff, and content. The *Crimson's* narrow field of vision was skewered in the *Journal's* claim to be "*the* University Daily," the definite article implying that the *Crimson* was too parochial to qualify for the title. A *Journal* pitch to potential subscribers announced, "Harvard Is Not Just Two Finishing Schools and Some Graduate Students. Read the Journal and See It Whole" (23 Apr.).

The most significant aspect of the *Journal's* drive toward serving the entire university was the inclusion of women. The first issue contained a Radcliffe column. The next day a front-page article announced that a Radcliffe editorial board had been created and approved; on 12 April page 7 was dedicated to "Radcliffe Correspondence," and beginning on 13 April, page 7 became "Radcliffe News," complete with its own banner, masthead, and articles that frequently spilled onto additional pages. Handing a full page of each issue over to an independent, female editorial board was a stunning innovation. Radcliffe material in the *Crimson* was limited to frothy topics such as dances and socials and to areas where the two colleges overlapped. What coverage there was tended to be patronizing: reporting on attendance at an anti-Nazi demonstration in Charlestown, the *Crimson* referred to "Harvard students" but "Radcliffe girls" (18 May), and an editorial describing a monthly film series sponsored by the German Department archly concluded, "The necessary off-stage color will be provided by a number of pretty, puzzled debutante faces, tense in their struggle with the German passive" (1 Mar.). For Monro, who would rejoice when Phillips and Harvard became coed and would encourage his daughters to become strong, independent individuals, the *Journal* was an early opportunity to include women where they had previously been shut out.

Reporting on the Outside World

The *Journal*'s commitment to covering news outside the ivied walls of Harvard coincided with Monro's belief that education imposed an obligation to participate in the world at large. He exploited the *Journal*'s eight-page format to expand news coverage, buttressing original stories with wire service articles. In comparison, early *Crimson* editors positively basked in their insularity, one of them asserting, "The columns of the Crimson are suited only for those communications which confine themselves to the bearing of the question on university men and especially the Harvard man" (Lawless 118).

A face-off between the newspapers' front pages on 9 April—the *Journal*'s debut issue and the *Crimson*'s crucial first issue after spring break—shows what each newspaper considered newsworthy, particularly off campus. Front-page topics in the *Journal* included the apparent suicide of a Harvard student; a City Council meeting about taxing local colleges; exclusive interviews with actor and opera singer Lawrence Tibbett, Boston Opera House doorman Bert Rowe, and Oxford Group leader Frank Buchman; and the withdrawal of an invitation to Ernst Hanfstaengl, Hitler's foreign press secretary, to serve as an official during his twenty-fifth class reunion.[3] *Crimson* front-page stories included the results of a student evaluation of the School of Engineering (generally unfavorable); a change in the scheduling of Class Day (always on a Tuesday, this year on a Wednesday), the varsity crew lineup, and—for those who were curious about the outside world—an interview with burlesque queen Sally Rand in Cleveland. Yet even the interview had a Harvard slant: Ms. Rand, complaining that her trademark fans could cost as much as four hundred dollars each, said a Harvard student had suggested she trim expenses by using smaller fans, an idea that illustrated "the practical side of the education received at Harvard."

The Aftermath of the *Journal*

Although the life of the *Journal* itself was brief, its impact was considerable. It still casts its shadow across the president's chair, where the plaque marking

Thorndike's presidency has been removed and leaves a gaping hole, presumably because his defection to the *Journal* erased him from institutional memory.

Many of the *Journal's* staff members made names for themselves as writers or in some branch of publishing. Thorndike became managing editor of the recently launched *Life Magazine,* then editorial director of *American Heritage,* then founder and editor of *Horizon.* Tilton went to *Time Magazine,* E. J. Kahn Jr. '37 to the *New Yorker.*[4] Peter Viereck '37 became a Pulitzer Prize–winning poet, political theorist, and history professor at Mt. Holyoke. Gladwin Hill '36 became a national correspondent for the *New York Times* (Ingram interview). Beverly Bowie '35 joined the staff of *National Geographic* (Brelis, "Monro Loaned"). Harry Kern '35 became managing editor of *Newsweek.* Boyd founded a suburban weekly newspaper, which eventually became the *Brookline Citizen.* Thomas O'Connor '35, who replaced Monro as *Journal* president, became a reporter for the *Nassau Transcript* in Farmingdale, Long Island, the *Los Angeles Post-Record,* and the *Los Angeles Daily News.* Iseman '37, who stuck with his plans to become a lawyer, had his senior honors thesis published by Harvard University Press and wrote numerous articles for law journals.

But the most significant vestiges of the *Journal* cropped up in the *Crimson,* which was galvanized by its rival's aggressive brand of journalism and absorbed some of its crusading spirit. One of the reforms it championed, albeit gradually, was a campaign to close down the tutoring bureaus, also known as exam schools or cram parlors. On 14 December 1936 *Time Magazine,* where former *Journal* editor Edwin Tilton '36 was now working, published an unsigned article describing cram parlor practices such as selling copies or summaries of copyrighted textbooks, charging high prices for breakneck sessions, and possibly providing prewritten themes, papers, and honors theses ("Councilors"). In response to the article, Harvard's Student Council urged college publications to stop running cram parlor ads, but for more than a year the *Crimson* continued to accept roughly two thousand dollars worth of advertising revenue from this dubious source. Then, on 18 April 1939, it published an arresting front-page editorial that began, "Lined up on Massachusetts Avenue, grinning obscenely down over Harvard Yard, there is a row of intellectual brothels." The editorial went on to announce that the newspaper would no longer accept advertising from the brothels ("Tutoring School"). *Crimson* president Blair Clark '40, who led the cram parlor crusade, wrote a letter thanking Monro for his "support and encouragement" in the campaign, adding, "I don't know anyone at Harvard who knows more about what the college daily could and should do, and . . . I consider your technical advice as almost biblical in soundness."

As Clark's letter suggests, Monro's ties with the *Crimson* survived his departure from the editorial board. As an administrator, he became a fixture at the newspaper's high school in-house days and scholastic conferences, and during tryouts he could be counted on to enumerate the benefits of working on the newspaper he had defected from.

But he also remained a stern critic, holding the *Crimson* to the same exacting standards that had led to the 1934 split. In 1948 he wrote a letter to the editor that added a sober note to the self-congratulatory seventy-fifth anniversary issue. First, he listed the advantages the *Crimson* enjoyed: "We look to the Crimson and we see at once the virtually assured circulation, the regular, if not munificent income; we know that by time-honored custom the paper is free from censorship; we see a daily published by able young men in a community given over to the fermentation of ideas. Where else in the world is there to be found a paper more favored by circumstance?" Then he accused the editors of ignoring the responsibility imposed by such extraordinary privilege: "The veteran newsman yearns for the freedom to tell his hard-won truth and save the world. Your college editor, with all the old-fashioned freedoms at his disposal, lets them go" ("Monro Deplores").[5]

By the time he wrote the letter, Monro was firmly entrenched in the administration and had said good-bye to his cherished dream of becoming a journalist. But his years on the *Crimson* and the heady months running the *Journal* were at least as formative as his family background and childhood influences. On the student newspapers he became part of an entity that could significantly affect society, and from then on, he repeatedly attempted to identify and merge with endeavors in which he discerned the same kind of potential.

I spent these years getting to feel like a writer.

—JOHN U. MONRO

3

INTERIM YEARS AND WAR YEARS
1935-1945

After commencement Monro was in limbo. Dottie had graduated and was hoping to open a school with a friend in September, and his buddies from the *Journal* had gone home or had begun working at their first jobs. But without his degree and with his final semester of course work to complete, he was hamstrung. He moved home to save money and found a part-time job at Phillips, checking footnotes for a translation being prepared by music teacher Carl Pfatteicher (Ruth Quattlebaum, e-mail, 17 Feb. 2005).

In the fall, hearing that there was an opening at the Harvard News Office, he went to see director Arthur D. "Art" Wild, who was exactly the kind of no-nonsense newspaper man Monro hoped to become. Wild had been working as a *Chicago Daily News* crime reporter when he was seated next to Harvard president James B. Conant at a banquet, and before the event was over, he had accepted Conant's spur-of-the-moment invitation to head the university's News Office (Brelis, "Ex-Student Monro"). Wild was equally brisk in offering Monro a position. Once he was collecting a pay check, Monro rented rooms at 5½ DeWolfe Street, just outside Harvard Square, and in the spring he enrolled at Harvard for his final semester while he continued to work. He took a writing course with historian and novelist Bernard DeVoto, submitting a short story and the first chapter of a novel, tentatively named "The Backwater." DeVoto was not a gentle critic; on the back of Monro's short story he scribbled: "The trouble with your style is its incredible stuffiness. Long, rolling words, long, stupefying sentences. Shed all that excess verbiage. Be plain, direct, simple, brief. . . . Give up (you would say abandon) the idea (concept) that long-windedness is funny (productive of a delightful agitation of the risibilities)."[1]

He did better in his major, earning honors for his thesis on eighteenth-century Scottish history (Brelis, "Ex Student Monro"), but in spite of his Scottish ancestry, he found the project boring and pointless, especially compared to the exciting world of journalism he glimpsed from the News Office. Once he had completed his course work, he was free to seek employment anywhere he wanted, but instead of pounding the pavement and setting up job interviews, he hesitated. Throughout the summer of 1935 he marked time, working at the News Office, visiting home, and escaping to South Freeport, usually in the company of his future father-in-law.

WILLIAM HARNDEN FOSTER

William Harnden Foster hailed from a long line of railroaders who were also avid hunters. These two interests often converged since repair work sent railroad men into habitat that was ideal for upland game birds. It was Foster's good fortune to shape a career around these two lifelong loves. His illustrations of trains for *Scribner's* and other publications eventually won him a job with the railroads themselves ("Story"), and his dramatic oil paintings of New York Central trains were reproduced on advertisements, posters, and widely distributed company calendars. He parlayed his love of hunting into a position with *Hunting and Fishing* and *National Sportsman* ("W. H. Foster"), first providing illustrations and eventually becoming editor of both magazines (Barry 52). But Foster's main claim to fame among sportsmen was his role in inventing skeet. Looking for a way to stay in practice from one grouse season to another, he and several hunting buddies got together in 1910 and learned to toss clay targets so that they approximated the conditions of field hunting. Foster further refined the sport, based in part on suggestions from readers of *National Sportsman*, then sponsored a contest to come up with a suitable name ("Skeet" 639–40). During each six-hour drive to Maine, Monro learned a bit more about this interesting man and even developed a mild enthusiasm for skeet himself.

GETTING AHEAD BY STAYING PUT

By the end of the summer Monro had decided to stay at the News Office for the time being. It would mean postponing his professional ambitions, but he wanted to be available during family emergencies. Claxton's health was deteriorating so seriously that in spite of his strong sense of duty, he had recently stepped down from the local school board ("Former Official"). Sutton would probably be needing help with his schoolwork at Phillips; he had flunked Latin the previous semester and had passed the makeup exam largely because of John's coaching (P. Monro 39). In addition, after eight years of courtship Dottie was eager to set a date for their wedding. Writing to him in July, she reminded him of this bit of unfinished business: "I hope we *can* be married within the year, darling. It would mean so much to me" (31 July 1935, DP).

Continuing at the News Office offered some professional benefits as well. Once it became clear that he was staying on, Monro became a photographer for the *Harvard Alumni Bulletin,* giving him the chance to pursue a hobby he had already become interested in. He also worked as Harvard correspondent for the *Boston Evening Transcript* and saw his copy in print on a regular basis ("News Office"). In 1936 Harvard's tercentenary year provided almost limitless opportunities to write about the university's past and present, and every June he wrote a lengthy "Year at Harvard" review as well as a separate story on each event connected to commencement.

It is easy to see why Monro later characterized his years at the News Office as the time that he spent "getting to feel like a writer" (Brelis, "Ex-Student Monro"). There was no denying, however, that much of the work was tedious. Releases about guest speakers and interviews were almost 100 percent quotations, although Monro took even these pedestrian assignments seriously, obtaining copies of the lectures as well as attending and taking notes. He relieved the monotony by creating snappy leads to introduce arcane subjects. Reporting on the donation of a mollusk collection to the Museum of Comparative Zoology, he began: "The influence of Harvard's name moves often in a curious fashion over the globe. It crops up in unexpected places, and among strange peoples. But rarely, one ventures to guess, has it moved more curiously or more effectively than it has on a tiny three-quarter-jungle island in the Philippines" (News Release).

No wonder he continued to look longingly at big city newspapers, particularly after hearing from friends who were working in far-flung places. Tom O'Connor, who had presided as president over the *Journal*'s final days, was rapidly turning into a brilliant young journalist, at least according to his self-promoting letters. By 1935 he had moved to Los Angeles—borrowing money from Monro to get there—and was a reporter for the *Post-Record.* He boasted that he had demanded a raise, doubled his salary, and quickly become the paper's golden boy: "I get every good story that comes in, get sent on all the big jobs, get bragged about by the managing editor to the publisher. . . . I'm getting enough by-lines so when I meet reporters from other papers they mention stories I have written. . . . There's a hell of a lot of satisfaction in it" (letter, 7 Oct. 1935, DP).

WELL-KNOWN, HIGHLY REGARDED, SORELY MISSED

Monro's world was upended by his father's death, at home, on 12 May 1936. Claxton was barely fifty-one years old, but he had been plagued with illness at least as early as the fall of 1930. Exploratory surgery in the winter of 1935–36 revealed that he had incurable liver cancer, so he returned home, dosed himself with morphine, and waited for the inevitable. For the final months of his life he was a shadow of his strong, energetic former self. Ever the faithful son of Harvard, he contributed to his thirtieth-anniversary class report. Without mentioning his illness, he stated with quiet pride that his position as chief chemist left him "with time and energy for little else, in common with most of the world in these hectic days" (*Class of 1906: 30th* 80–81). By the time the report appeared, he was gone.

The official cause of death was carcinoma of the liver (Death Register), but Claxton Jr. firmly believed that his father had contracted cirrhosis from exposure to the dye chemicals he was so expert at manipulating (P. Monro 6). Church and civic commitments, financial worries, frequent transfers and domestic relocations, exposure to dangerous materials, incessant travel from one mill to another, long hours, an irregular schedule, delinquent medical and dental care, the zealous pursuit of overtime—these factors may not have killed him, but they surely wore him down and made him susceptible to illness. It was a painful early lesson for Monro on the toll that insufficient funds could take, and it is understandable that he spent one of the most productive periods of his career developing procedures for dispensing financial assistance where it was most badly needed.

Inevitably, Claxton's death overshadowed what would otherwise have been two joyous events. First, in June Claxton Jr. graduated from MIT with a degree in business and engineering administration. Diploma in hand, he took a job in the market research division of J. Walter Thompson Advertising Agency and packed his bags for New York (Mary MacGregor, e-mail, 1 Apr. 2006).

Then, on 21 July, John and Dottie were married in a quiet ceremony at the Foster home ("Monro-Foster"). In their wedding photo Dottie, wearing a white satin gown and bridal veil, stands very close to John, looking up—way up—at him while he peers fondly down at her. After a honeymoon in New York City, Dottie went to South Freeport for the remainder of the summer, and John returned to work in Cambridge. In the fall they moved into their first home together, an apartment at 1648 Massachusetts Avenue (lease, 1 Sept. 1936, DP), a few minutes' walk from Harvard Square and the News Office.

Once they were settled, they sent a copy of their wedding photo to Hezekiah, who had moved in with his daughter Edith when Claxton died. His reply to the photo was characteristic, lacing gratitude with criticism and counseling moderation even in marital bliss: "You gave me a very sweet surprise by the lovely gift of yourselves in the photograph of the dear 'Bride and Groom' and I want to thank you. Because I had begun to wonder if ever I was to be so favored—They are fine and so 'true to life'—I venture to congratulate you! . . . May the New Year bring you all reasonable but unspeakable joys that life can bring you" (28 Dec. 1936, DP).

Monro had been right in assuming that Sutton's academic woes were not over. His grades, which arrived shortly after Claxton's death, included failures in English, history, and French, and Phillips did not permit students to make up three failing grades. Frances responded to the first crisis of her widowhood by renting out the family home in Andover, moving to the same Cambridge apartment building John and Dottie were living in, and enrolling Sutton at Cambridge High and Latin, whose students frequently won scholarships to Harvard or MIT. Her strategy succeeded, and although Sutton had to repeat his junior year, he graduated in June 1938 and was accepted at MIT. Soon after Sutton's graduation, Dottie discovered she was pregnant, and Ann Monro was born on 21 January 1939.

In New York Claxton's career in advertising was meeting with heavy competition from an unexpected source. One evening he went to a prayer service at Calvary Episcopal Church and was surprised and moved when members of the congregation took turns telling stories about God's presence in their lives, a practice known as lay witnessing. It was at the heart of the Oxford Movement, a six-step program for salvation that originated in England and that Calvary's pastor, Sam Schumacher, strongly believed in (P. Monro 37–38).[2] At Calvary Claxton found not only a religious vocation but his future wife. When he met Victoria "Vicki" Booth Demarest, she was trailing in the wake of her mother— also named Victoria—a beautiful and charismatic evangelical preacher who had come to Schumacher's service to check out the competition. Claxton was greeting guests at Calvary's door and persuaded Vicki to return for the young adults group he was leading that evening (Vicki Monro, telephone interview, 8 Aug. 2005). Soon afterward they began courting.

Sutton had also found a soul mate after biking out one weekend to Northampton with a friend who was dating a Smith student. Sue Carlton, another Smith student, had recently lost her mother and could empathize with Sutton's mourning over his father's death. Soon Sutton was returning to Smith on a regular basis, and Sue was visiting him in Cambridge and Andover (P. Monro 43).

EXPANDED RESPONSIBILITIES

In 1938 Monro became editor of Harvard's weekly *Summer School News,* handling all aspects of its production for a single payment of one hundred dollars (Mather). Now a seasoned journalist, he also began to exercise more initiative, proposing articles on subjects he deemed important. He was especially supportive of an affordable housing campaign being promoted by the Cambridge branch of Labor's Non-Partisan League. A $4.5 million federal project, which promised low-rent housing for six hundred families and five hundred jobs during the two-year construction period, had been proposed by federal and city housing authorities and approved by the city council but was languishing on Mayor John W. Lyons's desk. Monro spent hours attending meetings then writing and placing articles in the *Christian Science Monitor* (4 May 1939), the *Cambridge Tribune* (5 May 1939), and the *Boston Sunday Advertiser* (7 June 1939). Setting journalistic objectivity aside, he contributed speeches, position papers, and a housing bulletin to the campaign (DP).[3]

Another subject that he pursued on his own initiative was Camp William James, a work-service farm that had recently been created at a former Civilian Conservation Corps (CCC) camp in Sharon, Vermont. The founders, led by Dartmouth professor Eugen Rosenstock-Huessy, hoped that the camp would become the prototype for a permanent national service program to replace the emergency measure CCC (Preiss xi). An obvious precursor of the Peace Corps, the camp was staffed by recent Princeton and Harvard graduates who had temporarily chosen rustic living over prestigious jobs or graduate school, and it was named after William James, in honor of his assertion that young people in modern society required an experience that was "the moral equivalent of war." Monro's front-page story in the 23 November 1939 *Boston Transcript* was an impressive scoop: the camp received little additional publicity until 29 December, when an article about it appeared in the *New York Herald Tribune.*

On 31 October 1941 Dottie's father was covering the New England bird dog championships for *American Field* when he suffered a heart attack and died on the spot ("W. H. Foster"). Foster was only fifty-five and died in mid-stride. He had just begun to read the galley proofs for *New England Grouse Shooting*, a book-length study he had been writing and illustrating for years. Monro, who had grown fond of Foster during their car trips to Maine, was struck by the suddenness of his death and its subliminal warning that important work should not be delayed.

MONRO AND THE GALLOPING GHOST

Foster's death was made even more traumatic by the United States's impending entry into the war, which put at risk the simple pleasures his art celebrated. John and Dottie's situation was a case in point. John had already left the News Office to join the navy, and Dottie, four months pregnant, faced the possibility that he would be overseas when their second child arrived. Nonetheless, Monro's eagerness to enlist in the navy was predictable, given the valiant military record of the Clan Munro, the many Monro seamen strewn across the generations, General Eben Sutton's pride in his military service, and the quasi-military nature of Camp Abnaki.

Unfortunately, Monro's first posting was something of an anticlimax. He was assigned to Boston's First Naval District Office of Public Relations, where he turned out press releases that felt more like his old job than a valiant contribution to the war effort. When the Japanese attacked Pearl Harbor on 7 December 1941, the entire office staff immediately requested sea duty. Unimpressed by this wave of patriotism, the district admiral refused to dismantle the entire office and let only half the staff leave (Brelis, "Ex-Student"). Monro fell into what he considered the lucky half and was sent to Northwestern for two months of training.

The trip to Chicago was the first of many for Monro. He loved the city, especially the jazz clubs and the black neighborhoods, both of which he explored during his free time. At the end of his training program he returned home, and for months the only excitement that came his way was an occasional out-of-town assignment. Even after he was notified of his posting, he remained landlocked, impatiently awaiting orders to report for duty. One positive outcome of the navy's foot-dragging was that he was home for the birth of Janet on April Fools' Day 1942. By this time even domestic events had taken on a military tinge: the birth announcement was a cartoon of a smiling infant sitting bolt upright in a baby carriage that flew a "Big E" pennant, for the USS *Enterprise,* to which Monro had been assigned. The message read, "Lt. and Mrs. John Monro USNR announce the launching of Janet Monro April 1, 1942" (DP).

Monro was still cooling his heels when Sutton graduated from MIT on 27 April, at the end of a semester abbreviated by the war. His grades had been so marginal that for a while his graduation was in doubt, but his then-unique major in statistics and industrial engineering made him a valuable wartime property, so a faculty committee recommended that he receive his diploma on condition that he enlist and put his expertise to immediate use (P. Monro 43). He joined the navy, and in July he and Sue Carlton were married in Scarborough, New York, near the Carlton family home (Munroe 390).

Controlling Damage aboard the Big E

Finally, in August 1942 Monro was ordered to report for duty as damage control officer aboard the twenty thousand–ton aircraft carrier the USS *Enterprise* (Navy Order, DP). The ship, dubbed the "Big E" after the navy's "Excellence in Efficiency" award, had escaped destruction at Pearl Harbor only because of a run-in with bad weather. The carrier had been delivering fighter planes to Wake Island and was due back in port on 6 December, but rough waters postponed its arrival by a day (Ewing 15–16). By the time Monro reported aboard, the *Enterprise* was the only carrier still operating in the Pacific, the others having been either seriously damaged or sunk.

Monro's title as damage control officer put him in charge of firemen, shipfitters, machinists, and carpenters, among others. The operations manual gave no indication of the high drama that damage control involved, saying only that it embraced "the entire system of maintaining watertight integrity, controlling stability, repairing damage, providing for defense against gas, and caring for injured personnel." The ship's air officer, Monro D. Blitch, stripped away the verbiage, explaining that he and the damage control officer shared responsibility for the flight deck. When things were going smoothly, Blitch was in charge, but "if during an attack bombs or enemy planes damage or clutter up the flight deck, the responsibility for restoration to normal operating conditions reverts to the [damage control officer]" ("Planes").

Soon after Monro's arrival, he saw for himself just how inadequate the official description was in a real-life situation. In late October 1942 a Japanese attack near Santa Cruz inflicted heavy damage on the *Enterprise,* leaving it exposed in enemy waters. Because some damage control crew had been wounded or killed, additional manpower was needed to conduct low-profile repairs quickly. When the ship anchored at Santa Cruz, a group of Seabees (Construction Batallions), who had been trained to build air bases, landing strips, and roads, was pressed into service. They pitched in, clearing debris, mending holes, and pumping out water, but the repairs were not nearly finished by 11 November, when the carrier was scheduled to head for Guadalcanal. Twenty Seabees agreed to go along and continue the repairs. Once the fighting began, they took up battle positions on deck. Monro described the peril of the situation: "We rigged temporary patches below the waterline, and strengthening these patches was hazardous work. Even if no enemy planes were around, we were in submarine waters and [the Seabees] were working at or below the waterline by the hull. . . . They worked hard, very hard. We were damn glad to have them" ("Andover Man").

The tense, limbo-like atmosphere of the damage control crew during an attack was captured by Commander William Stafford in *The Big E: The Story of the USS Enterprise:* "In action there is nothing for a damage controlman to do until the ship has been hit. Spread out in small subdivisions of repair parties throughout the ship, surrounded by their equipment, blind, unoccupied, totally dependent on the good judgment of the captain and the competence of fighter pilots and gun crews, they can only wait" (141).

There was a lot of damage to control on the carrier: in all, the ship participated in forty-five offensive engagements, and after absorbing its first enemy bomb attack off the Solomon Islands in August 1942, it was attacked fifteen times. To the crew it seemed as though the Japanese pursued the Big E with special zeal, on the lookout for its blocky island silhouette, which distinguished it from the other ships in the fleet (Al Santisi, personal interview, 7 Apr. 2005). After the Japanese claimed to have sunk it no less than six times, the American press dubbed the ship the "Galloping Ghost" ("Big E Carrier").

Dud bombs, which were common on both sides, could also cause serious damage, such as the one that landed on the deck in March 1945, its phosphorus head bursting into flames when it hit the iron railing before it could be rolled over the side (Santisi, interview). Friendly fire was another danger: a few days after the dud bomb, four kamikaze planes diving the *Enterprise* were shot down, but in the melee "an antiaircraft shell from a nearby ship exploded over the deck of the Big E, spreading shrapnel and causing serious fires on the deck" ("USS *Enterprise:* Galloping" 16).

Even in the absence of enemy or friendly fire, a carrier was a dangerous place to be. Takeoffs and landings were particularly perilous times on deck. Shipfitter Frank Albert described the precision required for successful takeoff: "Timing had to be perfect. The bow had to raise as the plane left the ship or the aircraft would plunge into the sea. Every once in a while one of our [bombers] crashed in the ocean with their heavy bomb load" (98).

Timing was even trickier during landings, because only thirty seconds separated one plane from another. Albert recalled some of the ways that landings could go wrong: "Many planes came in low on fuel, shot up, no hydraulic system, wounded pilots or gunners. . . . When a plane crashed, which was quite often, the pilot was removed with the help of the deck hands and the plane was pushed into the sea. . . . If a plane landed where the pilot would forget to cut off the safety of his guns after a dog fight, then the guns would discharge spraying shells across the flight deck as the plane jolted when the tail hook caught in the resting gear" (99). Landings became more difficult after December 1944, when the Big E became the navy's first night carrier and its pilots began using radar. Planes returning from night flights had to land in the dark, visually guided only by the dim running lights along the runway. The risk was deemed worthwhile because the night strikes were extremely successful: during the first few flights the Japanese mistook enemy planes for their own and actually turned on their lights to facilitate landing ("Planes").

Another technological breakthrough, less glamorous than radar but essential to damage control, was a new type of fire-retardant chemical foam, far superior to water for extinguishing fires caused by bombs and explosions and less likely to jam than the product made by the ship's foam generators. The only catch was that nobody knew exactly how to use it. To demystify the foam for himself and his men, Monro turned a three-day stop in Hawaii into an intensive fire-fighting clinic. Using the time-honored technique of trial and error, the crew figured out the most efficient way to combine the contents of the five-gallon black-and-yellow cans with water, then practiced extinguishing fires with the foam until they could do it in their sleep (Santisi, interview; Dreyer, "Eulogy," South Freeport). "We made a lot of mistakes with the foam because it was new, but we got to where we could take a can of powder and fill a compartment with foam in a minute," recalls shipfitter Bob Terreberry (telephone interview, 27 Apr. 2005).

Photographs of the *Enterprise* engaged in battle or in the immediate aftermath show the decks awash in foam. It was pivotal in containing the fire that broke out during a March 1945 battle off the coast of Japan, as Stafford describes: "Below in Central Station Monro, the Big E's damage control officer, coolly went about his business. He knew where every fire, every hole, every casualty was, and how it was, nearly as soon as it happened. And he knew what to do. He ordered more foam brought to the flight deck to blanket and smother the flaming fuel, foam that would not have been available if he had not been foresighted enough to 'requisition' at midnight several times his quota the last time in Pearl [Harbor]. . . . He had the hot magazines sprinkled, the overheating bomb elevator filled with foam. He ordered the burning planes on deck dragged away and apart, and attacked separately with fog and foam" (449).

Once he returned to civilian life, Monro loved to tell the story behind the "midnight requisition." When the foam was being distributed, he wangled a double ration, possibly by means of a well-placed gift of a bottle of liquor. During the three-day battle all of the foam, including the unauthorized part, was needed to extinguish the fires. In the aftermath Admiral William F. Halsey sent a message from the flagship complimenting Monro and asking how many barrels of foam he had used. "Forty barrels," Monro clicked back. "But you were only allowed twenty," Hasley protested. "Yes, sir," Monro clicked back—and promptly signed off, ending the exchange (Michael Shinagel, personal interview, 26 Oct. 2004).

As the requisition incident proves, Monro took a commonsense approach to emergencies in which by-the-book procedures simply would not work. In April 1945, for instance, a kamikaze plane hit the *Enterprise* at the waterline on the port side. Shipfitter Norman L. Zafft examined the huge gash and found that the tanks had been seriously ruptured and were exposed to the elements. The official procedure required returning to dry dock for repairs, a time-consuming move that would leave the wounded ship vulnerable to further damage or attack. His boss had a better idea, Zafft recalls: "Monro gave orders to move equipment and ships stores to . . . the starboard side of the ship. After this was accomplished, he ordered the quarterdeck officer to announce, 'All hands move to the starboard side of the ship.'" All members did and the ship listed to the starboard. The hole in the side of the ship was exposed and the repair ship came along and made repairs. Thus saving a trip back to dry dock in Pearl Harbor or the States" (letter, 3 Mar. 2005).

Monro and his men figured prominently in the Big E's final engagement, on 14 May 1945. A kamikaze pilot flew his plane straight down the ship's forward elevator shaft, where it exploded, hurling the shaft more than four hundred feet in the air and igniting a fierce fire that penetrated five layers below the flight deck. The damage control crew, fourteen men short because of casualties, put out the fire in only seventeen minutes (Stafford 496). It was the following day before the bodies of the men trapped in battle stations below decks could be retrieved (Santisi, interview). The crippled carrier headed to Bremerton, Washington, for repairs, and it was still in dry dock in August, when Hiroshima and Nagasaki were bombed. On 2 September Japan officially surrendered, and the war was over.

Once the ship reached the West Coast, the crew was given a month's leave, and Dottie and the girls took the train out so that they could all travel home together. As they changed trains in Chicago, the ticket agent told Monro, who was wearing his uniform, that all the sleeping compartments were full. Monro went to the men's room and pinned on all his medals, then returned to the ticket booth, where the agent miraculously discovered that sleeping berths were available for the entire family (Dreyer, e-mail, 1 June 2005). At the time Monro had a Combat Action Ribbon, Presidential Unit Citation, Navy Unit Commendation, American Campaign Ribbon and CV-6 Medal, Asiatic Pacific Ribbon with seventeen battle stars, WWII Victory Ribbon and Medal, Philippine Presidential Unit Citation Badge, and Philippine Liberation Ribbon with star (Olson).

Monro was back on board when the *Enterprise,* minus its planes and aircrew, joined the Victory Fleet on its ten thousand–mile trip through the Panama Canal, up the East Coast, and into New York Harbor for the first Navy Day since the beginning of the war. Right behind the USS *Missouri,* on which the treaty with Japan had recently been signed, the Big E led the seven-mile procession of ships. The 578-foot "Homeward Bound" pennant streaming from its mast measured the longevity of the carrier's uninterrupted service, one foot for each day at sea ("Big E Docks").

After all the hoopla, the *Enterprise* was refitted for troop transport and joined the Magic Carpet program, bringing GI's home from Europe. Even though he was one of the few married crew members, Monro volunteered for the program and was made navy transport officer.

Monro's damage control expertise came in handy during a December crossing, when the *Enterprise* was headed for New York with five thousand American soldiers eager to reach home for the holidays. A late-season hurricane suddenly blew up, badly battering the ship. Flooding pushed the carrier's bow hazardously low, and the hull seams, repaired after the final kamikaze attack, burst open. Realizing that it was essential to alleviate the stress and raise the bow level immediately, Monro advised the captain to order the ship turned around so that its stern faced the waves. Then he sent shipfitters, with safety lines attached, onto the forecastle to weld steel plates over the compromised seams: a time-consuming and hazardous procedure because only a few beads could be welded into place each time the plates briefly rose above the waterline. As the ship approached Staten Island Pier on Christmas Eve, the swells were still so high that even with tugboats running interference and both its huge anchors released, it narrowly missed hitting the pier straight on (Banks 10).

The Magic Carpet program concluded in the spring of 1946, its mission accomplished. On 15 June Monro was given two months' leave then released from active duty with the rank of lieutenant commander (Navy Release, DP). To the medals he had shown the railroad agent in Chicago, he now added a Bronze Star, presented to him by Halsey in a ceremony on board the *Enterprise* while it was docked at Boston Navy Shipyard on 6 November.

A Way of Teaching

More impressive in their own way than Monro's medals and awards were the tributes of his men. Bob Terreberry, a seventeen-year-old dropout when he enlisted, is certain that he could never have become a first-class fitter without Monro's guidance. "J. U. was one of the greatest people aboard ship," Terreberry said, using a nickname that seems to have been unique to the *Enterprise* crew. "There wasn't a valve he didn't know. He was always walking around the ship, finding short cuts, seeing what was wrong, seeing how we could fix it." On his rounds Monro thought up practical but effective fire-prevention techniques; he had his men run foxtails along the tops of all the pipes and wires, getting rid of dust and lint that would accelerate the spread of a fire (telephone interview).

Terreberry considered Monro the very best kind of teacher and mentor. "We knew he was from a university, but he was quiet about it. He was an educator; he had a way of teaching. We went to school five days a week." Monro showed him some shortcuts along the catwalks underneath the flight deck as well as an inconspicuous hatch that went directly into the ammunition locker. When the ship was hit in March 1945 and the ammunition was in danger of exploding, Terreberry used the access to get to the gun mount and turn the sprinkler system on.

To keep his crew's skills honed after the initial firefighting clinic in Hawaii, Monro set up drills and simulations of battle damage, fires, collisions, and abandon-ship conditions. Sometimes he set off smoke bombs to make the simulations more realistic, and he insisted that the men know how to get in and out of every compartment on the ship. Drills below decks were conducted in darkness so that the men would know how to move toward safety when the lights went off during an attack (Santisi, interview).

Like a good teacher, Monro sometimes gave pop quizzes. One of his favorite tricks was to stroll the decks during the midnight shift and brake, by a half-turn, one of the many risers the man on duty was supposed to check regularly. Because the adjustment was not visible to the naked eye, Monro would quickly discover who was being sloppy. "But he would correct you in a nice way; he would never chew you out," Terreberry recalls.

Al Santisi also remembers Monro walking the ship at night, talking to the men on duty and helping them stay awake: "He gave 24 hours a day to his job; he knew damage control inside and out." Nobody could figure out when he slept, and he gave the impression of constantly being in motion (interview). Always slender, he had become downright gaunt by the time the war was over, weighing only 145 pounds (Dreyer, interview, 3 Aug. 2005).[4]

Yeoman W. W. "Bill" Norberg noted Monro's dedication, describing him as "one of the few people I've ever known who'd throw self completely into the task at hand, day by day, and never seek recognition." Such dedication left little time for small pleasures, as Norberg observed when he delivered documents to Monro's office and noticed that his Christmas presents remained unwrapped. "Year by year the stack grew. Why? There was work to do; frivolities were for after the war," Norberg explained (letter, 24 May 2005).

Many of Monro's shipmates were impressed by the calm way he went about his highly stressful job. In Stafford's account of the April 1945 kamikaze attack, he described Monro's almost preternatural composure: "Lean, dark, Monro, sitting like a beatle-browed spider at the center of his communication network at Central Station, initiated the necessary repairs with the calm precision of a digital computer" (486).

One development on the *Enterprise* foreshadowed Monro's deep commitment to civil rights. On 20 May 1944, nine days after he became secretary of the navy, James Forrestal wrote to president Franklin D. Roosevelt, saying that if the navy was to become truly integrated, sea duty had to be made more accessible to black sailors, most of whom had been serving on shore duty since general service ranks were opened to them in 1942. To that end he identified twenty-five large ships, including the Big E, and directed them to make sure their crew was at least 10 percent black (Goodwin 523). The next batch of crew members to come on board included a black carpenter, and Monro was ordered to make sure the carpenter bunked with the white sailors. Realizing that ordering his men to accept their new shipmate would be futile, he explained the situation to the carpenter and suggested that he bunk in the carpenter's shop for now and claim he was doing so to keep an eye on his equipment. The senior officers had taken to playing cards in the shop, but Monro approached them about the new arrangement, and they agreed to end the card game when the carpenter wanted to turn in. Card players and carpenter coexisted until he distinguished himself in a particularly danger-ous firefight and the white sailors asked him to bunk with them (Wilkinson 123).[5]

THE HOME FRONT

Monro's military service kept him away from home for almost four years—precious years during which his daughters were growing and changing. In his absence Dottie talked to the girls about him and kept a scrapbook of the *Enter-prise*'s exploits. Janet recalls that they said good morning and good night to his picture every day and that during car trips they sang the yearning ballads of the day, with their wartime subtexts: "I'll Be Seeing You," "Now Is the Hour," and "There's a Long, Long Trail A-Winding" (Phil and Janet Dreyer, personal inter-view, 9 Feb. 2005).

The activities and whereabouts of troops and ships were carefully guarded se-crets, so friends and relatives of servicemen had to learn to live with uncertainty. Monro was even more out of touch than most servicemen because the *Enterprise* returned to the mainland only once before it came home for good. When the ship docked at Bremerton, Washington, in July 1943 for a major overhaul, most of the men left for home on thirty-day leave, but Monro stayed put, while Dottie and the girls took the long cross-country train trip to spend his leave with him (interview).

In addition to her anxiety about John's safety, Dottie struggled to coexist with her forceful mother-in-law, into whose home she and the girls had moved when it became clear that the war was not going to end quickly. Wartime or no, Frances expected John to write letters to her, and she would gloat loudly over hers on the days that Dottie did not receive one. To make matters worse, the four-bedroom house on Chestnut Street was bursting at the seams: for a time Frances's mother also lived there, and in the early summer of 1945 Sutton's wife, Sue, moved in with their baby son, Peter. When Monro signed up for the Magic Carpet program, instead of returning to her mother-in-law's Dottie moved in with her sister, Helen, and her husband, James Scobie, who were now living just down the street.

When he finally got home, in the summer of 1946, Monro found that many changes had occurred in his absence. In late 1943 his brother Claxton, who was in the seminary when the United States entered the war, had graduated then married Vicki Booth Demarest ten days later. They were living in Nyack, New York, where Claxton was rector of Grace Episcopal Church. John liked Vicki at once and told Claxton on more than one occasion that she was the best thing that had ever happened to him.

After attending Officers' Training School in Newport, Rhode Island, Sutton had applied his engineering skills to improving the performance of Allied torpedoes, whose erratic behavior had been a serious concern aboard the *Enterprise* and other potential victims of friendly fire (P. Monro 43). Sue and Sutton now had two sons and were living in Orono, Maine, while Sutton studied for a master's degree in mathematics at the University of Maine (40).

THE AFTERMATH OF THE WAR

Monro's time aboard the *Enterprise* had a permanent impact on him, and echoes of his years at sea sounded throughout his life. He suffered partial hearing loss as a result of the numerous bombings and explosions, and as he aged, he became increasingly deaf. It was this difficulty that eventually forced him to discontinue classroom teaching.[6]

He also paid a price for the calm facade that had so impressed his shipmates. In South Freeport, where most leisure-time activity took place near, in, or on the water, he showed no interest in boating, saying that he had had his fill of it in the navy (Dreyer, interview, 3 Aug. 2005). He was selective about the war stories he told, focusing on funny or human interest episodes rather than pain or suffering. He kept his medals in a drawer and joked that he had won the Bronze Star not for an act of courage but for "turning off the water so the ship wouldn't sink," an allusion to the repair strategy he had worked out after the April 1945 kamikaze attack (Dreyer, e-mail, 1 June 2005). But one day as he was looking at a photo of the *Enterprise* under attack, he said softly, "Most of the guys in this photo didn't make it" (Dreyer, interview).

The trauma at the heart of damage control duty came back to haunt Monro in 1960, during ceremonies aboard the recently christened USS *Enterprise* CVN-

65, the navy's first nuclear-powered aircraft carrier. When he got home from the event, he seemed troubled, and eventually he told Dottie what had happened. During the ceremonies he had been on the bridge observing a series of flight operations, when suddenly a steam catapult misfired, sending it into the water and automatically triggering a "Man Overboard" drill, complete with ear-splitting claxons and alarms. For Monro it was like tumbling, via a horrifying time warp, back to the *Enterprise* during a life-or-death crisis, and it was days before he could get a good night's sleep (Dreyer, interview).

But if it sometimes haunted him, his military service was also a source of great pride. In spite of the death and destruction he had witnessed, he believed that there had been a noble side to the war and that fallen soldiers were heroes. This belief animated his condolence letter to the mother of Larry Wyffels, a young carpenter who had shown him the ropes when he first came aboard and who had been killed shortly afterward in the Battle of Santa Cruz. Monro wrote: "Of all the officers and men I know, he was perhaps the most determined of all to fight this war hard for the things he believed in, for freedom and decency. . . . In his daily life he showed that a man can be brave and generous and honest in a world turned hard with war" (15 Jan. 1943, DP).

Monro even considered a career in the military at one point, applying to the navy for permission to begin graduate studies to that end. His request was denied, probably because he was not a "ring-twister"—a graduate of Annapolis (Brelis, "Monro Loaned"). Undeterred, he diligently cultivated his navy affiliations, becoming a reserve officer on 1 June 1949 and being awarded the rank of captain in 1953. For several years he worked with Edward P. Stafford on a history of the *Enterprise,* but at some point he turned his materials over to Stafford, who brought the project to completion with the 1962 publication of *The Big E: The Story of the USS* Enterprise. In the book Stafford thanked Monro for devoting "scores of hours of his own limited spare time to collecting and indexing the books, papers and pictures which provided the majority of the material" on which the book was based (484).

Monro also supported efforts to preserve the Big E itself. In the immediate aftermath of the war it seemed inconceivable that the vessel would not be saved. Secretary of the Navy James Forrestall described it as "the one ship that most nearly symbolizes and carries with it the history of the Navy in World War II," and President Truman pledged to preserve it as "a visible symbol of American valor and tenacity in war" ("Truman Saves"). But memories are short, and postwar finances were tight. When the Magic Carpet program ended, the Big E was mothballed at the Naval Supply Depot in Bayonne, New Jersey, and after several failed attempts to fund its preservation, it was sold for $561,000, towed to a ship-yard in Kearney, New Jersey, and expertly but unceremoniously scrapped in 1958 (Ewing 100–107).[7]

Monro kept one souvenir of the war: "a round piece of aluminum about eight inches in diameter, three inches thick with several very serious gouges out of it . . . about as nondescript and worthless a piece of metal as you could imagine." In spite of its unprepossessing appearance, it held pride of place on his desk and was among his personal effects when he died. It was a piece of the propeller cowling from the kamikaze plane that had put the *Enterprise* out of action for good (Dreyer, "Eulogy," Cambridge).

Shortly after his return, Monro confided to Frederick Noss, his pastor at An-dover's South Congregational Church, that he had not expected to survive the war and that he now believed he owed it to his fallen crewmen to make a differ-ence with the life that had been spared (Augusta Noss Howe, personal interview, 23 Sept. 2005). The scarred metal disk was a physical reminder of that moral imperative, and in the years to come Monro repeatedly explained his decisions by stating, "I wanted to make a difference" or "I wanted to be of use." It was es-pecially apt, therefore, that his next career move was in the service of veterans who, like him, had made it home from the war.

4

ADMINISTRATOR MONRO
1946-1958

Monro spent the first few months of civilian life in South Freeport with Dottie and the girls, repainting the cottage, stoking the woodburning stove for heat, and working sporadically on what he jokingly called "the great American novel about the war." The project must have taken some courage, given Bernard DeVoto's savaging of his earlier attempts at fiction (Brelis, "Monro Loaned"). But he soon realized that the novel was seriously stalled—a disappointment that strengthened his resolve to become a real newspaperman at last.

Having tentatively accepted a position with the New York newspaper *PM*, he made a fateful stop at Harvard to say good-bye to friends, colleagues, and coworkers. Chester "Ace" Hanford, the dean who had urged him to withdraw from Harvard at the height of the *Crimson/Journal* competition, suggested that he check out the recently created Veterans Bureau, where director Wilbur J. "Bill" Bender '27 was helping veterans take advantage of the GI Bill.

Bender offered Monro the position of assistant counselor, and in spite of the tempting job awaiting him in New York, Monro said yes, recognizing the position as a perfect opportunity to honor his fallen shipmates (Brelis, "Ex-Student"). What many saw as a bureaucratic tangle of government and military red tape, he viewed as a grand adventure and a noble experiment. The four thousand veterans enrolled at Harvard College in the fall of 1946—75 percent of the undergraduate student body—comprised a group he thoroughly admired. "Never in Harvard history have we had so mature, so hardworking, and so effective a student body," he later said of that class ("Southeastern Massachusetts Institute Speech").

Monro served as assistant counselor for less than a year; in June 1947 Bender replaced Hanford as dean of the college, and Monro replaced Bender as counselor for veterans (McCabe). He downplayed his accomplishments at the bureau, saying that Bender "had the office beautifully organized by the time he left. You might say I presided over the denouement of the veteran's program at Harvard" (Brelis, "Monro Loaned"). But in fact Monro's tenure was far more than a holding action. Under his leadership a veterans' pediatric service was created, offering free emergency treatment, exams, immunization, diagnosis, hospitalization, and medication to veteran students' children. Characteristically, he took a hands-on approach, supervising construction of the clinic in a former barroom and showing up at the end of his office day to wield a hammer and saw ("Pediatric"). He claimed to be saving the university money by doing the work himself, but the truth of the matter was that he loved being in the thick of things. When World War II benefits expired in 1956, he told a *Time Magazine* reporter that the veterans had "knocked out the playboy era of American colleges. They set a pace that is still with us—and it is here to stay" ("Education: End of an Era").

CHICAGO RECRUITMENT

It may have been the diversity the veterans were adding to Harvard; it may have been the satisfying memory of gradually integrating the black carpenter into his damage control crew or the postwar yearbook in which he counted only two black members among Harvard's graduating seniors (Wilkinson 123). But whatever the reason or constellation of reasons, in 1948 Monro took the first step in his commitment to black education, joining a few other administrators in an effort to bring more black students to Harvard. For the next three years, while he was still running the Veterans Bureau, he traveled frequently to Chicago, whose diversity, bustle, and lively jazz scene he had grown to love during his training at Northwestern. Explaining his reasons for targeting Chicago, he said, "I liked the city, and it had a large Negro population which sent almost no students our way" ("Grand Lodge").

He soon learned that sheer enthusiasm went only so far in recruiting minority students: in three years his efforts yielded only one black student who applied and was admitted to Harvard. Early on the principal of an all-black high school had predicted his failure. Monro described the encounter: "This determined, forceful and experienced woman backed me quickly into a corner, told me she had never known a Negro to go east to Harvard without being hurt and spoiled, doubted I would find any candidates, and urged that I please not arouse any false hopes in her school. She turned out to be discouragingly right" ("Grand Lodge").

On the bright side, in Chicago he encountered the organization that he came to consider the best vehicle for achieving meaningful educational equality. The National Scholarship Service and Fund for Negro Students (NSSFNS), which was founded the same year Monro began recruiting, identified promising black students through the National Merit Scholarship exam, helped them apply to colleges where they stood a chance of succeeding, and saw that they got financial support, often making up the shortfall between what they needed and what the college offered. While Harvard's campaign foundered, the NSSFNS was so successful that it began working in segregated southern high schools, placing six hundred black students in interracial colleges in a single year. Monro soon joined the organization, serving on the board of directors and the awards committee ("Grand Lodge").

When Monro was made assistant to Provost Paul H. Buck in 1949, he immediately began to badger his new boss for more aggressive recruitment of black students. He dismissed his own scattershot efforts in Chicago as useless: "[We] get only chance [black] applicants . . . not very many or very good ones. On our part, we have not bothered to approach the Negro populations for good men; and they, of course, are largely unaware of our interest or the big opportunity." Monro recommended that Harvard work with black leaders in major metropolitan areas to identify promising high school seniors and offer them financial assistance; he proposed a goal of ten black students recruited to each freshman class (Ferede 11). In 1953 he finally persuaded Harvard to collaborate with the NSSFNS. Black enrollment figures began to pick up, and by the late 1950s more than half the college's black applicants were reporting that they had worked through the scholarship service (Karabel 400).

One of Monro's stops in Chicago was the Francis W. Parker School, which became a permanent source of inspiration for him. The tiny progressive school sent many of its graduates to the Ivy Leagues, due in large part to principal Herbert W. Smith, a 1912 Harvard alumnus who diligently cultivated his old school ties. Parker was a school after Monro's heart. It sought to be egalitarian, keeping the identity of scholarship students confidential to prevent embarrassment, and requiring the female students to wear uniforms to prevent their clothing from becoming class markers (Richard Freeman, telephone interview, 12 Dec. 2005). Its founder and namesake, Francis W. Parker, valued education as a seedbed for democracy and tolerance, and upon his death John Dewey said Parker's influence on modern education was equaled only by that of Horace Mann (Monro, "Francis W. Parker 75th Anniversary").

Parker students were encouraged to think for themselves, and their occasional flaunting of rules and conventions amused Monro, who so frequently sidestepped, ignored, or creatively interpreted regulations himself. He claimed that during his first visit to Parker, four seniors called on him at the tony University Club, still wearing the paint-streaked dungarees in which they had been working on the school's Christmas Toy Shop.[1]

IT DEPENDS ON WHAT YOU MEAN BY "DIVERSITY"

Thanks in large part to schools like Parker, Monro could claim that his recruitment efforts in Chicago were making Harvard geographically diverse, even if racial diversity was proving elusive. A popular academic trend in the 1930s, geographic diversification had been warmly embraced by Harvard president James B. Conant, who made it the lynchpin of Harvard's National Scholarships. The program, which began on a limited scale in 1934 and was formalized in 1936, aimed to recruit students from underrepresented regions, particularly the South and the Midwest, thus balancing out the many students from the Northeast and turning Harvard into a "national university."

The regional approach was consistent with Conant's belief that genius could flourish anywhere, and he optimistically assumed that geographic diversity would morph into class diversity. As he put it in his first president's report: "We should be able to say that any man with remarkable talents may obtain his education at Harvard whether he be rich or penniless. . . . The privately-endowed institutions must keep the way clear for the gifted youth of limited means" (qtd. in Monro, "Helping Him" 378). Profiles of the students that Monro and other recruiters wooed to Cambridge illustrate both the promise and the limitations of regional recruitment.

John Merrifield '54

When Monro visited New Trier High School, in Winnetka, Illinois, in 1950, senior John Merrifield had already talked to recruiters from Princeton and Yale, but on a whim he signed up for a fifteen-minute appointment with "the guy from Harvard" (personal interview, 18 Nov. 2008). Merrifield's father, a maxillofacial surgeon, had headed a dental lab in South Africa before coming to Chicago, where he set up practice as an oral surgeon, started a cleft palate clinic at Northwestern, and worked pro bono at Children's Hospital. Merrifield's mother was one of only three women in her class at Cornell Medical School, and she had met her husband on a Grenfell Cruise, which sent ships loaded with medical supplies and volunteers up the Labrador coast, setting up clinics at villages along the way (interview).

Merrifield was a good illustration of the limitations of Harvard's diversity campaign. Granted, he was from the Midwest and attended a public high school. But affluent New Trier was not your average high school, and his privileged background did not set him apart from the prep school graduates who were already overrepresented at Harvard; the scholarship he received was honorary because his family could afford to pay his expenses. Moreover, Merrifield was no exception: of the 161 National Scholarships awarded through 1940, only 2 recipients came from a working-class background; 53 percent were from business or professional backgrounds, 14 percent from teaching or administrative backgrounds, and 10 percent from farming families. Geographic diversification was also slow to arrive: in 1948 a third of the National Scholarship students still hailed from within twenty miles of Cambridge (Keller 33).

Ronald Messer '54

Ronald Messer was the real thing: a midwesterner from a typical public high school and a working-class background who never would have made it to Harvard without financial assistance. The youngest of three children, he grew up knowing that money was tight. His father, a meatcutter, had introduced him to the mysteries of the trade so that he would always be able to support himself. The only other contribution the family could make to his financial assets was a metal box for sending home his laundry, to save the cost of having it done on campus (personal interview, 18 Nov. 2008). Messer arrived with a one-year five hundred–dollar scholarship from the Harvard Club of Chicago and a matching Harvard National Scholarship. He cut every cost and earned every penny he could, asking for a room on the top floor of Grays Hall, since the rent dropped fifty dollars for every floor the student climbed to get to his room. He got a part-time job cutting meat at a supermarket, then Monro helped him locate two additional part-time jobs, recognizing him as the kind of student who could truly diversify the student body and deserved all the help the college could provide.

Even success stories like Messer's reminded Monro that individual recruitment, no matter how ambitious, would not make higher education significantly more accessible to a wide range of students. Centralized efforts such as the NSSFNS represented one promising option. Another was a wholesale reform of financial aid policies, which were using scholarships to compete for the most gifted students, many of whom could pay their own way. Even as he continued to recruit, Monro was put in a position to begin formulating such a reform, first at Harvard and then on a national scale.

FINANCIAL AID RECONSIDERED

When Monro became assistant provost in 1949, his first assignment was to evaluate the college's financial aid program, which was being administered jointly and inefficiently by the Scholarship Committee and the Student Employment Office. The inflationary postwar economy, which had doubled student expenses by 50 percent since 1940, had left the college underfunded, GI program funding was dwindling as the veterans graduated, and the endowment was producing only two thirds of what was needed to provide scholarships for 20 percent of the incoming freshman class ("Scholarship Funds").

A committee chaired by Monro, working in tandem with a student committee, warned that unless the financial aid program was expanded and reorganized, only wealthy students would be able to afford Harvard (Monro, "Helping Him" 378). The committees recommended that new, improved financial aid packages include scholarship assistance, work opportunities, and low-interest loans; low-cost housing was later added to the mix (Fouquet). It was clear that the new program needed a centralized command center, and Monro, with his understanding of veterans' affairs, his recruiting experience, and his leadership role in researching the financial aid issue, was the logical choice to head it. Knowing that the consolidation would raise some hackles, Provost Paul Buck announced the creation of the center and left the rest to Monro, suggesting during a Saturday strategy meeting that they aim for a Monday opening.

Working around the clock, Monro missed the impossible deadline by only two days. On Wednesday, 1 March 1950, Harvard's Financial Aid Office opened at 54 Dunster Street (Barter), the building where he, Dottie, and the girls had been living since he joined the Veterans Bureau.[2]

Get a Job or Start a Business

The student employment component of financial aid brought Monro far more grief—and more challenges—than either scholarships or loans did. He dreamed up so many innovative work opportunities for students that the term "JUM-jobs" was coined to describe them. When the Student Employment Office, at his urging, created sixty student porter positions for the 1951–52 school year, two hundred students applied for the right to make beds and clean rooms in three of the college houses ("Two Hundred"). Students could earn as much as a thousand dollars, well over the cost of tuition, by choosing such lonely roles as night watchman or night switchboard operator ("Manpower").

By 1957 Student Employment had corralled most of the job opportunities available to students, with one notable exception: businesses that young entrepreneurs operated from their rooms, jeopardizing both Harvard's nonprofit status and its real estate tax exemption. Reluctant to snuff out student initiative, Monro set about bringing the student businesses into the financial aid fold. He was familiar with student entrepreneurs from his prep school days at Phillips, where many "scholarship boys" like him had earned money running concessions for local businesses such as laundries, linen services, and newspaper delivery (Allis 429–30). To supervise the new program, Monro chose Dustin "Dusty" Burke, whom he had recently hired as director of student employment. In the spring of 1957 the program received a capital investment of seven thousand dollars and won the lucrative contract for the university's weekly linen service. The following August, Harvard Student Agencies (HSA) was incorporated, with Monro and Burke both serving as officers.

The agency and its members met with resentment from local merchants, on-campus publications, and some student entrepreneurs who did not care to be supervised. The *Crimson* took exception to the *Harvard Student Calendar*, a weekly HSA publication that was distributed to every residential room on campus and gave the *Crimson* serious competition for advertising revenue. Inevitably, wild-eyed or ill-conceived projects caused problems. One student, clearly ahead of his time, proposed selling condoms in the Student Union. Another submitted a plan to sell firewood to dorm residents, unaware that nobody could remember when—or if—the chimneys had been cleaned. In an effort to honor the student's interest in temperature control, Burke suggested that he run the refrigerator rental service instead (personal interview, 30 Mar. 2005).

In spite of the difficulties, HSA thrived. Today it claims to be the world's largest student-run corporation, employs more than five hundred students, and is best known for its forty-eight best-selling *Let's Go* travel guides (Harvard Student Agencies). Burke credited Monro with HSA's success, saying: "He had tremendous courage, and was always willing to go against the grain and do something nobody else would do. Creating the HSA was the kind of new thinking he did all his life" (interview).

The Monro Doctrine

As creative and innovative as he was in fostering student employment and entrepreneurship, Monro's major contribution to financial aid dealt with the nuts and bolts of determining how much and what kind of assistance each student should receive. His 1953 article "Helping the Student Help Himself," published in the *College Board Review,* described the complex formula he had developed to calculate financial aid packages at Harvard.

Citing the difficulty of measuring financial need, he suggested that the College Board create a committee to come up with "some generally accepted standards" for determining need and awarding aid. Such a move would be a major expansion of the board's mission, which up to this point had been administering college entrance examinations, not financial aid. But Monro insisted that the time was ripe for such a study because, as recruitment became more competitive, colleges were "fishing in the same suburban pools," using scholarships to compete for attractive students rather than giving them to needy students who would otherwise miss out on college altogether (351).[3]

The system that Monro had been tinkering with during the past three years was remarkable for its thoroughness, its fairness, and the balance it struck between equitable procedures and sensitivity to special cases. In a particularly impressive passage he explained how he calculated a reasonable family contribution to a student's assets. The rule of thumb at the time was to use 15 percent of net family income, after subtracting a certain amount for every child in public school and a higher amount for every child in prep school or college. Dissatisfied with this reductive approach, Monro asked parents for more data: employment specifics, ages of children, information about other dependents, past and future income, business expenses, extraordinary expenses, value of real estate holdings, mortgage amount, cash value of life insurance policies, outstanding debts, how much of their son's expenses they estimated they could cover the following year, and whether they would like a financial aid award to include a job and/or a loan if the scholarship did not cover all expenses.

Using this information, Monro and his staff deducted expenses from income to arrive at what he called a "family remainder." This figure, after being progressively taxed, was added to the family's assets, also progressively taxed, to produce a "required contribution," and once finalized, it was matched against the student's needs, which were calculated in an equally painstaking way ("Helping the Student" 355). The procedure was undeniably labor-intensive, especially compared to the simple "15 percent of income" format. But remembering his parents' struggles to put three sons through college, Monro felt the expenditure of time was thoroughly justified because it stretched scholarship money as far as possible and put it into the emptiest pockets.

In the fall of 1954, after months of the kind of research Monro had suggested, the College Scholarship Service (CSS) of the College Board was created, and Monro was named chair. Made up of the board's ninety-four member colleges—including all the Ivy League colleges—the CSS amassed financial aid data that had formerly been submitted to individual colleges, often with much redundancy. The data were then distributed to the colleges specified by the student. The Parents' Financial Statement that the CSS adopted was a slightly simplified version of the format Monro had developed at Harvard ("CEEB"). To discourage the competitive bidding Monro deplored as wasteful and counterproductive, the CSS published the member colleges' financial aid offers.

A year later CSS added a new service. Based on the data it collected, it would compute a student's financial need and forward the results to colleges that signed on for the service. Colleges continuing to do their own computations were urged to use the newly developed CSS manual, which relied heavily on Monro's procedures for estimating assets and determining need, now known as the "Monro Doctrine."

It is difficult to appreciate Monro's impact on financial aid practices and even more difficult to measure the esteem in which he is held by his successors in the field. Whenever the history of financial aid is recounted, Monro is praised as one of its pioneers. In 1976, in celebration of its seventy-fifth anniversary, the College Board gave Monro both the Distinguished Service Award and the Edward S. Noyes Award for Outstanding Service to the College Board, calling him "the Father of Modern Financial Aid Practices." In 1984, on its thirtieth anniversary, the College Scholarship Service gave him its own distinguished service award. In 2004, on its fiftieth anniversary, the CSS created the John Monro Memorial Award to recognize educators "who exemplify John Monro's goals of recruiting talented, needy, and underrepresented students into higher education, using needs analysis as the means to accomplish the goals of access and equity" (*College Scholarship Service* n.p.). Phillips headmaster John Kemper summed up Monro's contribution simply and memorably: "Probably no single man in the United States has done more to ensure that fine boys from poor families can have the same chance at a college education as anyone else."[4]

PHILLIPS REVISITED

During this remarkably productive period Monro revived his connection with Phillips Academy. In 1955 he was elected to a three-year term on the Alumni Council, and as his term was set to expire, alumni voted to make him a charter member of the board of trustees (Allis 583). His fellow board members, most of whom were businessmen, valued his expertise as an educator and relied on him to explain educational theory without subjecting them to academic claptrap (Helen Eccles, personal interview, 18 July 2006). One grateful member of the board used a nautical image to sum up Monro's contribution to the group, calling him "a kind of rudder in educational policy and institutional direction, which has kept us on an even keel and enabled [us] to avoid the shoals on which so many schools have foundered" (qtd. in Stott).

An additional role he accepted was the obligation to repeat, as often as necessary, the school's mission to accept "youth . . . from every quarter." At one board meeting the trustees were congratulating themselves on a recent rise in standardized test scores among incoming the freshmen. Several trustees agreed that it would be ideal if Phillips could draw all the best students. Monro disagreed, objecting: "That's all very well for a while—you can't turn your back on bright kids. But the value-added idea is very important for a place like Andover. We obviously want to take all kinds of kids. If we don't take some people with low [standardized test scores], I'm going to be ashamed of us" (Theodore and Nancy Sizer, personal interview, 3 July 2006).[5] Championing another kind of diversity, he supported the merger between Phillips and all-girls Abbot Academy in 1973, urging reluctant members of the board to recognize it as "the most significant and humanizing event in the long history of this old school" ("Old

Lessons"). When Barbara Landis Chase became the first female headmaster, Monro congratulated her, writing that as the father of daughters, he was "impressed, delighted, and reassured for the future of a truly great school" under her leadership.

A MAN WHO NEEDS NO INTRODUCTION

At Harvard Monro was becoming known as the man to go to for an appropriate, entertaining speech. As he had shown in his address to the Men's Fraternal League while he was still a teenager, he had a knack for exploiting the specifics of an occasion and lacing his speeches with humor, often poking fun at himself.

Harvard's commuter population was an audience with whom he felt a special rapport, having commuted to Concord High School and attended Phillips as a day student. He recognized commuting as a particularly austere form of financial aid that could jeopardize full participation in college life, and during his editorship of the *Crimson* he had argued that commuters deserved parity with residential students.

He spoke at the commuters' annual dinner two years in a row. In 1951 he took a lighthearted approach, pretending to explain how the commuter was abnormal but in reality showing that it was the resident students' lifestyle that was bizarre. Describing the commuter, he said: "His daily program, by ordinary student standards, is a mess. The commuter gets up in the morning and goes to bed at night. He is an odd sort of college student who eats breakfast. . . . There are things he misses around Harvard that it does no harm to miss. Most important, probably, he doesn't have to read the *Crimson,* and is smart enough not to believe it anyway" ("You Can Always").

The following year he began by peppering his speech with rapport-building jokes. He pointed out that Dudley Hall, now serving as Harvard's commuter center, had a particularly virile pedigree: "Old Tom Dudley . . . had three wives and his last child was born when he was just seventy. Also, when Old Tom took time out from his duties at home, he got to be Governor, and he got Harvard College its first charter" ("Second Commuters' Dinner Speech").

He praised the commuters for maintaining their identity and keeping Dudley Hall as their quarters, despite a recent recommendation that they be disbursed among the resident houses for meals and social activities. Then he invited them to become leaders in a movement to introduce group tutorials into the house system. Specifically, he suggested that they create small groups combining freshmen students and upperclassmen tutors. This was a clever idea because such study groups could not exist in any of the residential houses, which were either for freshmen or for upperclassmen but never for both. For once the difference between the commuters and the residential students gave the commuters an advantage, and Monro urged them to seize it: "Does this not suggest to you that Dudley, alone of all the houses, stands naturally ready to conduct the experiment? . . . I shall say no more. If you are worthy sons of Tom Dudley, you will know how to take it from there."

Six years later, in 1958, Dudley Hall was renamed Dudley House and made the commuters' house, with its own tutors, athletic teams, social events, and support services; to complete the transition, Delmar Leighton stepped down as dean of the college to become Dudley's first housemaster. Because Monro identified so completely with the commuters, it was fitting that their victory triggered a major change in his own status. On 1 December he replaced Leighton as dean of the college, a position that would catapult him into national prominence during a time of social foment and serve as the jumping-off point for his journey South.

What a new Dean does for his first year is make mistakes,
hang on for dear life, and learn a new lesson every day
about his college.

—JOHN U. MONRO

5
DEAN MONRO
1958-1962

If you are looking for a clear description of Monro's duties as dean, you will
not find it in the official *Records of the Dean of Harvard College,* even though
they stretch back to 1889. Instead, you will get a motley list of roles the dean is
expected to fill: "teacher, friend, counselor, and disciplinarian to undergraduates." Monro described the job in more colorful terms: "The Dean . . . is the man
whose job it is to stand on that hot boundary between the interests and standards
of the institution, on the one hand, and the interests and rights and welfare of
the individual" ("Leighton Speech").

Unlike Yale, where the dean of the college oversaw both academic and social life, Harvard split those duties between the dean of the Faculty of Arts and
Sciences, who supervised both graduate and undergraduate academics, and the
dean of students, who supervised student life (Samuelson, "Monro's Altruistic
Instinct"). This arrangement left the dean of the college to carve out a space between his two fellow deans. The territory Monro coveted was the rocky terrain
of educational policy, and he succeeded so thoroughly in infiltrating it that *Time*
credited him with upgrading "the vague deanship to make it one of Harvard's
most influential offices" ("Act").

Monro's lack of a graduate degree was a handicap, but in his defense he could
point to wunderkind Dean of Faculty McGeorge Bundy, who did not have one
either. In lieu of a graduate degree Monro brought to the job a unique perspective shaped by his experiences as a student, News Office writer, counselor for
veterans, assistant provost, and financial aid director. He saw the two sides of
the deanship as complementary rather than contradictory because educational
theory shed light on many of the problems that sent students to his office or
caught his attention.

In fact, one of his early failures occurred precisely because he ignored the link between academics and residential life. Attempting to create a tutorial program for non–honors students, he had already proposed that a yearlong course be listed in the catalog when a housemaster pointed out that the plan would work only if it was conducted at the house level. Properly chastened, Monro concluded, "All of us are specialists and workers, but all of us are citizens too; and the House, though paying heed to the problems on the academic side, is really a center where men learn to deal with one another, in short to be effective members of a community" ("Leighton Speech"). This early lesson in the consequences of proposing change in a vacuum shaped Monro's later, more collaborative administrative style; henceforth, with a few notable exceptions, he took pains to consult those who would be most affected by a policy before he made up his mind about it.

DEFINING THE DEANSHIP
Freshman Seminars

Both in the classroom and in the Financial Aid Office, Monro had witnessed adjustment problems among overcommitted freshmen, whom he described as "spinning madly with one toe on the ground." To make the first year of college less frantic and more meaningful, Monro proposed to the Committee on Educational Policy a roster of freshman seminars based on student participation rather than the traditional lecture format ("Monro Suggests"). As a model he pointed to David Riesman '31, whose social science students were required to participate in classroom panels and critique their cultural environment ("CEP May"). In May 1959 a pilot freshman seminar program, proposed by the committee and approved by the faculty, enrolled 10 percent of the freshman class in the kind of seminar Monro had described ("Faculty Approves"). A year later the faculty voted to double the program and extend it for another three years; those teaching seminars included Radcliffe president Mary Bunting, Bundy, and Monro ("Report on Freshman Seminar").

Monro had been teaching the freshman writing course since 1953, and he was eager to try out the new formula he had thrown his weight behind. Unlike most of the seminar descriptions, which attempted to draw the best and brightest students, Monro specified in the catalog that his expository writing seminar was open to "students whose experience in writing had been meager, as well as students whose preparation had been thorough" (*Freshman Seminar Catalogue,* *1959–1960*). He taught the seminar twice and later recalled it as a near-idyllic experience. "In the spring, we took it easy, sat on the grass at Radcliffe, and enjoyed the flowers," he told the *New York Times*'s Linda Greenhouse. "I got closer to those kids than to any others in the college. It made me very happy" (82).[1]

For his twenty-fifth anniversary class report Monro expanded on the satisfaction he was drawing from the seminar and other aspects of his job: "I commit myself easily to education because I see education at the heart of our democratic process, sharing a large part of the task of assuring each young person the chance to develop his own talents and of awakening and strengthening each individual mind and spirit" (*Class of 1934: 25th Anniversary Report*, 939–40).

Digging for Hidden Treasure

In the fall of 1959 Monro directed the seventh in a series of College Board colloquia on college admissions issues. For four days he joined administrators, College Board staff, and admissions and financial aid officers at Arden House, Columbia University's conference center in Harriman, New York. His foreword to the published proceedings reveals how deeply his emotions were becoming engaged in the plight of minority students. Unlike other directors, whose forewords were studded with cozy recollections of the Arden House gathering, Monro urged a wider audience to look over his shoulder and into his heart while he examined the speakers' papers. "Anger and urgency assail me, as I read these excellent papers again before publication," he wrote. "Anger that so rich and fat a country as ours, dedicated to the worth of individual personality, should still, so desperately late in history, be starving the educational and personal development of tens of thousands of able children whose only fault is that they are poor, or the wrong color. Urgency because, as these papers make clear, we have begun to trace most of the twisted strands of our problem and know at last how to attack it" (foreword, *Search* v). Twenty years later College Board president George Hanford hailed the symposium as "the first concentrated deliberations on the special problems of young members of minority groups" (*Minority* 5).

Monro again compared hidden talent to buried treasure when he spoke at the annual College Scholarship Service (CSS) meeting in October 1960. With the stern criticism reserved for his favorite causes, he took member colleges to task for doing so little to implement the reforms that had seemed inherent in the creation of CSS a decade earlier: scholarships were still being awarded "for embellishment purposes" rather than going to students who truly needed financial assistance, and his formula for calculating family contribution was being used to siphon funds to students who could have gotten by with loans or jobs. Searching for buried talent, Monro warned, would not be easy. It would require new testing methods since standardized tests were poor indicators of how these promising but unconventional students would do in college. Given the complexity of the task, he recommended that a serious effort to find promising students begin as early as the third grade ("Responsibility of the Colleges" 5).

Reforming ROTC

In the same way that Monro continued to both criticize and identify with the financial aid community, he remained loyal to the military in spite of its flaws. In June 1960 he presented a paper at a conference on the future of Reserve Officers' Training Corps (ROTC) programs. At the time critics were suggesting that ROTC be restricted to the summer months or be moved off college campuses altogether, but Monro disagreed. Instead, he recommended that useless drills be replaced by "increased physical rigor, development of personal courage, identification of students with armed forces, and experience with real Service problems and facilities," such as the Boston Navy Yard, Fort Devens, and Hanscom Air Force Base. He insisted that ROTC belonged on campus because colleges and military services could learn a lot from each other and because, "by one of the most vital traditions in our democratic society, we subject our military establishments to civilian influence and controls" ("ROTC").

PARTNERING WITH THE PEACE CORPS

Realizing that most of the students milling around Harvard Yard did not share his enthusiasm for ROTC, Monro encouraged other forms of national service, and when John F. Kennedy signed the Peace Corps into being on 1 March 1961, Monro was eager for Harvard to be in on the ground floor. So was director Sargent Shriver, who believed that Harvard's prestige would lend credibility to the fledgling organization. Former Brandeis dean of students Joseph Kauffman was named the corps' program director, and he asked Monro to persuade the necessary people to offer Harvard as a training center. Employing one of his favorite strategies, Monro achieved his goal by offering to do much of the work himself, becoming chair of Harvard's Advisory Committee on Peace Corps Training. Harvard contracted to prepare forty-six Peace Corps volunteers—only a few of them Harvard students— to teach in secondary schools in Nigeria, which was frantically trying to bridge the gap between its fourteen thousand classroom openings and its three million school-age children (Stossel 229).

Harvard's preexisting links with Nigeria made it an ideal training site. In 1959 Frank Keppell, dean of the Harvard Graduate School of Education, had been named to the Ashby Commission, created to develop a master plan for Nigerian education as the country became independent (Robert Binswanger, telephone interview, 4 Apr. 2006). Harvard was already corresponding with a Nigerian college about sending a small group of students there in the near future (Ballard, "Dean Stresses"), and Monro was well acquainted with a federal program that was helping Nigerian students attend American colleges.

As advisory committee chair, Monro traveled to Washington, DC, several times during April 1961, conferring with other educators, administrators, government agencies, and Peace Corps staff about the final details of the program (Lottman). His familiarity with crisis management proved helpful during the Peace Corps' infancy, when everything had to get done in a hurry and all but the most rudimentary planning was an unaffordable luxury.

In A Moment in History: The First Ten Years of the Peace Corps, on-site Peace Corps representative Brent Ashabranner described the chaos that plagued the Nigerian program in particular. In its recent bid for independence, Nigeria had chosen to become a loosely knit federation of states rather than a country with a powerful centralized government. Foreign affairs minister Jaja Wachuku, determined that the nascent country not appear overly beholden to the United States, found one excuse after another to postpone the cabinet's vote on the Peace Corps program. He was still stalling in early July, when Ashabranner, who had been waiting for official approval, reluctantly let Harvard and UCLA training program representatives visit Nigeria to gather information for the program, assuming it ever got off the ground (65).

As soon as Ashabranner relented, Monro flew to Nigeria, where he spent two weeks examining facilities and comparable programs, seeking advice from local educators, and arranging for the volunteers to train and practice teach through University College, Ibadan (UCI, soon to become the University of Ibadan). In a lengthy memo summarizing his findings, he laid out a series of priorities and potential problems. He warned against replacing university-based training programs with a centralized government-run program, a change that was already being discussed in Washington. He also emphasized the importance of on-site training, identified isolation as the main morale problem the volunteers would face, and recommended assigning them in clusters (memo to Brent Ashabranner, 15 July 1961, DP).

Monro had great respect for the local educational experts, warning that volunteers had to understand they were coming to Nigeria not as tourists, heroes, or agents of change but as teachers "in a school system which is already well organized, indeed which has some schools a good deal better than some U.S. high schools" (2). In fact, before Nigeria became independent, UCI was considered one of the best universities in the British Commonwealth (Polgreen).

On 21 July 1961 the Nigerian cabinet finally approved the Peace Corps program. Three days later the volunteers—collectively known as Nigeria 1 Training Group—arrived at Harvard (Ashabranner 68). Given the short lead time, it is no wonder that Monro later described the training program period as "that first wild summer" ("Moral Values"). Harvard's quick turnaround made it the only training site to meet Shriver's original, and wildly optimistic, goal of having volunteers in Nigeria by early fall.

Monro had a significant impact on the shape of the training program itself. According to Mike Shinagel, who later became advisor to Harvard students accepted in the corps: "John was the organizing force for the project, and he could use the bully pulpit of his office . . . to get things done. He helped to coax, cajole, commandeer, and convince faculty to join the program and arranged the logistics locally" (e-mail, 31 Jan. 2006). Among the Harvard faculty members he successfully cajoled were Martin Kilson, of Harvard's Center for International Affairs, for the African problems course; Paul E. Sigmund Jr., from the Government Department, for the international affairs course; and Ted Sizer, from the Graduate School of Education, for the comparative education course and the overall training curriculum. At his insistence two of the courses—on Nigerian problems and the Nigerian educational system—were taught by a faculty member from UCI.

Monro also exploited Harvard's clout to demand a five-month training period rather than the three-month model followed at UCLA and the University of Michigan, the two other training sites for Nigeria-bound volunteers. Ashabranner protested that five months of training would take too big a bite out of the two-year service period and try the volunteers' patience, but "Harvard was very hard to argue with, in those days, at least," so Monro got what he wanted (79).

Monro had no official role in selecting Peace Corps candidates, but as usual, he found ways to cut through red tape for unconventional applicants. One such volunteer was David Hibbard, who had taken a leave of absence from medical school and spent the previous summer with Operation Crossroads Africa, building a road to a school in rural Nigeria. His fascination with African affairs had brought him to Harvard for a summer school course on the subject, and when he read a notice about the Peace Corps training program, he knew he wanted to be part of it. Too late to go through official channels, he made his way to Monro's office and explained his situation. Several days later Hibbard received a cable from the Peace Corps inviting him to join. Serendipitously, he ended up teaching at the same school to which he had helped build a road the previous summer (telephone interview, 3 Apr. 2006).

Damage Control Revisited

Monro's expertise in damage control came in handy during the early days of the volunteers' on-site training, when an indiscreet postcard written by a member of Group 1 created an international furor. The eye of this particular storm, Margery Michelmore, was a twenty-three-year-old Smith graduate who had left a job at *Reader's Digest* to join the Peace Corps (Bramson 5). One Saturday morning in mid-October she wrote a number of postcards to friends back home, one of which described "the squalor and absolutely primitive conditions rampant in both cities and the bush. . . . Everyone except us lives in the streets, cooks in the streets and even goes to bathrooms [sic] in streets" (qtd. in Ashabranner 82). Somehow the postcard went astray, and by lunchtime the unflattering text had been mimeographed and widely distributed within UCI, where the volunteers were continuing their training.

On the day in question Group 1 volunteer Aubrey Brown was rearranging the furniture in his room. As he worked, he gradually noticed that the noise and activity in the open courtyard was increasing, and when he went down to lunch, he came across a copy of Michelmore's message. When he went down to dinner and chose a seat, the dormitory president tapped him on the shoulder and said, "We have a place for you," pointing to a table in a distant corner. The table had been set for four—the number of volunteers living in that particular dorm. A seasoned activist by the time he arrived at Harvard, Brown took the meaning of the gesture and returned to his room without eating. Later that night a Nigerian student knocked on his door, said he realized Brown had not eaten dinner, and invited him to have tea and biscuits in his room (Aubrey Brown, personal interview, 17 July 2006).

Elsewhere on campus the UCI students demonstrated, rioted, and scrawled messages such as "Yankees go home!" on the doors of the volunteers' dorm room (Ashabranner 82–83). The Students' Union passed a resolution demanding the volunteers' deportation, calling them "agents of imperialism" and branding the corps "espionage-inspired" and "a scheme to foster neo-colonialism" ("Postcard to Friend"). Murray Frank, the Peace Corps director of Nigeria's Western Region, gathered the volunteers at his house, where they huddled for a day and a half, debating a course of action. Eventually, it was Brown who came up with a plan, rooted in his experience with nonviolent resistance: he told the Nigerian students in his dormitory that he would not eat until they joined him for meals. When he refused the trays of food brought to his room, they eventually relented and joined him in the dining hall; the strategy worked in the other dormitories as well (Frank). On 6 November newly elected UCI student body president Abidoye Babalola announced that the university's Nigerian students had resumed "cordial relations" with the remaining volunteers ("Rift").

Back in Cambridge, Monro sought insight regarding the controversy by talking to a newly arrived Nigerian student, who told him that "the main thing that outrages the Nigerians from schoolboy to Prime Minister, is 'mockery' by foreigners, or the suspicion of ill-concealed contempt on the part of whites" (letter to Leon Bramson). Speaking out on the incident, Monro sympathized with the Nigerian students but defended Michelmore, describing her as "fine and dedicated." He pointed out that the Harvard training sessions had included material about culture shock and local conditions. Byron Stookey Jr. '54, the training session administrator, counted at least fifteen Nigerians who had described local conditions to the volunteers while they were still at Harvard (Ballard, "Monro").

Monro may very well have seen a positive side to the incident, which supported his belief that comfortable Americans could understand poverty only when their noses were rubbed in it. In a round-table discussion shortly after the event, he bluntly stated that it would be good for the volunteers to find out "what it's like to live in a country where half the babies are dead before they're three" (Ballard, "Dean"). Michelmore herself admitted as much. In a comment that was rarely quoted because it lacked shock value, she wrote on the postcard that her confrontation with poverty had been valuable: "It really is a revelation, and once we got over the initial horrified shock, a very rewarding experience."

Ending the Partnership

Once the volunteers were launched, Monro did all he could to support the Peace Corps and preserve its connection to Harvard. He chaired the local advisory committee, spoke at a Hillel Round Table in World Affairs (Ballard, "Dean"), and gave the keynote address at a daylong Peace Corps conference at Boston's Statler Hilton Hotel, one of fourteen conferences taking place across the country as the corps headed into its seventh month (Roberts). But the first training program at Harvard also turned out to be the last. In late October, long after the time frame for a second summer of training had come and gone, Monro made the announcement himself, saying only that there had been "a friendly disagreement" between the college and the corps (Fenton, "Harvard Drops"). The sticking point was the corps' decision to conduct all its training in the United States, a policy Monro found so objectionable that he reluctantly recommended Harvard withdraw as a training site.

Buttressing Monro's belief in the importance of on-site training was an interim report submitted by David Seeley, the Harvard graduate student who had supervised the Nigerian segment of the training program. From his front row seat for the Michelmore incident, Seeley described the difficulty of preparing volunteers for third world conditions. He recommended that volunteers be chosen for their ability to adjust to drastically different surroundings, that stateside training include a realistic—perhaps even pessimistic—picture of the destination country, that training personnel live on-site before training began, and that, because "even the most vivid presentation is no substitute for living here," on-site training include practice teaching and copious opportunities to talk informally with residents (Seeley, *Interim*).

Ironically, the Peace Corps eventually reversed itself on the training issue and agreed with Monro: by 1969 more than half of the Peace Corps training was taking place in the destination country (Ashabranner 255), and today all of it does.[2] His other recommendations fared less well: a three-month training period, rather than the five months he had demanded, soon became the norm (79). His recommendation that educational institutions continue to run the training programs was ignored: in the late 1960s training was taken over by private companies (255).

Other Roads to Africa

Even after Harvard had withdrawn as a training site, its students continued to apply to the Peace Corps, and travel to Africa through two other volunteer programs Monro had been instrumental in bringing to campus. The longer-running of the two was Operation Crossroads Africa, a church-affiliated summer program founded in 1957 by Presbyterian minister James H. Robinson. In 1958 there were 60 Crossroaders; by 1961, when the Peace Corps came on the scene, Operation Crossroads was sending 225 volunteers to fourteen African countries ("Crossroads Head"). According to Byron Stookey, Monro's support of Crossroads was crucial to its acceptance on campus, especially in light of rumors that Robinson had Communist affiliations (personal interview, 3 Apr. 2006). At Monro's invitation Robinson made three recruitment trips to campus in 1960 and 1961, and the students who signed on for the program frequently decided to pursue more volunteer work, more time in Africa, or both. Crossroads was an ideal feeder for the Peace Corps because an undergraduate could spend a summer with the program then go on to the Peace Corps after graduation, as Dave Hibbard had done.

Crossroads served as the inspiration for Project Tanganyika, the other volunteer-in-Africa program on campus. It was the brainchild of Peter Goldmark '62, who returned from a particularly boring summer to hear classmates raving about their experience with Crossroads. He worked up a proposal for a similar program and took it to fellow members of the Phillips Brooks House, Harvard's student-run public service organization. As a member of the board that had to approve the project, Monro supported the students' initiative, insisting only that a faculty member accompany them. After a hectic month of orientation on campus, the group left for Africa on 20 June 1961, before the Peace Corps training program had even begun ("Project Tanganyika").

DEAN MONRO AND THE SUBWAY SCHOOL

In addition to the Peace Corps and the other projects Monro volunteered for while he adjusted to the deanship, he began teaching writing at University Extension. He was drawn to extension schools in principle because their philosophy satisfied his appetite for inclusion and his belief in the liberating power of education. Although the rest of Harvard often fell short of his expectations, the extension program was a lifelong source of pride, like a favorite child who could do no wrong. It was also a valuable training ground, since its diverse student body prefigured the wide range of students he would encounter at historically black colleges.

From the beginning extension students were remarkable for the focus and determination they brought to their studies. An article in the *Boston Transcript* for 15 June 1910 emphasized the atmosphere of diligence in one philosophy course: "At the stroke of eight every lecture evening notebook was spread and until nine o'clock not a glance wandered towards the clock, nor were there any signs of wavering interest. The students were all voluntary seekers of knowledge who elected philosophy as an aid in constructive thinking" (qtd. in Shinagel 17).

A half-century later the students in Monro's classes were just as eager to tap into the transformative power of learning. Ruth Voutselas was a good example. The eldest of eight children raised during the Depression, she grew up convinced that college was out of the question for her. After high school graduation she married and raised a family (Gove 2). It was not until 1960, when the youngest of her three children started school, that she began to think about furthering her education. A friend told her that about the extension program, and before she knew it she had earned more than half the credits she needed to graduate.

Voutselas met Monro in the fall of 1963, when she took his Expository English class to fulfill a writing course requirement. She was an insecure writer, but Monro's pragmatic advice demystified the process for her, and she found additional lessons embedded in his behavior, interpreting his soft-spoken manner as proof that you did not need to shout down an opponent to win an argument (personal interview, 20 Jan. 2010). By the time she received her degree, in 1967, Voutselas had become a curious and insatiable student. She took graduate courses at Northeastern and Boston College, went to China to study education in a totalitarian society, and chose a career working with emotionally disturbed children in the public schools. Recently retired and looking back on how her life had changed since she entered Monro's classroom, she concludes, "Having a family was a joy, but until the Harvard Extension School opened up, I was only half full" (e-mail, 15 Aug. 2010).

Monro loved working with students like Voutselas, and he relished the heterogeneous class lists, which could include anyone "from a Ph.D. to a high school dropout." Near the end of his career he pointed to the extension courses as the most satisfying teaching he had done at Harvard (Brooks). His affectionate label, the "subway school," suggests that he identified with these students just as he did with the undergraduate commuters and the former servicemen who came to Harvard through the GI Bill. All three groups had to fight their way from the margins to become full-fledged members of the university community, and Monro wanted to help them do it.

His rapport with the extension students was so strong that he sometimes shed his customary reticence and shared his emotions with them. In a letter to the *Boston Herald* Beth Rosenbaum, a former student, described one evening when Monro came to her section meeting and produced several sheets of crumpled paper he had retrieved from his wastebasket. He said he wanted to use them to discuss the importance of revising. The first sheet was a formal letter notifying a student's father that his son was being expelled from the college. Monro told the class, "I thought about that boy's father out there, and I just couldn't send this letter, so correctly dictated by one of my staff." The second sheet was the final version of the letter, which, according to Rosenbaum, "said everything about Dean Monro and his view of society" and began with the words "You and I have a problem."

Curriculum Development

Monro liked the relative ease with which the curriculum could be updated and new courses created in the extension school. When he joined the program, writing courses were conducted as lectures, with virtually no discussion or give-and-take. Monro thought the hardworking extension students deserved better; what they deserved, he decided, was much more interaction and faculty feedback. At first he tried to incorporate student participation into the lecture format, but the large hall was not conducive to give-and-take, so he overhauled the course structure completely, dividing the students into groups of twenty for the second half of every class. According to John Adams, the administrative assistant in charge of scheduling, the new format was a logistical nightmare but well worth the effort, since the dropout rate, which had been high in the lecture format writing classes, declined significantly in Monro's classes (Adams, letter, 2 Jan. 2005). President Derek Bok identified Monro's extension program writing course as one of his most valuable contributions to Harvard: "At that time, students were sorely lacking in ability to communicate their ideas, particularly on paper. John saw that need and did something about it. Since that time, thousands of students have taken advantage of the program."

Extension at Sea

In 1960 University Extension gave Monro an unexpected opportunity to renew his ties with the U.S. Navy. The Polaris University Extension Program, which eventually became the Program for Afloat College Education (PACE), began as a series of college courses that went to sea with the crew of the Polaris atomic-powered submarines based in New London, Connecticut. On board the crewmen watched classes filmed via kinescope at the studios of WGBH, Boston's public television station. Back on land they attended section meetings then took a final exam if they wanted to earn college credit (Shinagel 85–87). After a successful first year, a two-year collegiate curriculum designed specifically for the Polaris Fleet was launched (88). Eventually the program was offered on surface ships and at naval bases, and some of the courses were also used at Harvard's Urban Studies extension program in Roxbury and broadcast over WGBH (93, 91).

Monro's contribution to the naval program was the first-year, two-part Expository English course, designed in collaboration with graduate student Shaun O'Connell, who tried out the course at the Polaris base while Monro sat in on several classes. In 1965 O'Connell filmed thirty half-hour classes, and the course became an official part of the program, with O'Connell listed as the lecturer and Monro as the supervisor (*PACE Program*). O'Connell was an excellent choice for the PACE course because he had spent three years in the air force before coming to Harvard, where he was teaching Freshman English and studying for a graduate degree in American studies. Not only could he identify with the seamen who would be taking the PACE course, but he adjusted easily to what he called Monro's "barracks commander style," classifying him as the kind of "at-the-helm" leader portrayed by Gregory Peck in *Twelve O'Clock High* (personal interview, 16 Nov. 2004).

A Handpicked Team

For his extension courses Monro was free to pick teaching assistants—known at Harvard as section men—based on their writing or teaching skills, rather than their graduate degrees or areas of expertise. Gravitating toward men he was comfortable with, he ended up with a congenial social unit as well as an effective teaching cadre.

A less generous man than Monro might have envied Dean Brelis '49, who when he became a section man had already written a highly praised novel and become a successful journalist—two of Monro's cherished aspirations, which were becoming more remote with each passing year. Brelis's leadership of guerrilla resistance efforts in the mountains of Burma earned him a Bronze Star and the rank of captain and lent authenticity to his thinly veiled autobiographical novel, *The Mission* (Marquard). When Monro invited him to join his team, Brelis had worked as a reporter for *Life* and a foreign correspondent, then a bureau chief, for Time-Life and was back at Harvard on a Nieman Fellowship ("Dean Brelis").

It must have given Monro special pleasure to invite Donald Nickerson to become a section man, because he added precisely the kind of diversity the Harvard Scholarships Program had been designed to cultivate. A graduate of Needham High School, Nickerson received a scholarship from the Harvard Club of Boston and found it difficult to make friends with classmates who had prep school backgrounds (e-mail, 12 Jan. 2010). After teaching high school for three years, he had returned to Harvard for a graduate degree in education. As a section man, he discovered the camaraderie he had missed as an undergraduate.

Mike Shinagel came to Harvard under the GI Bill—in his case the Korean War GI bill—with a Woodrow Wilson fellowship in hand and a year of graduate study under his belt. When he went to the Office of Graduate and Career Plans looking for a job, he was offered an associate directorship in the office. Shinagel racked up administrative or semi-administrative experience while he completed his degree: he was a freshman advisor, a departmental tutor, a member of the college admissions staff, and student Peace Corps advisor from 1962 to 1964 (Shinagel 120).

By the time Byron Stookey '54 became a section man, he and Monro had worked together frequently, reading applications in the Financial Aid Office and setting up several co-op houses for erstwhile commuters. Stookey directed the freshman seminar program during its pilot phase and was administrative dean of the Peace Corps training program.

* * *

LIFE BEYOND HARVARD YARD

When he was not working late or hanging out at the Wursthaus with his section men, Monro immersed himself in suburban family life, which now centered around Winchester, particularly its First Congregational Church. Through several of the church youth group's activities, younger daughter Janet had become close to Philip Dreyer, a neighbor who soon became a de facto member of the family and something of a surrogate son for Monro. Monro and Dreyer liked many of the same things, including soccer, music, and photography, but by far the strongest bond between them was their interest in teaching. Once Phil told Monro that he intended to become a high school physics teacher, they embarked upon a lifelong conversation about education. Janet also realized that teaching was in her future—she had known since she was seven years old that she wanted to work with young children.

As future teachers, Phil and Janet put serious thought into selecting colleges, and Monro, who had guided the admissions deliberations of so many strangers, now had to gauge how much (or how little) to participate in the deliberations of two young people who were very close to his heart. He offered advice but did not push them; ultimately, Janet chose Mount Holyoke, and Phil went to Harvard (Dreyer, e-mail, 13Apr. 2010).

Meanwhile, Monro's brothers were making progress in their own spheres. Sutton had earned his master's degree at the University of Maine, then enrolled as a doctoral candidate at the University of North Carolina. There he and Herbert Robbins developed the Robbins-Monro algorithm, a theory of sequential analysis that was recognized as the most reliable method of quality control to date. After a brief stint with the navy during the Korean War, Sutton went to work for Bell Telephone Laboratories, first in Manhattan then in Allentown, Pennsylvania. Feeling comfortable in the area, he and Sue bought a twenty-eight-acre farm in the Lehigh Valley, and it became the family home for more than three decades. From the farm Sue was helping to establish a library to serve rural communities nearby (P. Monro, e-mail, 17 Nov. 2008).

As for Claxton, he was following in Grandfather Hezekiah's footsteps and developing into a respected clergyman with a streak of social activism. During his ministry at Calvary Episcopal Church in Nyack, he led a successful building campaign, created many parish organizations, strengthened the youth ministry, and helped create an ecumenical local youth union. He also worked toward civil rights, persuading the local YMCA to accept black members (MacGregor).

A SPEECH FOR EVERY OCCASION

As dean, Monro was asked to speak even oftener than in the past, and he prepared painstakingly for each occasion, doing background research, writing several drafts, rehearsing, and timing himself. On 20 May 1962 he returned to Francis W. Parker, the Chicago school that had so charmed him in 1949, to mark the dedication of a new building. Browsing through old yearbooks, he homed in on one activity: the eighth-graders' construction of a clubhouse in the school's backyard in 1911. He borrowed the youngsters' simple dedication and applied it to the handsome new building being launched five decades later: "We want the house to stand as a symbol of what the school means to us and what we would mean to the school. . . . We wish everybody to take pleasure in the house" ("Francis W. Parker Dedication").

Just before summer break he traveled to affluent Bloomfield Hills, Michigan, to attend commencement at Cranbrook Academy of Art. Urging the seniors to escape the "upholstered rut" of their comfortable middle-class existence, he warned that privilege harbored its own pitfalls: "We are too comfortable, stuffed with food and with other people's ideas, a nation of spectators, wary of real controversy." The only way to escape this peril, he told them, was to see the world through a different culture, and that involved risk ("Cranbrook Commencement Address").

To dramatize his point, he described several Harvard students who had taken the kind of risk he was recommending. The most compelling was Lawrence Ekpebu, who had left his village in the Nigerian bush to study medicine at Harvard so that he could go back home to care for the sick. No matter how hard he studied, however, he could not pass his science courses. Ultimately, after consulting with Monro, he switched his major to government and went home to teach rather than heal. Ekpebu had taken a risk in coming to Harvard, and by some measures he had failed, but Monro did not see it that way: "Lawrence Ekpebu knows in his bones about Africa. He has learned the hard way about America. Now he is the master of two widely different cultures and so knows a critical truth about humanity and our human problems."

Monro urged each graduate to embark on a series of small risks rather than waiting for a single, dramatic incident to present itself: ask for a roommate who is different in fundamental ways, take a tough science course, study a foreign language rooted in an unfamiliar culture, pick an extracurricular activity or summer job that is a stretch rather than a familiar routine. As the Cranbrook seniors scattered for the summer. Monro flew to Miami and a chance encounter that would eventually spring the latch of his own "upholstered rut" at Harvard.

6
MOVING TOWARD MILES
1962-1964

Returning from Cranbrook, Monro wasted little time mourning the absence of the Peace Corps training program at Harvard; instead, he flew to Miami and attended a weeklong conference of the American Teachers Association (ATA). There he met ATA president Lucius Pitts, who was winding up his first year as president of Miles, a hardscrabble, historically black college on the outskirts of Birmingham, Alabama. After Monro addressed the group, Pitts challenged him to match his "pretty speech about educational theory" with action and come see for himself what a black college was like (Long). The two men spent a good deal of time together during the conference, and Monro resolved to take Pitts up on his offer as soon as he could get away (Monro, letter to Merrifield, 1992).

A FAMILIAR, SAD STORY

Monro did not need Pitts to introduce him to the challenge that faced blacks seeking higher education; he had repeatedly met it face to face. As a member of the National Scholarship Service and Fund for Negro Students board of directors and awards committee, he knew that budget constraints frequently forced the board to turn down worthy applicants; one student was in such dire need that each board member personally contributed fifty dollars to create a scholarship for him when the organization's budget could not be stretched to include him (Monro, "Grand Lodge").

But the lesson that made the deepest impression on him came from Harvard's few black students, who described the "dreadful new pressures" they faced at a predominantly white institution. It began when an associate dean told him that all the black freshmen were sitting at the same table during lunch. He asked them to come to his office, and in the discussion that followed, one student compared leaving his dormitory room every day to "going over the top," a military phrase for trading the comparative safety of the trenches for the exposure of the battlefield. The student explained: "Sometime during the morning or sometime during the day I'm going to catch it from behind. . . . There are very tough moments here that you don't know about. And so, come lunch time there's a bunch of us like to take off our shoes and just be folks, if that's all right with you" (Aubry 20–21).[1] Monro did not try to break up the black lunch table again, and he sometimes sat there himself, first asking if he could "intrude." The reply was invariably, "Sure, we'd be happy to have you intrude." It was a lesson he never forgot, and it made him particularly receptive to the challenge Lucius Pitts flung out in Miami.

Lucius H. Pitts

Lucius Holsey Pitts was the seventh of eight children born into a sharecropper family. His mother died when he was young, and the family moved to Macon in search of better job opportunities. By the time Pitts graduated from high school, he was a seasoned preacher in the Colored Methodist Episcopal (CME) Church, having been named after one of its founders, Lucius Holsey (Conley).

While attending Paine College and working as a dishwasher, Pitts suddenly went blind and had to drop out of school. Eventually, he partially regained his sight and returned to school, working as a teacher for $47.50 a month. After graduating from Paine, he went to Fisk, where he served as assistant dean of the chapel and earned a graduate degree in religious education. He was formally ordained as a CME minister, and after a decade of teaching, preaching, and youth work, he moved to Atlanta in 1955 ("Tribute" 2).

From Atlanta Pitts became increasingly immersed in the civil rights movement. In 1958 the Rev. Martin Luther King Jr. asked him to become the Southern Christian Leadership Conference's first executive director, an invitation he declined in favor of heavier involvement on the local level (Eskew 194). He was executive secretary of the Georgia Teachers and Educators Association, vice president of the state's National Association for the Advancement of Colored People (NAACP), and president of the Georgia Council on Human Relations, which collected dues for the NAACP (Egerton 108).

One of his most important assets as a civil rights spokesman was his strik-ing physical appearance; according to social science professor Neil Friedman: "Dr. Pitts was a man of erect carriage and great dignity. He looked every inch of his 6'2" height. He was very black. His high forehead glistened in the sun. His white hair, natural and sparse in front, reminded me of a light snowfall on a dark night" ("1968" 156).

The Miles presidency offered Pitts little in the way of external trappings: his pay cut and the absence of a job for his wife would slash their joint income in half, and the family of six would be trading their comfortable house in Atlanta for a four-room rental (Egerton 108). Moreover, Miles itself was in dire straits. In October 1958 it had lost its regional accreditation from the Southern Associa-tion of Colleges and Schools (SACS), partly because the less stringent Grade B formula previously used to evaluate historically black colleges had been abol-ished. Miles's deficiencies were highly visible: the library and science facilities was inadequate, few faculty had graduate degrees, and the three wooden class-room buildings—which resembled military barracks because they had been built from army surplus—were so decrepit that the evaluation team had demanded they be either veneered or torn down (*Miles College: The First* 33). Nevertheless, after four months of consideration, Pitts agreed to come to Miles, saying he had been "forced by [his] own conscience to do it" (Egerton 109). Disingenuously, he claimed that commitment to black education would spell the end of his political activism, whereas he knew full well that in assuming the presidency of Miles he was buying into its long history of social engagement.

THE CIVIL RIGHTS TRADITION AT MILES

Miles began making a name for itself in the civil rights arena as early as 1940, when the Southern Negro Youth Congress established an active chapter at the college and invited Miles president W. A. Bell to join its advisory board (Mc-Whorter 151). During his presidency, which ended when he suffered a fatal heart attack in January 1961, Bell permitted activism to continue on and off campus.

In the aftermath of the 1954–55 Montgomery Bus Boycott, Miles graduate Autherine Lucy enrolled at the University of Alabama, an act that tested the Su-preme Court's *Brown v. Board of Education* ruling. Everyone, including Lucy, was surprised when federal judge Herbert Grooms gave the case class action status and ruled that the university could not exclude students on the basis of race (Mc-Whorter 96). Lucy's presence triggered protests, mob demonstrations, firecrackers, rock throwing, attacks on cars and buses, and racist chants ("Hey hey ho ho / Where in the hell did that nigger go?") and made her "the first black student in the history of desegregation to be greeted with organized violence" (99).

Miles as "Militant Youth Arm"

Miles's role as what Diane McWhorter calls the "militant youth arm" of the local civil rights movement began in 1960, under the leadership of Frank Dukes and student government president Jesse Walker. Dukes, a Korean War veteran who had recently returned from Detroit after being laid off by General Motors (Eskew 195), was unsparing in his indictment of Birmingham, saying, "In terms of human indignities, conditions are worse here than in the war-torn areas of the world" (qtd. in Osborne 400).

Dukes's brand of activism did not include taking unnecessary risks. When the Rev. Fred Shuttlesworth urged Birmingham students to stage lunchroom sit-ins like those in Greensboro, North Carolina, Dukes persuaded them to substitute a round-the-clock prayer "Vigil for Freedom." On 29 February 1960 twelve placard-carrying demonstrators showed up at downtown Kelly Ingram Park and were promptly arrested, fingerprinted, photographed, and released without being booked or charged. The police did release the names of the students to the *Birmingham News,* however, and on 12 March, demonstrator and Miles football star Robert Jones, his mother, and his sister were attacked in their home by eight men wielding pipes, clubs, and blackjacks studded with razorblades (McWhorter 153). The attackers had disappeared by the time the police arrived, but the next day, when deputies came to the hospital where Jones's mother had been sent with crushed hands, broken legs, and a sliced-open scalp, she identified two of them as assailants (Salisbury 28).

"Don't Buy Where You Can't Eat"

The first major civil rights development Pitts faced as president began in December 1961, when a group of student leaders headed by Dukes formed a committee to plan "a spectacular Negro demonstration" (Eskew 195). They intended to boycott the segregated downtown stores, having learned from marketing research

Dukes had cleverly obtained from the Chamber of Commerce that the stores operated on a profit margin of 12 to 15 percent, significantly less than the 25 percent accounted for by black customers (McWhorter 255).

When Pitts learned about the boycott, he called the student committee in for a talk. "He told us he wasn't going to fight us; he was going to advise us," said Dukes. "He wanted us to protest, but in an organized fashion and in a way that hopefully wouldn't get us killed." Pitts persuaded the students to postpone the boycott and work with local businesses toward a solution, then he got the business owners on board by hinting that if they cooperated, he might be able to head off a demonstration planned for the following weekend (Dukes).

Once the two sides got together, the store owners learned that they were facing a mere boycott rather than a demonstration, and they began to stall. After several unproductive meetings the students concluded that the owners had no intention of cooperating, and the boycott began. In the end the delay Pitts had urged benefited the boycott, postponing it to mid-March, the peak of the busy pre-Easter shopping season. Students from Miles, Daniel Payne College, Booker T. Washington Business School, and Birmingham-Southern maintained a visible presence in the stores (Osborne 400), with additional manpower coming from Shuttlesworth's recently created Alabama Christian Movement for Human Rights (ACHR) (M. L. King 51). Flyers and posters sported slogans such as "Wear Your Old Clothes for Freedom" and "Don't Buy Where You Can't Eat" (Eskew 198–99).

As black shoppers disappeared from the downtown shopping area, Public Safety Commissioner Bull Connor vented his fury by choking off the city's contribution to the county surplus food program. He also countermanded the mayor's permission for Miles to conduct a "Miles of Dimes" book-buying drive for the library (Osborne 401), a move that backfired when a news services reported the story and contributions to the book drive came pouring in from across the country (Kahn 43).

The boycott achieved its short-term goals, seriously curtailing department store sales and demonstrating the scope of black buying power. Pre-Easter sales were 12 percent lower than the previous year's (Eskew 201), and participation was an impressive 90 percent at the height of the campaign (Osborne 398). There were admittedly a few steps backward: several stores fired the few black employees on their payroll (McWhorter 272), and most of the segregated water fountain signs that had been taken down during the campaign reappeared as momentum ebbed. (Eskew 201). Nonetheless, the boycott set a precedent by uniting the black community in a direct action campaign. It also made the segregationist politicians and business owners so nervous that the Chamber of Commerce created a Senior Citizens Committee to head off potential disruption during the upcoming SCLC conference and asked Pitts and other black leaders to join (M. L. King 52). When Monro met him in Miami, Pitts was no longer a newcomer to Birmingham but a force to be reckoned with in the civil rights arena, "a man of the masses who could speak to the classes" (McWhorter 246).

THE ALPERT-LEARY IMBROGLIO AT HARVARD

Every year after his meeting with Pitts, Monro found himself dealing with a problem at Harvard that made great demands on his time and patience. The largest controversy to land in his lap during 1962–63 was the furor over drug experiments that made Timothy Leary a household name.

Leary, who had yet to coin his mantra "Tune in, turn on, drop out," was not the star of the drug drama but merely the sidekick to Richard Alpert, an assistant professor of clinical psychology and education. In March 1962 members of the Harvard Center for Research and Personality accused Alpert, assisted by Leary, of using graduate students in their experiments with the hallucinogenic drug psilocybin and administering it in the absence of a medical doctor (Smith). After investigating, the state Department of Mental Health allowed the experiments to continue on condition that a licensed medical doctor be present whenever drugs were taken; Harvard also permitted the experiments to continue, provided that undergraduates not be used as subjects, even though there was no evidence that they ever had been.

On 27 November 1962 the *Crimson* published a joint letter from Monro and Dana Farnsworth, director of University Health Services, warning undergraduates that "mind-distorting" drugs were "known to intensify seriously a tendency toward depression and to produce other dangerous psychotic effects." Asked what had triggered the letter, Monro told a *Crimson* reporter that within the previous three weeks he had received "definite evidence" that undergraduate "interest" in mind-altering drugs was on the rise and that students were obtaining illegal drugs (Russin). At this point nobody was explicitly linking the Alpert-Leary experiments to the warning by Monro and Farnsworth, nor had anyone claimed that actual drug use among Harvard undergraduates was on the rise.

Two weeks later, in a phone interview with *New York Times* reporter Fred Hechinger, Monro indirectly implicated Alpert and Leary, tracing the growing appeal of drugs among undergraduates to their "intellectual promotion" by scientific experimenters who did not "realize how inflammable undergraduates can become" ("Use" 1). He also gave credence to the possibility of increased drug usage by Harvard students, saying that there had been multiple reports of "private psilocybin parties" for undergraduates, which some suspected were being hosted by the graduate students Alpert and Leary had used in their experiments (3). The day Hechinger's article appeared, Alpert and Leary released a statement to the *Crimson* targeting Monro as though he were the sole author of the warning letter. They surmised that he was "apparently the focus of pressure exerted by persons alarmed by rumors about drug usage" and called his description of the drugs' dangerous effects "ill-informed." They announced that they had shifted the site of their research from the university to an independent association since the drugs they were studying were "too powerful and too controversial to be researched in a university setting" ("Leary and Alpert").

In April 1963 Leary was relieved of his teaching duties, and on 27 May, with Monro in attendance, President Nathan Pusey announced that the Harvard Corporation had voted to terminate Alpert's contract because he had used an undergraduate in his research, in spite of his having told Monro he had not done so (Ram Dass, letter, 19 May 2006). The following day an unrepentant Alpert admitted that he had used an undergraduate in his drug research but added that more than two hundred undergraduates had asked to participate, and concluded, "I do not feel that this single exception constitutes bad faith on our part" (Fenton, "Ousted Educator").

Spring and Summer in "Bombingham"

While Monro was struggling with the Alpert-Leary episode, the violent events in Birmingham that began in the spring of 1963 were drawing the horrified attention of readers and TV viewers nationwide. The marches, beatings, water hoses, jailings, bombings, and attacks by police dogs made a mockery of Birmingham's long-standing title the "Magic City" and spawned the far less flattering nickname "Bombingham." Miles could claim a good deal of credit for the events because Martin Luther King Jr. acknowledged that the previous year's department store boycott had been a major factor in his decision to come to Birmingham.

Looking beyond the earlier boycott's meager results, King had recognized its strengths, which were ripe for appropriation: united forces, a clear goal, careful planning, appropriate tactics, canny leadership, effective communication, widespread participation, and sympathetic national press coverage. King used the boycott as a template for planning Project C (for *confrontation*), which targeted the downtown department stores and relied on the marketing research Dukes had obtained. Like the boycott that Miles had spearheaded, Project C capitalized on the pre-Easter shopping season. Even the work clothes that King, Shuttlesworth, and SCLC's Ralph Abernathy wore in the Good Friday march were reminiscent of the original boycott's motto, "Wear Old Clothes for Freedom." The strategies employed in Project C soon outgrew the boycott model, incorporating marches on city hall, lunch counter sit-ins, violation of a cease and desist court order, and, most famously, recruitment of children in the demonstrations. But in the amorphous early stages King exploited the earlier boycott as a powerful research and development tool to shape his own more highly publicized protest.[2]

Many Miles students and faculty members became foot soldiers in the 1963 demonstrations. Miles chemistry professor Jonathan McPherson and Rev. Abraham Lincoln Woods, a recent Miles graduate and teacher whose activist roots stretched back to the 1950s, were among the demonstrators jailed for refusing to leave a segregated lunch counter. King's executive assistant, Wyatt Walker, recruited Miles students for special duties, such as blowing dog whistles to see if the K-9 dogs could be tempted to break away from their handlers—they could not—and setting off false fire alarms to decrease the power of the hoses aimed at the demonstrators (McWhorter 391). Sabotaging the hoses was an important job: when attached to monitor guns, which directed two hoses' worth of water through one nozzle, the powerful blasts peeled the bark off trees, whipped the clothing off demonstrators, tumbled children head over heels (277), and hurled the reed-thin Shuttlesworth against a wall so hard he was hospitalized with chest injuries (M. L. King 93).

Pitts, after doing all he could to prevent Project C, became deeply involved in its daily workings. First, he agreed to serve as a local advisor to King, Abernathy, and other out-of-town leaders (Eskew 233). As the violence escalated, he repeatedly represented the "traditional Negro leadership class" in biracial attempts to end the demonstrations. For a brief time, in the vacuum created by Shuttlesworth's hospitalization in early May, Pitts replaced him as "Birmingham's ranking civil rights leader" (McWhorter 412).

A DRAMATIC FIRST LOOK AT BIRMINGHAM

By the fall of 1963 Monro's family life had settled into a comfortable routine. He and Dottie were living in a stately brick house at 65 Francis Street, on the edge of Harvard Square. Their elder daughter, Ann, had graduated from Colby College and married high school classmate Robert Becker, then accompanied him on his naval posting to Rota, Spain. Phil Dreyer and Janet had married promptly after their graduations from Harvard and Mt. Holyoke, respectively, and moved to New Haven, where Phil was working on his master of arts in teaching degree at Yale and Janet was teaching second grade (Dreyer, interview, 9 Feb. 2005). Both of Monro's brothers had found niches where they would remain for the rest of their professional lives: Claxton was rector of St. Stephen's Episcopal Church in Dallas, and Sutton was teaching in the industrial engineering program at Lehigh University.

With his usual skepticism toward comfort and stability, Monro chose this moment to take Pitts up on his offer to come see black education in action. The date Monro arrived to participate in a faculty workshop at Miles, 4 September 1963, was opening day for city schools reluctantly facing court-ordered desegregation. When five black students showed up at three different schools that morning, they were met outside by rock-hurling demonstrators and by massive absenteeism in the classrooms (McWhorter 495). The entrance to Miles was patrolled by a shotgun-toting guard, and twelve students were on call in case the president's house needed special protection ("Doing Something" 86). The dreadful climax of the year's events—the 15 September bombing that killed four young black girls in the basement of the Sixteenth Street Baptist Church—was less than two weeks away (McWhorter 521).

Almost twenty-five years later, in an address to the Miles College assembly, Monro described his first visit to Birmingham. Pitts had invited him to come to a downtown church, where a statement protesting the school desegregation fiasco was being drafted to send to the mayor. Monro told it this way:

> There were about 15 of us in the church basement, discussing the paper, when we heard a loud explosion nearby. It startled me, but to the other people there, mostly Black ministers, it did not seem that much of a surprise. They hauled out small radios, and quickly the news came that a bomb had been set off at a home, Arthur Shores' home, up on "Dynamite Hill."[3] Dr. Pitts said, "Shores is a friend of mind,

and I'm going up the hill to see what I can do." It was not far, and within minutes I found myself walking very fast to keep up with Lucius Pitts, in the midst of a great crowd of angry and determined Black men and women streaming toward and up the hill. Looking around I became aware I was absolutely the only white person anywhere around. And it also occurred to me to grab Lucius Pitts by the arm as we walked along, to make the point, "I'm with *him*. He's my friend!" As we neared the top of the hill, just below Arthur Shores' house, we could hear sporadic gun-fire, and it turned out the police had brought up their armored truck and set up a strong point at a cross-roads. And there was a fairly steady exchange of fire going on. . . . [Pitts] went inside and I sat on the steps and watched the huge crowd con-tinue to gather, and listened to the guns. . . . That evening, I got my own first-hand look at the fury, and unity, and determination of the city's Black community. And at their tolerance, even under stress. In all that time nobody made the slightest gesture toward me. I began to understand very well what strength in the commu-nity lay behind Dr. King's success. ("Miles College Assembly Speech" 2–4).

With stunning understatement Monro concluded, "I'd seen enough to know that this interested me very much." Before he left, he promised to help design a new freshman studies program at Miles and to return as often as necessary to see the project through.

THE PARIETALS CONTROVERSY AT HARVARD

Back at Harvard Monro found himself at the center of another campus tem-pest. It had begun in the spring of 1963, when two dorm parties became "fairly drunken, and vulgar," to use Monro's words. Within the first three weeks of the fall semester there were three violations of parietals—the regulations governing the presence of women in the residence halls—including a situation in which two Radcliffe students appeared to be living with their boyfriends, who were senior tutors in Dunster House (Keller and Keller 302). Shortly after that, Dean of Students Robert B. Watson, who worked with Monro, announced that his office was conducting an "extensive study" of parietal hours and was "seriously considering" reducing them (Paisner). At the time women were allowed in dorm rooms until midnight on Saturdays and until seven o'clock other evenings, with extended hours on special occasions (McLaughlin and Banks). Watson hinted that the revised guidelines would close a provocative loophole by restricting women to the living rooms of the suites: "It is not appropriate for a Harvard student to entertain a girl in his own room" (Paisner).

Monro was deeply offended by what he considered insensitive treatment of women at the rowdy spring parties, but he had little patience with the parietals issue itself (Samuelson, "Monro's Altruistic"). In 1961, when the Student Council had proposed allowing women in the residence halls until midnight on Fridays and holidays, he let his annoyance show: "The administration is weary of this constant nagging on the issue of parietals. Surely there are more important issues for the Student Council to worry about" ("Precedent"). Now, with the memory of Birmingham still fresh in his mind, the dorm residents' complaints struck him as even more petty than before.

Monro entered the fray with a 9 October 1963 letter to the *Crimson*, responding to a recent editorial against reduced parietal hours. He praised the editorial for "sharpening up our discussions of the basis of our regulations," explained his position, and urged students to join him in making the debate public. Later that month he copyrighted an unpublished article and distributed it to Harvard's senior tutors and administrators and their counterparts at other colleges. In the article "Sex Mores in Transition," psychiatrist Graham B. Blaine Jr. '40, of University Health Services, described a survey he had administered to students at several colleges, including Harvard and Radcliffe. Analyzing the results, Blaine concluded that permissive parietals had significantly contributed to an increase in premarital sex (Locke).

Once the survey went beyond Harvard, so did the controversy, with leering emphasis on Monro's earlier statement about "wild parties and sexual intercourse." On 1 November the lead paragraph of a UPI story read, "Sex parties behind the ivy walls of Harvard University . . . were disclosed by a Harvard dean" ("Behind"). The *Chicago Tribune* graced its story with the headline "Harvard Sex Orgies Disclosed by Dean," whereas in Las Vegas the six-inch headline screamed, "Harvard Sex Parties Taking over Campus."

After the sensational headlines appeared, Monro received little backup, from the administration on down. Pusey supported him within the Harvard community but refused to comment to the press. Radcliffe president Mary Bunting said that its parietals seemed to be working just fine ("Behind"). In a letter to the *Crimson*, economics professor John Kenneth Galbraith fumed that he was fed up with the "banal, depressing" debate and that the college should stick to its mission, which was to make sure the students received high-quality instruction, rather than attempting "to protect them from the natural penalties of indolence, alcohol, or lust." Some students called Monro's description of sexual activity in the dormitories highly exaggerated. Senior Erik Sundquist, perhaps a bit wistfully, observed, "The closest thing to a scandal at Harvard happens when the deans say one is brewing and the newspapers print it" ("Harvard Students").

In November Monro announced that housemasters and faculty would have to approve any changes to the existing regulations. Students, faculty, alumni, and administrators expressed their opinions in college publications as Monro had urged them to do. In this conciliatory atmosphere national coverage had already begun to peter out when the assassination of John F. Kennedy cut the controversy down to size and threw the campus, along with the rest of the world, into deep mourning.

But Monro needed more time to process what had happened. For a speech he had agreed to give in January 1964 at New York's Harvard Club, he used the parietals controversy to launch an analysis of "Moral Values in Education." He leavened his serious subject with his usual humor, claiming that national attention had been drawn to the controversy not by his statements but, rather, by the *Crimson*'s shift from headlines about "parietals"—a word journalists did not understand—to headlines about "college sex," a term journalists not only understood but reacted to with a "ritualistic, fierce, and fairly threatening tribal dance" that stifled rational debate.

But the humor barely masked Monro's feeling of alienation from the community whose values he had believed he was defending. He confessed that Galbraith's sharp criticism, followed by a faculty silence that implied agreement, had taught him "that professors did not sign on at Harvard to be cops. Even if a professor is a Housemaster he will not turn into a cop. In short, professors are poor cops. In short, most professors have a little piece of Galbraith in them." Another painful lesson he had learned was "how well the undergraduate community can keep its real attitudes a secret from the older generation—at least from this member of it."

While he regretted the tactical errors he had made, he defended his position, calling it a "right, though clumsy" effort. In defense of moral education in general, he denied that it was merely "kid stuff, all right for the family and the Boy Scouts and the school, but really not the business of a grown-up college faculty." He hinted that such laissez-faire was selfishness in disguise: "It may be observed that the policy of leaving young people alone to fend for themselves has the undoubted advantage . . . of saving the adults a lot of time for strictly adult concerns, like golf or book-writing. So it is a fairly popular policy." This swipe at self-absorbed, book-writing professors was clearly aimed at Galbraith, one of Harvard's most prolific authors. Monro's sarcastic tone, so different from his habitual sense of fair play, revealed how disappointed he was by his colleagues' lack of support.[4]

Birmingham on the Charles

At first the 1964 edition of Harvard's annual spring madness—in which students demonstrated in support of a cause, the more frivolous the better—seemed like a welcome diversion from the rancorous parietals debate. Things always got tricky when the event moved off campus, and this time it was guaranteed to do so because the students were campaigning to "Save the Sycamores" lining Memorial Drive. The congested road that ran along the Charles River was scheduled for a long-overdue widening, and rumors were flying that the venerable trees fringing its edges would be cut down in the process. In early May two thousand Harvard students streaming onto Memorial Drive and blocking traffic were challenged by police officers from Cambridge, Watertown, and the Metropolitan District Commission.

When four police dogs emerged from the police cars, the chanting switched from "Save the Sycamores" to "Birmingham, Birmingham," alluding to the police dogs used by Bull Connors's troops the previous summer. In case anyone missed the parallel, the students also sang "We Shall Overcome." Dean Watson, who had gotten the parietals discussions off to such a rocky start, was similarly ineffective when he ordered the students to disperse and nobody listened (Matejyzyk 1). A week later Monro stepped in to quell a smaller demonstration in Harvard Square, bellowing into a bullhorn, "Get out of here or get out of college" ("Harvard Square Riot"). For him the surface similarities merely underscored the vast differences between the Cambridge and the Birmingham demonstrations.

INCREASING DIVERSITY AT HARVARD

One valuable source of satisfaction for Monro during this trying period was his evolving relationship with Archie Epps, who became a close friend and protégée, as well as a key figure in increasing diversity at Harvard. Epps arrived on campus as a divinity school student in 1958, with a degree in psychology and philosophy from historically black Talladega College. His hometown of Lake Charles, Louisiana, had been racially mixed, and his father's profitable dry cleaning business had made it possible for him and his twin brother, Martin Luther, to attend the local Catholic schools (D. Martin).

Initially, Epps was not particularly interested in civil rights. He confessed: "I was not very sophisticated about race or much else. In the late '50s, the battle lines were just being drawn anyway." But he quickly became a leader within the small black community on campus. In addition to teaching a seminar on civil rights and black nationalism and bringing Malcolm X, Ralph Ellison, and James Baldwin to speak, Epps led and coordinated the Boston contingent of the March on Washington (D. Martin). Monro first called Epps into his office to discuss the Association of African and Afro-American Students (AAAAS), which a group of black students, under the leadership of Epps, had begun on an unofficial basis in 1962. Monro considered the organization an important addition to campus life, but he was unable to promote its official recognition because it did not meet the requirement that it be open to all students. After numerous strategy sessions Monro and Epps hit upon a solution: the new organization would be modeled after the finals clubs, whose restricted membership had never been an obstacle to official recognition (Epps).

In 1963 Monro suggested that Epps apply for an administrative opening in the career office, but he was told that he was not a suitable candidate because white students would not take advice from him (Gewertz). Monro told Epps, "Well, then, you'd better come in with me," and made him assistant dean of the college and one of Harvard's first black administrator (Flint).[5]

GROWING TIES TO THE SOUTH

Planning for the Freshman Studies Program took Monro to Miles once or twice a month during the school year (letter to Merrifield, 1992), and somewhere along the line he agreed to direct the English component of a precollege summer workshop that Pitts had recently set up. Monro was drawn even more strongly to the South when he became involved in the search for a new president at Tougaloo, a historically black college on the outskirts of Jackson, Mississippi. Because of an impending partnership with Tougaloo, Brown president Barnaby Keeney was a key behind-the-scenes player in the search, and he thought Monro would be perfect for the job. At Keeney's urging Monro met with the selection committee and indicated interest in the position; by 8 April he was one of five finalists (Wilder).

Monro had some reservations about the presidency, however, and in a 31 March letter to Keeney he described his growing belief that black colleges needed black leadership. The language of the letter indicates that he was still formulating his position, but he already had strong feelings about it: "I begin to think with some firmness" and "This conviction begins to run deep." By May Monro had made up his mind, and he wrote to chairman Bob Wilder, withdrawing his name from consideration. He insisted that recent civil rights victories strengthened his belief in the importance of black leadership because the type of "black scholar" the presidency demanded was more plentiful now than in the past. Moreover, he added, now was the ideal time for Tougaloo to realize its full potential under a black president, especially with "the new help in sight" that the Brown partnership promised. "When I think of Brown and Tougaloo," he wrote, "it seems very clear to me that the relationship will be most educational and meaningful for both institutions if President Keeney is in working contact with a Negro president at Tougaloo" (18 May 1964). On 4 June Keeney, who had received a copy of the letter, gamely acknowledged defeat, admitting that the committee had probably come to share Monro's opinion. But Monro's curiosity about Tougaloo had been piqued, and if not for Pitts's charisma, he might well have moved from Harvard to Tougaloo rather than to Miles.

Pitts and Monro had by this time become quite close, however, and when Pitts came to Cambridge in December 1963, Monro arranged a meeting with members of Phillips Brooks House (PBH), Harvard's student-run public service organization. As always, Pitts was on a mission. He worried that because the previous summer's violence had snuffed out so many civil rights opportunities, Miles students would become cynical in the absence of outlets for their idealism. He hoped that PBH would join Miles in a grade school tutoring program that summer.

Naturally, Monro relished the prospect of bringing some of Harvard's best, brightest, and most socially committed students with him to Miles. Besides, he was on a mission of his own. At the meeting was Jon Clifton '63, past president of PBH, who was spending a year working at Harvard before entering law school. Monro suspected that Clifton had the makings of a fine teacher, and he hoped the tutoring project would prove him right (Jon Clifton, telephone interview, 15 Sept. 2004). After Pitts described his plan, Monro turned to Clifton and asked simply, "Can you do it?" Clifton looked around the room, calculated the support he could count on from those who were present, added the names of other PBH members who would be interested, and said yes (interview). The lives of the students who chose to go South with Monro that summer were changed forever, and so was his.

AN UNFORGETTABLE SUMMER

Like most historically black colleges, Miles traced its origins to a church—in this case the Colored Methodist Episcopal Church, which in 1956 became the Christian Methodist Episcopal Church (CME)—but it was unusual in that its founders were themselves blacks, rather than white missionaries (*Miles College: The First Hundred Years* 12). When a rich coal deposit was discovered beneath the land on which it stood, the Tennessee Coal and Iron Company promptly negotiated a land swap and paid Miles a measly thirty thousand dollars to move to its current site in Fairfield, just west of the Birmingham city limits (15). The surrounding neighborhood, virtually unchanged today, consists mostly of modest bungalow-style homes owned by blacks. By the 1960s the area had been heavily mined (Jones, "Miles"), and the U.S. Steel Mill smokestacks, which were visible from campus, were wreaking havoc on the atmosphere; according to one eyewitness, "When the wind is out of the west, rust-colored smoke from the mills spews over the campus and much of the city" (Donovan).

When Monro and the Phillips Brooks House contingent arrived in June, Lucius Pitts had been president for three years. The campus was still ragged around the edges, although it boasted two solid, handsome brick buildings that added a touch of class: Williams Hall, built in 1907 and eventually designated a Jefferson County Historic Site; and Brown Hall, built in 1927. The rickety classroom buildings that had appalled the accreditation association had been remodeled, but the library building was still under construction, and fund-raising for the badly needed science center had barely begun. The sidewalks were cracked, and the grass and shrubbery were parched (Chisum 16). Pitts once interrupted an interview with a *Time Magazine* reporter to get the lawn sprinklers shut off, explaining, "I like to see the grass grow, but I have to watch the water bill" ("Miles's Mileage").

But the scruffy campus was bustling with activity. In addition to its own summer school, the grade school tutoring program, and the precollege workshop, the college was hosting a seminar on Africa; a church leadership training school; workshops for kindergarten teachers, supervising teachers, and church choir directors; and one of two Head Start programs in the area ("Calendar").[6] Nor were Monro and his cadre the only white faces on campus. The summer programs were filled with white college students and teachers hailing from places such as Brandeis, Lake Forest, Princeton, the University of California at Berkeley, the University of Colorado, the University of Michigan, the University of Virginia, and Yale (*Light in the Shadows*). In the fall Dartmouth junior Robert Schweisow was due to come to Miles as the first participant in Dartmouth's Southern Exchange program, and, as Monro well knew, a similar partnership between Brown and Tougaloo was imminent. By 1967 there would be at least a dozen such partnerships or exchange programs at historically black colleges.

The Grade School Tutoring Program

Thanks to Jon Clifton's preparations, the Cambridge tutors had cots to sleep on and fans to compensate for the lack of air-conditioning. They bunked either in faculty apartments or in rudimentary field houses, everyone pitched in to prepare meals in the home economics classroom, and a munificent one dollar per person per week was budgeted for living expenses (*Miles College–Phillips Brooks*).

When the dust settled, there were ten pairs of tutors—each consisting of one Miles student and one PBH student—to help local fourth-graders and a few third- and fifth-graders with their reading skills (*Miles College–Phillips Brooks*). The tutoring sessions, conducted in the morning at various sites throughout the region, were the heart of the program, but there were also field trips to libraries, the zoo, the art museum, a bottling plant, and a newspaper office. Late in the program each team hosted an open house for parents, and the final event was a celebratory "Kids' Day" at Miles, including games, singing, treasure hunts, picnicking, and a look at the tutors' digs (*Miles Chapel Center*).

Both Monro and Clifton repeatedly described the tutoring project as an educational program rather than a civil rights campaign. Clifton once insisted that the project was about "human rights rather than civil rights" ("Students to Tutor"), and Monro explained that because it was essential to protect the children from violence, the tutors had agreed not to demonstrate, regardless of their own attitudes toward civil rights ("PBH Teachers").

Their precautions were justified. The continued presence of federal troops in the South, residual hostility from the traumatic Year of Birmingham, resistance to the first year of court-mandated school integration (Cobb), and the signing of the Civil Rights Act on 2 July 1964 combined to produce a tinderbox atmosphere. The tutors were most vulnerable while driving to and from their tutoring sites because mixed-race groups were inflammatory by definition. "We felt like pioneers going out together," recalls Mary Oliver White, who graduated from Miles in 1965. Her sister Eunice Oliver Boswell, who graduated from Miles a year later, remembers that one morning a group of tutors were headed toward their work site when their station wagon stopped for a red light and a car pulled up alongside them. As soon as the occupants looked inside, one of them got out of the car and approached the station wagon, raising over his head what looked like an ax, as if to strike. The tutors' driver ran the red light rather than risk an attack (personal interview, 5 Mar. 2008).

To avoid unnecessary confrontations, the tutors usually went straight back to campus after the tutoring sessions and stayed there until it was time to head out the next morning. The college gates were locked at night, and a watchman was on duty round the clock, but Clifton, who realized that the watchman sometimes dozed, patrolled the campus himself and even had his father send him a shotgun (interview). Nor did the comparative safety of the campus protect the tutors from frequent bomb threats delivered by phone (Jack Fitzgerald, e-mail, 16 July 2003).

In spite of the risks, the tutors sometimes got restless and left campus for a bit of recreation. Several of them tried going bowling once, a few days after the Civil Rights Act was signed. Elisha "Major" Gray, Harvard '66, described the excursion:

We walked in together to a sparkling, huge bowling alley, which was thundering with rolling balls, crashing pins and cranking pinsetters. By the time we reached the desk to sign up, the place had become dead silent. All the pins had been set up, the balls returned. But nobody was bowling. They were all looking at us. We asked the man behind the desk to bowl, but he told us that establishment did not serve people like us. We reminded him of the law, and he reminded us that he didn't serve us. Out of the corner of our eyes, we saw some men begin to approach us, and we decided that discretion was the better part of valor. We walked through the exit as the rednecks followed, and in the parking lot we ran to the car, piled in and sped out of the lot. So did our pursuers in their pick-ups with rifles on their window racks. They followed us for about two miles. Then, as we stopped at a light, a battered old hot rod, filled with the meanest looking, tough black men pulled up beside us to indicate that they would escort us safely back home. (E-mail, 6 July 2004).

One potentially dangerous situation began as a gracious social gesture, when Charles Zukoski, a prominent white banker and president of the local Harvard Club, invited the PBH students to a reception the club was sponsoring. Edward S. LaMonte, Harvard '65, who answered the phone when Zukoski called, replied that the tutors had committed to do everything with their partners and asked whether the presence of the Miles students would create a problem. Zukoski promised to check with the board members and was mortified when they refused to include the Miles students. Taking things into their own hands, Zukoski and his wife, Bernadine, invited all the tutors to a cookout at their home in posh Mountain Brook (LaMonte, personal interview, 23 July 2003).

The presence of the tutors, whose four cars were conspicuous in the quiet neighborhood, attracted a good deal of loud car honking, and Zukoski nervously explained that such disruptions were often caused by "jalopies," unregistered cars used during violent confrontations because their owners could not be traced. There was no out-and-out violence, but the honking became more frenetic when the Zukoskis asked their guests to join in singing "We Shall Overcome" (LaMonte interview; Clifton interview).

On the job the tutors faced less dramatic challenges than violence. Some centers lacked basic equipment, so the tutors had to lug blackboards back and forth every day. Others had to pick up and drop off children from far-flung areas, adding hours to their schedule. At some sites the project's patchwork recruitment methods produced a group with wildly varying skills. One team described the outliers in their group, which met at a federal housing project. On one end was a fifth-grader who "was unable to pronounce any letters . . . did not know how to differentiate between printing and writing; [whose] vocabulary was limited to a few two and three letter words, and [who] could not read AT ALL." On the other end were several fifth-graders who required seventh- to ninth-grade material to keep them stimulated (Wilson and Ozawa). Working with such heterogeneous groups required sophisticated teaching strategies the tutors had not had time to acquire.

What the Children Learned

At least some of the two hundred–plus children who participated in the program profited from it, although most gains were not immediate or dramatic. One team saw few signs of improvement until the open house, when a parent said: "I used to think my daughter could never really read a complete sentence.

. . . I don't think she could even understand what she read. Now it seems that when she reads aloud, the words just flow out" (qtd. in Ferrell). A delighted grandmother said that every night she had to yell at her grandson, previously a reluctant reader, to stop reading in bed and turn out the light (Oliver and Gray). One team, discovering that their pupils knew nothing about phonics, decided to make that the focus of their sessions. They began by creating and demonstrating phonics flashcards then progressed slowly but steadily, so that by the time the children took a field trip to the zoo, they were using phonics to read the signs on the animals' cages (Scott).

It was hoped that, in addition to strengthening the children's reading skills, the tutoring project would serve as a model of interracial cooperation (*Miles College–Phillips Brooks*). Unfortunately, one crucial level of interracial cooperation was stripped away before the program even began: after word got out that the tutoring teams were integrated, not a single white child joined the program (Priscilla Ellis, personal interview, 16 Nov. 2002)—disappointing maybe, but not surprising, given that 85 percent of the black children in Birmingham were still attending segregated schools five years later (Egerton 125). On the other hand, because the PBH tutors were often the first white people with whom the grade school children had interacted on a regular basis, there were a few small steps toward interracial understanding (White and Boswell interview). A little boy sitting on Jack Fitzgerald's lap during a bus ride asked if he could run his hand through Fitzgerald's hair, so different from the boy's own—"I had some then," Fitzgerald quipped several decades later (e-mail). During one open house a parent claimed that "race had been forgotten in our classroom and the children had accepted [the PBH tutor] with total confidence; this view was enthusiastically seconded by all the parents" in attendance (*Miles Chapel Center*).

What the Tutors Learned

Many of the PBH tutors were profoundly affected by the summer at Miles. The decision to join the tutoring program had an immediate impact on the career plans of Priscilla "Prill" Ellis, Radcliffe '65. In line with her goal of becoming a psychiatrist, she had planned to take a summer course in organic chemistry that would keep her on track for medical school, but she had also enjoyed tutoring in a Boston development house the previous summer, so she postponed the chemistry course and went to Miles (interview).

Major Gray, for whom the tutoring team was the first racially mixed group he had ever joined, later worked as a Peace Corps volunteer in Niger and taught African Studies and African American history for two years in a low-income neighborhood in New York City (e-mail, 6 July 2004).

Susan (First) Pollock, Radcliffe '64, had been accepted to Harvard Law School when she decided to go to Miles. The tutoring project appealed to her because "it seemed like a wonderful way to get involved in making a positive impact, and making a statement in a positive (and non-violent) way." But face-to-face experience with racial tension brought her up short: "Driving in Birmingham, shopping in Birmingham etc., always worried that we would be arrested or attacked was a powerful experience." She helped create a scholarship program for the United Negro College Fund and does volunteer work for Girls Incorporated (formerly known as the Girls Clubs of America), which sponsors programs for disadvantaged girls (e-mail, 25 Aug. 2003).

As Monro had hoped, the summer at Miles piqued Jon Clifton's interest in teaching, and instead of going to law school, he became director of college guidance at the school where he had been volunteering and eventually became a Presbyterian minister.

The summer at Miles helped Jack Fitzgerald '64 "understand—in a very limited way, of course—what it meant to be the object of racism," and he put that understanding to work, serving on a commission that appointed his town's first black firefighter, demonstrating for a more equitable housing policy, and supporting the recruitment and retention of minority students at Knox College, where he taught sociology and anthropology (e-mail, 16 July 2003).

For Joseph Ozawa '67 the situation at Miles was complicated by the fact that he was Asian and therefore not clearly identifiable as either black or white. This indeterminacy made his presence provocative no matter which group he tried to join. He believes that the tutoring project taught him "that risk is part of commitment to our fellow human beings." As a clinical psychologist, he has courted risk in some of the world's most dangerous areas: Sri Lanka during the long civil war; Indonesia during the fall of the Suharto regime in the 1990s; Eritrea and Ethiopia in 1999, while the two countries were at war; and Burma during the military crackdown on the Karen population in 2001 (e-mail, 24 Sept. 2003).

For the Miles tutors, who collectively identified themselves as the Pitts Volunteer Organization, the tutoring program rarely provided the dramatic impact the Harvard-Radcliffe tutors experienced. More often, it moved them closer to goals they had already set for themselves. Sisters Mary and Eunice Oliver were typical. Both intended to become teachers, but with eight siblings at home, college was an expense the family could ill afford. The tutoring program, besides providing practical teaching experience, allowed them to attend Miles tuition free the following year. Both went on to teach: three years in public school, followed by thirty-two years in junior college and college, for Mary; and thirty-three years in the public schools, of which eighteen were spent teaching and fifteen spent counseling, for Eunice (interview).

Lelia Vickers, Miles '66, was drawn to the project because she liked getting involved in community affairs. Although she enjoyed the tutoring, she initially resisted a career in teaching precisely because it was one of only two careers open to black women with college degrees; the other was nursing. She eventually succumbed to the lure of academe, earned a master's degree in reading instruction, headed a developmental reading program at Winston-Salem State University, and served as dean of the School of Education at North Carolina Agricultural and Technical State University. She may be most notable, however, for resisting the legendary charisma of Lucius Pitts and politely declining his invitation to join the faculty at Miles (telephone interview, 27 Sept. 2010).

Summer School Courses

In addition to Monro, Clifton, and the tutors, the Harvard-Radcliffe group included two volunteers who became involved in the Miles Summer School—so involved, in fact, that both of them returned the following summer. Ed LaMonte, incoming PBH president, taught several sections of an American history seminar. At first the students struggled to deal with either historical facts or historical ideas, but LaMonte encouraged them to analyze material critically, and eventually they began to make connections with their own lives. When they examined social Darwinism, LaMonte noted, "The period of the Gilded Age was familiar to all the members; I presume Birmingham's experience with United States Steel accounts for this knowledge of the techniques of the 'Robber Barons.'" Jack Fitzgerald, outgoing PBH president, taught an anthropology course when the original instructor had to cancel at the last minute. He also helped Howard University professor Marvin Head teach the psychology of adolescence, giving lectures and conducting small group discussions. Fitzgerald sometimes disagreed with Head, a practice that first shocked and then fascinated the students, who found it "a lesson in the exchange rather than the repetition of ideas—a lesson which I have the impression they had not had frequently before" (8).

The Precollege Workshop

Once the tutors and other volunteers were settled in, Monro threw himself into the precollege English workshop (Chisum 17). Most participants were local high school seniors whose grades and standardized test scores indicated they would have difficulty handling college work; many were reading at a ninth- or tenth-grade level and needed intensive work on the basics of grammar, spelling, and punctuation. Two hundred such students had been urged to attend the workshop prior to entering Miles in the fall (Monro, "Summer" 79), and it was hoped that the workshop would reduce Miles's astronomical dropout rate: from a typical freshman class of 400, only 110 to 140 students graduated ("Dean Monro's Enormous Reward").

Miles was highly attractive to graduates of Birmingham's public school system. It was the largest four-year college for blacks in the state, the only one in Jefferson County, and the only four-year college within commuting distance of Birmingham open to blacks—an important consideration for students who lived at home and faced heavy family and work obligations ("Doing Something" 86). Virtually any student with a high school diploma was accepted, and half the teachers in the county's black schools were alumni ("Dean Monro's Enormous Reward" 389). In short students who were advised to take the workshop usually did because Miles represented their best, if not their only, chance to turn their lives around. Monro was dazzled by their dedication, which manifested itself in a 95 percent attendance rate ("Doing Something" 87).

The official literature described the summer program as a "basic skills workshop," but Monro, ever alert to the power of metaphor, called it "a booster-shot program." Students spent an hour each day on math, another on social studies, and two hours on English ("Summer" 79). As both director and a teacher in the English workshop, Monro worked at least as hard as the students did, since the Harvard undergraduates he had taught bore little resemblance to the summer workshop students. Even his experience with a diverse student body at University Extension had not prepared him to deal with the serious deficiencies most of the workshop students struggled with.

Monro decided to structure his workshop around paragraph writing, calling it, in typical military fashion, "the beach head for the six-week . . . campaign" ("Summer" 81). Because the students were creative and expert talkers, he turned paragraph writing into a conversation, proposing a subject to trigger discussion then letting the class talk freely while he kept track of things on the blackboard. After group brainstorming, the students worked on their own paragraphs. In dramatic contrast to the passive classroom behavior they were used to, the students were actively engaged virtually every minute of the class, and they loved it.

Unfortunately, their paragraphs showed all too plainly that in spite of their rich contributions to class discussion, when it came to writing they could not do justice to their ideas. As Monro put it: "Like all people, these students have an undisciplined flow of verbal sounds rushing around in their minds. The sad fact is that in 12 years of schooling many of them have not learned to subject this interior flow of sounds to any effective visual discipline when transcribing them onto paper" ("Summer" 82).

But what mattered most to Monro was that they did have ideas they were burning to express, a fact he learned when he told them to write about their hometown. One student began her essay: "I have always lived in Birmingham and I have always hated it and dreamed about the day I could leave. Then came the riots." Firsthand experience of the violence changed her mind, and in the essay's conclusion she claimed Birmingham as her permanent home: "I want to go to college and come back to change things." The essay exerted a pull on Monro that he could not resist. "It followed as the night the day that I would have to come back again after that summer," he stated. Lucius Pitts put it even more simply: "Those students pulled a chunk out of his heart" (qtd. in Greenhouse 84).

John's paternal grandfather, Rev. Hezekiah Usher Monro.
Courtesy of St. Paul's Episcopalian Church, North Andover.

Yearbook photo of John, age seventeen. 1930.
Courtesy of Phillips Academy.

Dorothy Foster Monro. 1934.
Courtesy of Janet and Philip Dreyer.

John and Dottie on their wedding day, 21 July 1936.
    Courtesy of Janet and Philip Dreyer.

Monro at Harvard, as assistant provost and counselor for veterans, 1949.
Harvard University Archives, UAV 605.270.5p, neg. F863.

Monro with Lucius Pitts and an unidentified third party.
Courtesy of Miles College Library.

Monro in his office at Miles, 1969.
Courtesy of Frederick Noyes.

Monro with students at Tougaloo.
Courtesy of Mississippi State Archives.

The Mansion, one of Tougaloo's historic buildings.
Courtesy of Tougaloo College Archives.

Harvard Foundation portrait of Monro.
    Courtesy of Stephen Coit and Harvard Art Museum/Fogg Museum, Harvard University Portrait Collection, Commissioned by the Harvard Foundation, 2007, H841.

Acrylic portrait of Monro at Tougaloo.
Courtesy of Johnnie M. Maberry Gilbert.

7
FINAL YEARS AS DEAN
1964-1967

Monro returned to New England when the summer workshop ended, but as the 1964–65 school year began at Harvard, the matters that demanded his attention paled in comparison to the issues taking such bold shape in the South. At the same time that he continued to find or create projects at Harvard that he believed in, he became increasingly absorbed in the cause of black education.

Although Monro had no regrets about withdrawing from the presidential search at Tougaloo, the vacancy was still on his mind. He had met former president Beittel at Miles that summer and talked to several Harvard teachers and grad students who had taught upper-level summer seminars and freshman tutorials at Tougaloo ("Students to Teach"). On 14 September he wrote to Wesley Hotchkiss, chairman of Tougaloo's board of trustees, asking how the search was progressing. A short time later the committee recommended that Acting President George Owens become Tougaloo's first black president and first alumni president. Owens promptly invited Monro to join the board of trustees, and Monro just as promptly accepted, also agreeing to help plan the inauguration.

Owens was not exactly the black scholar Monro had envisioned as Tougaloo's ideal president, but he had a lot going for him. His life up to that point was an inspirational story much like that of Lucius Pitts. A sharecropper's son, he had grown up in Bolton, Mississippi, attended Jackson State College, graduated from Tougaloo in 1941, and received an MBA degree from Columbia. He briefly held an executive position at Saks Fifth Avenue but soon realized that the business world had little room for a black executive, even one with impressive credentials. Dispassionately examining his options, he carved out a niche for himself in black education, and after six years as business manager at Talladega, he accepted the same position at Tougaloo (Posner). Since his arrival in 1955, he and his family had become fixtures at the college and in the black community ("Inauguration").

STUDENT INITIATIVE AT HARVARD

The summer Monro had spent with the highly motivated Birmingham students made him more sensitive to the apathy and entitlement so common among Harvard students. Hoping to engage them more fully, he helped create the Harvard Policy Committee (HPC), which gave them a stronger voice in formulating long-range educational policy. As dean, he served on the HPC, along with two faculty members and eleven students. Many faculty members and administrators, and even some students, viewed the new committee with skepticism, but from the beginning Monro took it seriously, faithfully attending meetings and engaging in discussions as if they mattered. Eventually, and partly as a result of his high-profile participation, the committee became a key player in shaping educational policy (Samuelson, "Monro's Altruistic Instinct" 5). Monro was also a staunch supporter of the *Southern Courier,* a newspaper created by Harvard students to provide accurate coverage of civil rights developments. He helped bankroll the paper by drawing seed money from the college's civil rights fund (Samuelson, "Monro's Altruistic Instinct" 3), and he served as faculty advisor along with Harvard Law School professor Mark DeWolfe Howe (Fenton, "Students").

One positive consequence of promoting student initiative was the friendship Monro frequently developed with student leaders, even those who initially viewed him as an adversary. Hubert Sapp '67 did just that when he saw Monro bellowing, "Get out of here or get out of college," to students involved in the 1964 "Save the Sycamores" campaign. Given Monro's size and the booming power of his amplified voice, he seemed the embodiment of heavy-handed authoritarianism. But Sapp soon realized that looks were deceiving. "We thought he was the heavy, but he was actually trying to contain things, get the students back into [Harvard] Yard, and keep the police from getting involved," he explained (personal interview, 30 July 2003).

As president of the Association of African and Afro-American Students (AAAAS), Sapp observed that, instead of obsessing about procedures and rules the way students expected administrators to do, Monro could be surprisingly casual about them. On one occasion, for example, Sapp and several other AAAAS members asked Monro for funding to attend a black student organization conference at Columbia. "We went in expecting to do battle," Sapp recalled, "but he surprised us by agreeing right away to all our requests" (interview). Together Monro and Sapp squelched the accusation that AAAAS, after being around for several years, was fostering resegregation by encouraging black students to isolate themselves. Sapp countered that the club's members belonged to many other groups but needed a place where they could talk, alone, about the issues that were particular to them. Monro used the same argument when describing to a *Crimson* reporter the crucial role the organization filled on campus (McDougall). Eventually, Monro would persuade Sapp to join him in the South.

DRUG CONTROVERSY AT HARVARD: ACT II

To Monro's annoyance the drug controversy that had begun in 1962 kept springing back to life, sometimes triggered by events only tenuously connected to Harvard. On 11 February 1965, the *New York Times* reported the arrest of three drug peddlers in the Harvard Square area. The pushers had no connection to Harvard, but the sentencing judge stated, "The use of drugs among students is depressing." *Times* reporter John H. Fenton seized on this remark to resurrect the issue of drugs on college campuses, using Harvard as a case study. Under the headline "Marijuana Users Disturb Harvard," Fenton assembled a mass of untraceable quotes and spurious statistics: the Harvard administration was "known to be alert to the problem" and was "understood to believe" that drug use was a manifestation of "youthful experimentation" rather than of addiction; Harvard students "estimate that from one-fifth to one-half the 12,500 persons studying at the university will have tried marijuana while at Cambridge" ("Marijuana Users"). In his nationally syndicated column Russell Baker used the bogus statistic to argue that young people in America were "using up life too fast" ("Observer"). On 28 February *Times* education editor Fred Hechinger repeated the statistic, admitted that it was probably inflated, then interpreted the unattributed phrase "youthful experimentation" to mean that Harvard administrators were blithely dismissing students' use of marijuana as harmless ("Drug Issue"). As spokesman for the college on issues of student behavior and misbehavior, Monro responded with a letter to the *Times* on 15 March. Pointing out that in journalistic circles repetition too often trumped accuracy, he upbraided Baker and Hechinger for parroting the questionable statistic, adding, "I can only hope the *Times* will not go on repeating the student estimate to the point where it becomes accepted as commonplace" ("Harvard Official").

A SECOND SUMMER AT MILES

While he wrestled with the hydra-headed drug issue, Monro remained active in the world of black education. He joined the Centennial Committee at Howard University, and his paper "College Programs for Disadvantaged Youth," delivered at the annual meeting of the American Council on Education (ACE), was included in *Expanding Opportunities,* a report published by ACE's Committee on Equality of Educational Opportunity. But the lion's share of his time and attention went to Miles, where he became a trustee (Kahn 52), making frequent visits to put final touches on the Freshman Studies Program. He successfully pushed to make Miles one of eighteen host campuses for the first year of Upward Bound, a federal program to help underprivileged high school students get into college. To make Miles more attractive as a site, he offered to run the new program himself (Whipple).

When he left for Miles that summer, he was joined by three Harvard-Radcliffe students, all veterans of the previous summer. Prill Ellis, who had just graduated from Radcliffe, worked with him in both Upward Bound and in the precollege English workshop; and Jack Fitzgerald and Ed LaMonte taught in the summer school. As a perk that only a true sports fan could fully appreciate, Fitzgerald, LaMonte, and Monro shared a modest bungalow known as the "Willie Mays House," after the pioneering black baseball star who had spent several years of his childhood there (Kahn 50).[1]

In the workshop Monro continued to adjust his teaching to fit the needs of the Miles students. To make the pedagogy even more challenging, the workshop was beginning to attract accomplished students, not just those who were struggling academically. Solomon Oliver, whose sisters Mary and Eunice had participated in the tutoring program, had a stellar high school record and was admitted to Miles unconditionally, but he decided to take the workshop anyway, and he was not sorry. He found it a stimulating combination of "substantial reading, writing, critiques of writing, and abstract thinking," and he met a fair number of students who had been accepted at more prestigious schools such as Morehouse or Talladega but who feigned interest in Miles so that they would be admitted to the workshop (telephone interview, 7 May 2008).

For the second year in a row Monro's reading list was heavily weighted toward black writers. He defended the noncanonical choices on several grounds, the first being that they fostered discussion of "critical issues in American social history, of especial importance for our students in Birmingham to know about" ("Summer" 84). An informal survey had convinced him that the workshop students were unacquainted with their literary heritage. In a group of about one hundred students only five had read Martin Luther King Jr.'s *Stride towards Freedom*, few had heard of Frederick Douglass, and about W.E.B. Du Bois they knew only that he had "turned Communist" (83).

Monro considered *Narrative of the Life of Frederick Douglass* especially appropriate for the workshop: it was "a short book, a young man's book," "an utterly convincing book," and one that "provide[d] the very best sort of raw material for classroom discussions of the corruption that comes with power" ("Summer" 85). When some teachers in the program complained that the book lacked literary merit or that they felt presumptuous discussing it with black students, Monro raised the issue with a group of students, who said they had found the book stimulating and had not been uncomfortable talking about it with white teachers (86).

Monro sided with the students, saying he was beginning to think that "graduate schools these days have too narrow a view of what is literature" ("Summer" 86). He insisted that the black writers on the reading list were so significant— and wrote so well—that "any course in American literature that does not include a study of Frederick Douglass, Booker T. Washington, W.E.B. Du Bois, and Martin Luther King Jr. stands convicted of ignoring truly great works in our national epic" (85). At a College Board conference later that summer he argued for the centrality of black literature in American education, not just in the black college curriculum or in black literature courses, a cause he would champion for the rest of his life. He had already begun assigning black writers such as James Baldwin and Ralph Ellison to his University Extension students, urging them to search out other black writers as well (Gove).

Three years later, in a speech at the New School for Social Research in New York, he mocked the esoteric courses that found their way into college catalogs in which works by black writers were either totally missing or treated as something less than literature: "We teach every exotic thing you can think of in our great universities: Northern Welsh Literature, Middle Irish, Origins of European Romanticism, Andean Archeology, Beowulf . . . . The Minor Works of Rousseau. We spend endless amounts of time on the *Iliad*, the poeticized story of a two-penny comic-opera war fought 3,000 years ago in the Dardenelles. But for our own terrible racial epic, one of the most agonized struggles in human history, involving millions of men and women over four centuries—our learned faculties cannot begin to see it" ("Negro" 9).

Monro traced his conversion to a spirited conversation with Betty Gates, the dynamic black professor at Miles who would be running the English component of the Freshman Studies Program during its pilot year. When he showed her a tentative reading list he had drawn up for the first semester of the course, she challenged the presence of a Shakespeare play, saying, "Your Harvard is showing, John." He replied, "Well, Harvard and Miles have to meet someplace." She shot back, "Why?" Realizing he had no good answer, he dropped the Shakespeare, although it eventually found its way into the sophomore curriculum (Greenhouse 87).

Before he left for Harvard, Monro agreed to return the following summer, to direct Upward Bound again and to run the entire precollege workshop, including the math and social studies components. Every year he found it more wrenching to leave and became more attached to the students, who had worked so hard all summer for the right to become freshmen: "My mind keeps going back to . . . boys and girls who have to bus it across town, one hour or two hours in the morning to get to class, one hour or two hours at night to get home. But still they come, with faith and hope in their hearts. After all, people do live only once, and if you don't get a fair start then you never do discover who you are and what's in you to do. In the end, that's what Miles College is all about" (qtd. in *Light*, n.p.).

That summer another factor contributed to Monro's reluctance to leave Miles: the pilot version of the Freshman English course was being taught in the fall, and he would have loved to participate in it. He took some consolation in the fact that two of his companions were staying on—the first in a long line of students and colleagues he would lure to the South as either a stimulating professional way station or a permanent home. After her second summer at Miles, Prill Ellis, whose plans to become a psychiatrist had already been delayed by her participation in the tutoring project, was beginning to think that teaching might be her vocation, so she stayed to teach the Freshman English course and to get a longer look at the teaching life than the summer activities offered (interview).

Ed LaMonte, who was headed to the University of Chicago to begin graduate studies in social science, had worked in the president's office following Pitts's second heart attack in eight months (Egerton 111). As autumn approached, Pitts began looking for a permanent administrative assistant, having been warned by his doctor that he risked a relapse unless he continued to reduce his workload. LaMonte said good-bye, went home, and packed his bags for Chicago. The night before his departure he received a frantic phone call from Pitts; his administrative assistant-to-be had accepted a more lucrative offer at the last minute, and Pitts begged LaMonte to delay graduate school for a year and fill the vacancy. Asked for his opinion, Monro told LaMonte that he should work with Pitts, where he would do more good in a year than many people could accomplish in a lifetime (personal interview, 23 July 2003).[2]

THE DRAFT DEFERMENT ISSUE

In Cambridge, Monro's pride in his military service complicated his response to a controversy that began in the spring of 1966, when Harvard became one of twelve hundred sites administering an optional Selective Service exam. Students' exam scores, along with their class rankings, were sent to local draft boards, where they could be used in decisions about granting or denying deferment. Harvard's prestige, as well as its status as a testing site, put it in the spotlight, as colleges across the country struggled with the policy. As usual, Monro encouraged student initiative, telling the *New York Times* that if a student asked that his class ranking not be sent, "I won't send it" ("Draft Sets"). In a follow-up letter to the editor he added that students who decided not to provide the information to the draft board would have to accept the consequences ("Harvard Dean").

After a student referendum indicated that 72 percent of the participants disapproved of class ranking as a basis for deferment, Monro unsuccessfully pressured the faculty for an open discussion about the matter, repeatedly raising the issue at faculty meetings (Samuelson, "Draft Debate"). The agenda for the 6 December faculty meeting included a resolution to declare the student deferment "unjust," but debate was squelched when a motion to table the resolution was swiftly passed ("No Argument"). Monro promised to raise the issue at the January 1967 meeting if nobody else did (Samuelson, "Monro Moves"), but philosophy professor John Rawls beat him to it, proposing a resolution to condemn student deferments. Almost the entire meeting was spent debating his proposal, and though the final vote—to postpone the resolution indefinitely—was inconclusive, the controversy had finally been aired in a public forum, after three months of faculty silence (Samuelson, "Faculty"). The vote preserved the college's existing policy regarding class rankings, which was the result Monro had hoped for, but even more important to him, the openness of the discussion prevented further fraying of the lines of communication.

He had been thinking a lot about those lines of communication since his return from Miles, where his rapport with the students was growing so strong. Long before the student referendum on draft deferment went unanswered, Monro had broached the communication theme during his September address to the incoming freshmen. He told them: "In all history, I think, no two generations have ever wanted more to talk together, or needed more to talk together than your generation and mine. And no two generations have had a harder time doing it" ("How to Live" 14). To improve intergenerational communication, he encouraged the freshmen to take advantage of his open-door policy and assured them that he would listen carefully to what they had to say.

THE MCNAMARA FRACAS

Overlapping the draft deferment controversy, and freighted with the same strong feelings about the Vietnam War, was a campus visit in November 1966 by Secretary of Defense Robert S. McNamara, who had been named first honorary associate of the university's Kennedy Institute of Politics (Fenton, "Harvard Men"). Eager to pit him against a prominent opponent of the Vietnam War, the Students for a Democratic Society (SDS) invited McNamara to debate *Ramparts* managing editor Robert Scheer (Lerner). The institute's director, Robert Neustadt, and graduate student Barney Frank '62, its director of undergraduate affairs, took the decision out of McNamara's hands, declining the invitation on the basis that, as part of their appointment, honorary associates were assured all their comments would be off the record (Samuelson, "Mill Street").[3] At their 2 November meeting SDS members voted to hold a "disruptive demonstration" outside of Quincy House, where McNamara was scheduled to appear. The housemaster and faculty associates voted to ban demonstrations on house property, making demonstrators who refused to disperse subject to disciplinary action (Lerner). Discussions between the institute and SDS broke down the week before McNamara's arrival.

On Monday, 7 November, a decoy car was sent to the front of Quincy House, and McNamara left by the back entrance. But the demonstrators learned about the ruse, and by the time McNamara emerged from the building and got into the waiting car, a crowd of some three hundred students, about equally divided between SDS members and their opponents, had assembled on Mill Street. The demonstrators sat down in the street to block McNamara's route, then surrounded the car and began rocking it (Fenton, "Harvard Men"). McNamara got out of the car, climbed onto the roof, and offered to answer a few questions, warning, "We're in a mob and I don't want anyone hurt." At that point SDS had achieved its goal: a direct confrontation with McNamara and an opportunity to force him to defend his views. SDS acting chairman Michael Ansara '67 produced a microphone, and the questions began.

The exchange quickly became hostile, and the police intervened, dispersing the crowd (Fenton, "Harvard Men" 8). Frank hustled McNamara into nearby Leverett House, where they took a tunnel and emerged onto what is now John F. Kennedy Street. From there McNamara was driven to the Littauer Center for Public Administration Building, where he attended a seminar being conducted by professor of government Henry Kissinger. McNamara appeared undisturbed by the confrontation, calmly completing the day's itinerary "with no visible signs of irritation" (Barney Frank, letter, 25 July 2007). But years later, in an interview with biographer Deborah Shapley, he admitted that the episode had shaken him badly: "It was a terrible situation. There was a great danger of people getting hurt or actual loss of life" (qtd. in Shapley 377).

Up to and including the demonstration, Monro had been involved only tangentially in the episode, although Frank had told him about the SDS "disruptive demonstration" vote. Given his preemptive participation in events with even a hint of potential for student unruliness, his hands-off attitude suggests that he believed everything was under control. He may also have wanted to convey confidence in Harvard's house system and the institute's ability to handle the visit. But once the demonstration occurred, he took on the familiar role of damage control officer and official spokesman for the college. First, he wrote a letter to McNamara, apologizing in the name of the college for "the discourteous and unruly confrontation forced upon you" ("Harvard Apology"). A day later McNamara received another letter of apology, signed by twenty-seven hundred of Harvard's forty-nine hundred undergraduates (Fenton, "Harvard Men"). McNamara replied to Monro in a letter of his own, protesting that the apology had been unnecessary. He identified with the demonstrators, stating: "I understand both the intense interest of the students in the vital issues of our time and their desire to express that interest in a manner which commands public attention. . . . Occasionally all of us allow our zeal to exceed our judgment, but such behavioral aberrations should not be a basis for curbing dissent—dissent is both the prerogative and the preservative of free men everywhere" ("McNamara Replies"). All three letters were printed the *New York Times*.

Monro introduced the embarrassing incident at the next meeting of the administrative board, even though it was the board's policy to avoid issues involving political protests. It was decided that the demonstrators would not be disciplined, but as chair, Monro warned, "If this happens again, action will be taken" (Samuelson, "Mill Street").

In a move that surprised SDS members, Monro attended their next meeting. He refused to condone "the assumption by this organization to take physical charge of a man because you disagree with his politics," but said that he was always willing to discuss matters, and he invited all interested members to have dinner with him and discuss the incident. After he left, several SDS members admitted that they had already spoken with him individually. Twenty-two students signed up for the dinner, which took place the following week (Samuelson, "Monro Speaks").

Thanks to Monro's fence mending, the administration and SDS worked together much more effectively in February 1967, when the Kennedy Institute hosted its second honorary associate, U.S. ambassador to the United Nations Arthur J. Goldberg. Monro was involved from the beginning, attending four lengthy meetings with SDS leaders and presenting their demands to Robert Neustadt and dean of faculty Franklin Ford. SDS wanted a public, on-the-record appearance by Goldberg, during which he would respond to follow-up questions, and Goldberg readily agreed, saying that the original arrangements had been the weaker for "a failure to provide facilities for this kind of expression." SDS leaders, after grousing that they should have been notified of Goldberg's decision in advance rather than reading about it in the *Crimson*, helped work out the details of the event. On Sunday, 12 February, the appearance went off without a hitch, and Monro could congratulate himself on succeeding in his role as go-between.

DRUG CONTROVERSY AT HARVARD: ACT III

Late in March 1967 the *Crimson* reignited the drugs-on-campus controversy with a two-part series called "Drugs in the Yard." In the first installment a house proctor was quoted as stating that the use of marijuana and LSD among freshmen had greatly increased since the previous year, and reporter James K. Glassman estimated that, on the basis of exchanges with "students, proctors and psychiatrists," 25 to 30 percent of the freshman class had smoked pot ("Use of Drugs"). Predictably, the *Boston Globe* trumpeted the unverified percentage of pot smokers in its headline ("Dean Doubts 25% Use 'Pot' at Harvard"), and buried the *Crimson*'s breezy qualifier in the final paragraph of the story: "Just how widespread drug use has become is hard to say. There are no statistics on the subject, and reliable ones would be nearly impossible to get" (qtd. in Mahoney).

Because the *Crimson* articles dealt with drug use among freshmen, dean of freshmen F. Skiddy von Stade Jr. '38, joined Monro in speaking for the administration, but because Monro was better known—and because he was linked to the sensationalism of the Alpert-Leary episode—he was the face the press attached to the controversy as well as the "dean" mentioned in the *Globe* headline. On campus he did what he could to keep the issue from mushrooming into another standoff between students and administration. He explained that although the college could suspend students caught using drugs, instead they were usually referred to a University Health Services psychiatrist. He added that the administrative board always considered the details and merits of each case before deciding on a course of action. Once the *Crimson* stories broke, other members of the board, including von Stade, pressed Monro to state the official policy on drug use, a step he felt would discourage debate and deflect attention from the flexible application of the policy (Glassman, "Deans Attempt").

Finally, he gave in and wrote a brusque letter, addressed to "Gentlemen of 1970," for publication in the 19 April 1967 *Crimson*:

> The Dean's Office has been repeatedly pressed by a number of members of the Freshman Class for a statement of the College's administrative position with respect to the use of drugs, including marijuana and LSD. If it will help anyone, I am pleased to clarify our position.
>
> As anyone bright enough to be at Harvard knows perfectly well, possession of, or distribution of, marijuana and LSD are strictly against the law, and taking the drugs involves users in psychological dangers and contacts with the criminal underworld. The college is prepared to take serious disciplinary action, up to and including dismissal, against any student found to be involved in the use or distribution of illegal and dangerous drugs.
>
> In sum, if a student is stupid enough to misuse his time here fooling around with illegal and dangerous drugs, our view is that he should leave college and

make room for people prepared to take good advantage of a college opportunity. ("Gentlemen").

The letter was widely publicized and admired for its no-nonsense firmness. Among its fans was Abigail Van Buren, who reprinted it in her nationally syndicated "Dear Abby" column. But the letter's confrontational tone was uncharacteristic of Monro. Gone were the sophisticated strategies he normally employed to woo a hostile audience. Gone, too, was the dean who had respectfully addressed the "Gentlemen of 1970" the previous fall, inviting them to join him in improving communications between their respective generations ("How to Live").

The simplest way to account for Monro's uncharacteristic approach is sheer chronology: each time the drug issue resurfaced, he confronted it with a shorter fuse. But other factors were at work too. The letter sounded angry because he *was* angry: he resented being pressured into writing it, believing as he did that that there was nothing to gain, and possibly a good deal to lose, by doing so. In addition, the current controversy had been created by the *Crimson* from whole cloth, a fact that offended his strong sense of journalistic ethics and tapped into his emotionally charged relationship with the newspaper. Finally, it rankled him that the drug controversy would give a bitter taste to his final days at Harvard. A month earlier the *Crimson* had run a headline that shocked the Harvard community far more than his terse letter to the freshman class: "Monro to Resign July 1 as Dean of College."

THE BIG MOVE

As early as 1964, Monro was toying with the idea of going to Miles for good (O'Connell interview; Stookey interview). By the summer of 1965 he knew it was what he wanted. One day the following winter he was sitting with Pitts in his kitchen, discussing the Freshman Studies Program. Pointing out that it was almost finished, Pitts half-jokingly suggested, "Why don't you just come down here and run it?" and without skipping a beat Monro replied, "I thought you'd never ask" (letter to Merrifield, 1992). Assuming that Monro would take a leave of absence to get the program on its feet, Pitts was stunned when Monro said he and Dottie would move to Alabama for good (Greenhouse 86).

For a time Monro kept his decision to himself and dealt with the problems that came across his desk—the draft deferment issue, McNamara's visit, and the stories about drug use on campus—as though he would be at Harvard forever. He told President Pusey about his plans in March 1966, a full year before the public announcement took place. The generous advance notice was appropriate, given their close personal and professional relationship. Pusey had appointed Monro dean, and during Pusey's brief stint as acting dean of arts and sciences, they had worked closely on many issues. He had supported Monro's positions, even the unpopular ones, although he had refused to speak to the press about the parietals controversy. Monro had been especially grateful for such loyalty during that difficult period, telling members of the Harvard Club of New York, "Even if all the undergraduates think your name is mud, and half the faculty thinks you have lost your mind, and the rest of the world thinks you are a fairly simple-minded, if well intentioned boob, none of this matters a damn if a man named Nathan Pusey is in your corner ready with the smelling salts between rounds" ("Moral Values" 4).

There was no need to discuss the move with Dottie, who had long ago realized that her husband was being inexorably drawn to Miles. It went without saying that she would support his decision totally and uncomplainingly. But moving would be a far bigger adjustment for her than for him, especially since she had not joined him during his frequent visits to Birmingham. The only people she knew at Miles were Pitts, who had come to Cambridge several times, and the Harvard folks Monro had talked into joining the Miles faculty. She would also have to adjust to being far from family. Since their move to Evanston, Illinois, where Phil was working in his doctorate at the University of Chicago, Phil, Janet, and the children had made the icy trek to Cambridge for Christmas. Ann, who was now divorced, was living in Woburn, an easy drive from Cambridge, and Helen and Jim Scobie, with whom Dottie had lived during the final months of Monro's active duty, were only a bit farther away, in Scituate (Philip Dreyer, e-mail, 6 July 2007). Moreover, Dottie did not delude herself that John would spend more time with her to compensate for their being far from family: the fact that he wanted a classroom built in their basement suggested that he had no intention of leaving his work at the office.

The Announcement

The world learned about Monro's plans on Thursday, 9 March 1967, at a joint press conference he and Pitts held at the New York Hilton. Announcing that as of 1 July Monro would become director of Freshman Studies at Miles, Pitts introduced him with a flourish, saying: "You ask for the moon and you get the stars. This time we got the moon *and* the stars (qtd. in Chisum 15).

When Monro took the floor, he struck a chord he would sound incessantly during the months and years ahead: "I want to disassociate myself from any idea that this is a sacrifice. I see it as a job of enormous reward" (Hechinger, "Dean Quits"). He could have saved his breath: just as the press had seized on the most lurid aspects of Harvard's campus controversies, they eagerly latched onto the broadest cliché to characterize his resignation. The trend began at the press conference, with Whitney B. Young, director of the National Urban League, saying, "At a time when most of our academic liberals are more interested in self-determination 10,000 miles away than one mile down the block, the Dean of the greatest university in the world is making a significant sacrifice" (Jones, "Monro to Resign").

Pitts was not much help in squelching the hero cliché; he said he doubted other academics would follow in Monro's footsteps: "I hope this will set a trend, but I have to admit that Monro is an extraordinary man and most people in his position are not likely to make such a change" ("Dean Monro: Position"). The *Christian Science Monitor* heard him—sort of—but refused to be convinced: "We understand what he means when he decries any suggestion that this is a sacrifice. But to lesser men it would be" ("In the Right Direction"). In a *Boston Globe* interview he expanded on the no-sacrifice theme: "Position doesn't mean anything. It's the function that matters. You have 400 freshmen who are behind academically, and you have to do something for them in their freshman year. That's when it matters." When the reporter asked about Monro's salary, he balked, probably because a pay cut could be interpreted as a financial sacrifice. "What a man gets paid is nobody's business but his wife's," he retorted (qtd. in "Dean Monro: Position").

Positive Press, for Once

Press coverage of the announcement was copious: the *New York Times* printed an interview that had taken place at Harvard earlier in the week, an editorial praising his move, and a front-page news story by Fred Hechinger. Articles appeared in *Time Magazine,* the *Saturday Review,* the *Nation,* all the Boston newspapers, and papers throughout the South. Both the *Times* and the *Christian Science Moni-*

tor parlayed Monro's news into an analysis of black colleges and the challenges they faced (Hechinger, "On the Ailing"). Across New England any connection to Monro, no matter how slight, merited coverage: an article in the *South Freeport Times* described the enduring local presence of the Foster family and emphasized Monro's citizenship-through-marriage ("Proper Sequel"). Edith Monro, John's aunt and the family's most avid genealogist, wrote a letter to the *Bristol Phoenix* detailing the presence of earlier generations of Monros in Rhode Island. Harvard's ROTC newsletter, the *Loudspeaker,* resurrected the details of Monro's career on the *Enterprise* and encouraged ROTC men to follow his courageous example (April–May 1967). When a longtime dining hall attendant at Harvard retired later that year, she reminisced about the famous people she had served, and listed Monro right up there alongside John and Joseph Kennedy Jr. ("Mrs. D"). As for the *Crimson,* the 10 March issue bulged with articles about Monro's announcement and its impact on the college, beginning with the lead story and a five-column front-page headline—an extravagant gesture more like Monro's beloved *Journal* than the comparatively staid *Crimson. Crimson* editors abandoned their customary adversarial stance and praised Monro's effectiveness as a student advocate and spokesman, concluding, "Miles may not yet fully realize what it is getting; but his presence there will be felt immediately, as will his absence here" ("Dean Monro").

What *Was* He Thinking?

The public reaction at Harvard was upbeat. Pusey stated that Monro had "given warm sympathy, searching thought and cool judgment to fostering the intellectual and moral environment of undergraduate life" (Spergel 21), and dean of faculty Richard Ford praised him for providing faculty and administration with "an essential interpretation of what is the best and most responsible student opinion" (Jones, "Monro to Resign").

But behind the scenes there was much head-scratching. Peter Gomes, who was in his second year at Harvard Divinity School at the time, recalls, "Nobody could understand it, since everyone believed that Harvard was the Emerald City, the only place the Holy Grail might be found, and that if it did happen to be elsewhere, it wasn't in Alabama." Nancy Deptula, Monro's administrative assistant, later confessed that his colleagues "thought he was crazy, absolutely out of his mind" (qtd. in Greenhouse 56).

Monro considered his decision perfectly logical, as he explained, in a letter dated 24 August, to his former advisee John Merrifield: "The move to Alabama made so much basic sense to me that I've been startled at the press surprise. Obviously, in a fundamental way, I've lost touch altogether with the main conditioning of the day. Been reading too much Thoreau, I guess. Anyway, I expect to have fun, and hope you'll drop in for a look." The letter practically bristles with eagerness, and the reasons are not hard to find.

First, Monro had always looked with skepticism on the layers of privilege in which Harvard's citizens were swaddled, and he used a startling image to suggest why one might do well to leave: "Our society has a great many traps. Once you start orienting your life around the expectations of pay, family, neighborhood, swimming pools, status, you're done—you've given your life over to a trap. Harvard is a fur-lined trap—it's one of the best. But that's a lousy way to decide how you're going to spend your life" (qtd. in Fuchs 20). As he had done in most areas of his life, Monro almost invariably chose challenge over comfort, which he viewed with suspicion through the lens of his Scottish-Yankee-Protestant heritage.

Besides, from a selfish point of view he was finding his position at Harvard less and less rewarding. In an interview with the *Crimson* published on 10 March, he implied that eventual burnout was inevitable: "My impression of the dean's office here is that after six or seven years it becomes a custodial position. This is a good time for a turnover to get a younger fellow with fresh ideas" (qtd. in Jones, "Monro to Resign"). Even more significant was his sense of diminishing returns as dean. Recent satisfactions, such as the Harvard Policy Committee and the *Southern Courier,* could not compare to earlier, groundbreaking work with the Veterans Bureau, the National Scholarships, the Financial Aid Office, the Peace Corps, and the commuter students. Less of his time and energy was going into projects he believed in, and more was being diverted to holding the line against attitudes he found distasteful. More than once he compared the deanship to "being the shock absorber in a Rolls Royce" (Gewertz).

He had also been badly shaken by the lack of support for his position on parietals; generalizing from that experience, he later said that he had felt like an outsider throughout his deanship: "I was never really prepared to be dean. I guess I never felt like an establishment guy" (qtd. in Greenhouse 84). His growing circle of friends in Birmingham underscored his sense of estrangement from his Harvard colleagues, and he listed the supportive local community as one factor that attracted him to Miles: "I like the town, I have been working there, and have a lot of friends working there and on the faculty" ("Dean Monro: Position"). Working in the summer program at Miles in 1966, Chuck Bunting was struck by the change he noticed in Monro: "It was clear that he was dying at Harvard and energized and alive at Miles" (e-mail, 12 Jan. 2008).

Of course, feeling like an outsider would not have been enough by itself to push him away from Harvard, since he had chosen that role, or been forced into it, so many times. At Phillips he had lived and worked off campus. At the *Crimson* he had alienated the administration and the masthead-only editors by jumping ship. In the navy he had been a sixty-day-wonder in a chain of command dominated by Annapolis "ring-twisters." As a writing teacher, he lacked a degree in English. As a dean eager to shape educational policy, he lacked a graduate degree. By choosing Miles, he was assuming another outsider role, that of a white northerner on a southern black campus.

Another important factor in his decision was his growing difficulty identifying with his student constituency, especially after he stopped teaching in the undergraduate program. "The dean's real function is to communicate honestly to the president and senior faculty what's on the undergraduates' minds," he later explained. "I wasn't doing that as well as I wanted to . . . . In fact, the chasm was getting pretty wide" (qtd. in Greenhouse 84–86).[4]

Although Monro had begun to feel remote from his student constituency, his colleagues noticed no change. Both Nancy and Ted Sizer, who was dean of the Graduate School of Education when Monro left, saw his departure as a heavy loss precisely because of his rapport with undergraduates. "So many people his age just couldn't talk to undergraduates in ways that indicated any empathy at all with what they were doing," Nancy explained. "But he saw where they were coming from and conveyed that message, especially in what he did" (personal interview, 3 July 2006).

The students themselves, both collectively and individually, continued to view Monro with affection and respect. After his announcement the Young People's Socialist League sent balloons inscribed "Good Luck, Dean Monro" floating over the Charles River (Greenhouse 82). What stood out about Monro for Peter Rosenbaum '67, president of Phillips Brooks House, was his "deep caring and conviction about righting some of the social injustices pervading our society. . . . He revealed this by example and by offering support; he never preached or pontificated. . . . I've always thought of him as the one Thoreau among all the faculty and administrators I came across" (e-mail, 5 June 2007).[5]

Many student leaders who disagreed with Monro on controversial issues nonetheless respected him. Mike Ansara '68, acting SDS chair during McNamara's visit to campus, recalls: "We sometimes were on opposite sides of a particular event but he was always a person of great integrity, quiet warmth, real support for students and someone I greatly respected. I was not profoundly surprised when he left to go to Miles. It was a decision made by an intensely moral man" (e-mail, 27 Oct. 2007).

Even those who did not know Monro well found his decision inspiring. According to Ed LaMonte's roommate, Peter Briggs '65: "Most of my generation of Harvard students were aspiring careerists, and it was a real eye-opener for us to see someone as successful as Dean Munro [sic] leave Harvard to go to Miles College. I think the man believed in education by example" (e-mail, 5 May 2006).

Midlife Crisis?

Monro's decision to go to Miles demonstrated some of the earmarks of a classic midlife crisis. Although he showed no signs of slowing down, time was slipping by, and, at the age of fifty-four, he wanted to exploit the rest of his life to maximum effect. He mused: "I'm . . . in the cancer and heart attack range. If I want to do anything, I've got about 10 years. I'm old enough to know that you can't change the world, but you can give it a heave" (Fuchs 22).[6]

"Giving the world a heave," as he inelegantly put it, was something that mattered deeply to him and that infused the midlife questions—Is this it? Is this what I want to do for the rest of my life? Is it enough?—with a sense of urgency. His early, even ancestral, influences emphasized the importance of making a contribution to society, and he believed that Miles was a better place than Harvard from which to do so. "The future of education is not at highly selective colleges like Harvard or Yale," he insisted, "but here at Miles, where we admit everyone with a high school diploma" (qtd. in Fuchs 21). With brutal honesty he questioned the efficacy and motivation of diversity campaigns like Harvard's: "You break your back getting some tough little kid from a slum to come here, you give him a full scholarship, and then he leaves in the middle of his freshman year because he just can't take it. He's unhappy, we're unhappy. You ask yourself, 'Did you do this for him or for yourself?' You just don't know" ("Monro Says").

Such doubts disappeared when he contemplated his role at Miles and the students he would be working with. Describing them to a reporter, he said, "The kids have an old-fashioned idea about college, which I find charming. They are not cynical. They believe the college can do something for them. They are serious in their hope it will" (qtd. in Donovan). Attempting to summarize the forces drawing him to Miles, Monro assumed the direct, stripped-down style he so admired in Frost, Hemingway, and Steinbeck: "I like the place. I like the people. I like what they are trying to do. There is something wonderful going on here. It's really hard to put into words—but you can feel it" (qtd. in Spergel 21).

SAYING GOOD-BYE

Harvard had been a presence in Monro's life since early childhood. Claxton's Harvard degree had been one of his proudest possessions, and Monro's undergraduate years had been full, happy, and rewarding. Except for his part-time job at the *Boston Transcript*, Harvard had been his only employer, and with the exception of his military service, he had lived his adult life within a ten-mile radius of the campus. Saying good-bye would not be easy.

But Monro rarely wore his heart on his sleeve, and he kept his feelings firmly in check during commencement week, when his imminent departure triggered a flurry of invitations and appearances. He delivered the Harvard greeting at the University's Joint Commissioning Exercises. On Class Day he helped present the annual Ames Memorial Award to Stephen L. Griffith and Joseph R. Schmidt, the two seniors identified by their classmates as exhibiting extraordinary leadership and commitment to service. At commencement he shared the podium with fellow honorary degree recipients, including Harry Truman; *Washington Post* journalist Carl Bernstein, whose Watergate exposé days were still ahead of him; Leonard Bernstein; artist Ben Shahn; Nobel Prize–winning scientists Lord Florey and Fritz Lippman; and Benjamin Mays, former president of Morehouse College ("Harvard Taps" 24). Among this stellar cast only Monro received a standing ovation (Dreyer, e-mail, 29 Sept. 2007).

The ovation was the seniors' homage to Monro, but he had already honored them a day earlier, channeling his feelings into a brief, heartfelt speech. Class Day, when each class gathered on its own, was the perfect occasion to talk to the seniors in particular, and he welcomed the opportunity, acknowledging the challenges he and they had jostled through, argued over, and eventually emerged from, sometimes as allies and sometimes as opponents. He urged them to become good citizens by putting back into the social system more than they had taken out ("Words of Farewell").

He pointed out that because the world had become so complex, good citizenship was best accomplished though institutions, and he wryly observed, "It is part of the difficulty of running a college nowadays that a number of students are all too well aware of how institutions run, and how people function, or fail to function, or function badly, within them." He did not provide examples, knowing that the seniors would come up with their own: they had used the *Crimson* and SDS to press for their causes and had assumed active roles in committees to which they were admitted, most notably the Harvard Policy Committee. They had been quick to criticize institutions that faltered, for instance, when the faculty waffled on draft deferment, when the Kennedy Institute mismanaged McNamara's visit, and when the dean's office took an autocratic position on parietals. He urged them to continue scrutinizing institutions critically rather than submitting fatalistically to them "as if they were an inevitable part of the natural order, like the ocean tides—reliable and imperturbable and impersonal" ("Words of Farewell").

He ended his talk by emphasizing what he and his audience had in common. Although this was one of his favorite rhetorical strategies, he had his work cut out for him this time. The seniors were young adults, and many of them were critical of Harvard, vehemently opposed to serving in the military, and insistent about their right to experiment with drugs and sexual behavior. He had worked loyally for Harvard as long as they had been alive. He remained married to his high school sweetheart and looked back on his military service with enormous pride. He had warned them against the dangers of drugs and inveighed against the folly of sexual experimentation. Nevertheless, he insisted that they stood on common ground. Calling them "the toughest, most alert, most responsible class" he had ever dealt with, he joined them in striking out for new worlds: "I am proud to share this departure, this Commencement, personally with you" ("Words of Farewell").

8
NEW HOME, NEW CHALLENGES
1967-1971

Monro was so eager to begin his new job that he begged Phil to drive him to Logan Airport the moment commencement festivities were over. In the car Dreyer listened patiently while Monro, preaching to the choir, insisted once again that going to Miles was an enviable opportunity rather than a sacrifice (Long).

The college was much spiffier than it had been when Monro arrived in 1964 with the Phillips Brooks House contingent in tow. Now the physical plant included a glass and concrete cafeteria–student union, the brand-new $500,000 Taggart Science Laboratory, apartment-style housing for eight faculty families, and three houses, one for the Pitts family, one for Dean Richard Arrington's family, and one—still not quite finished—for John and Dottie. Venerable but decrepit Williams Hall had been renovated, several other old buildings had been given a cosmetic coat of paint, and the freestanding library was plump with forty thousand volumes (Pitts, "Presidential").

The college's bottom line had also improved slightly, but Pitts still struggled to make ends meet, estimating that it would take two dormitories, a Health and Physical Education Building, a five million–dollar endowment, and ten thousand dollars of additional annual income to compete for gifted faculty and students (Pitts, "Presidential"). Even though the CME church spent half its budget on its educational affiliates (Kahn 45), the amount it gave to Miles scarcely covered a month's expenses ("Miles's Mileage"). As a private college, Miles received no regular government funding, and other sources of support were severely limited by its continuing lack of accreditation.

Monro's arrival almost immediately improved the bottom line with outside funding earmarked for his program. When Harvard law professor Mark DeWolfe

Howe, Monro's co-advisor to the *Southern Courier*, died suddenly of a heart attack, his friends and colleagues donated $100,000 to Miles in his memory, specifying that it go to the Freshman Studies Program. This early infusion of cash was soon followed by a three-year, $346,000 grant from the Ford Foundation, with the stipulation that it go to the new program (McClung 349).

TENSION OFF AND ON CAMPUS

In addition to its financial and accreditation problems, life at Miles was complicated by the specter of racial tension that still haunted the region. Local landlords displayed little southern hospitality toward white teachers coming to Miles. On three separate occasions Merle McClung was shown apartments that suddenly turned out to be rented when he identified Miles as his source of income (354). White teachers who succeeded in renting apartments often encountered hostility once they moved in. In the working-class neighborhood where Bob Lowe moved into a two-family house, his neighbors began crossing the street to avoid him (telephone interview, 28 May 2008). Safety as well as convenience dictated Monro's on-campus address, especially in view of the publicity he had received; as Jeff Zorn, who came to Miles in 1968, bluntly put it, "The Klan knew just who he was" ("Monro, a Great Educator").

As Monro's administrative assistant, McClung got a close look at some of the racial pressures Monro customarily kept to himself. One day McClung was working on a report when he saw Monro, who was going through his mail, curse and toss a letter into the wastebasket. His curiosity aroused, McClung asked to see the letter. It read: "Such nigger lovers like you behind all this racial trouble does not help 'cause we in the South will overcome too. And when the revolution and shooting starts you may be in the top 10. We don't have any more use for you dam Yankees than we do these dam niggers" (qtd. in McClung 354). McClung asked how often such letters appeared, and Monro replied that they were frequent but that he had "more important things to worry about." Then he set about preparing for his English class (McClung, e-mail, 11 July 2003).

Monro realized that unless he was careful, he could easily ratchet up the tension, because racial friction frequently coalesced around the young white teachers who were attracted to the Freshman Studies Program. One such controversy flared up shortly before Monro arrived, when social science professor Walt Draude was fired for ignoring the college stricture against inviting local high school students to campus. Sixteen white faculty members boycotted their classes in protest, objecting as well to what they considered Pitts's autocratic management style. Neil Friedman, director of the Freshman Social Studies Program, told a *Newsweek* reporter, "I can't remember when we've ever voted on anything in a faculty meeting." Pitts obligingly illustrated Friedman's point by telling the same reporter, "I'll let people talk about things all they want—and then I'll tell them how it's going to be" ("Boat Rockers").

Monro's attitude toward his place at Miles helped relieve the tension his presence might otherwise have aggravated. He rejected the role of "Great White Hope," a title that Dottie teasingly used when she wanted to irk him (Shane Crabtree, personal interview, 8 July 2003). He also refused a leadership role, having decided during Tougaloo's presidential search that black colleges needed black leaders. "I couldn't be president of this place. I couldn't be dean. But I think there is a fine opportunity for white teachers to make an effective contribution in a subordinate role," he explained (qtd. in Thomas and Nunnelley 22). He insisted that black teachers were the only legitimate role models for activism, and he warned white teachers against impinging on their territory. "That is not their role; when they come they are guests and it is not their privilege to insurrect," he stated. He pointed out that by their very presence white teachers were demystifying integration for their students, an important preliminary to effective civil rights engagement ("Negro Colleges" 78).

Pitts praised Monro as an exemplary white presence at a black college: "Whites who come to a black college need to come as John came—naked. Naked in the sense that he's come not just to give but to receive, as a participating learner and contributor." Even Columbus Keepler, an army veteran and one of the most passionate student activists on campus, described Monro with grudging respect, noting that he did "a good job of looking at the black struggle and leaving out his own Harvard standards" (qtd. in Kahn 92, 58).

PROMOTING INSTITUTIONAL STRENGTH

Another attitude that accelerated Monro's acceptance at Miles was his unswerving belief in black colleges as crucial centers of institutional strength. Suggestions that black colleges be phased out infuriated him. "I regard the idea as idiocy," he snapped ("Negro Colleges" 77). In particular he bridled at "The American Negro College," a recent article by Harvard colleagues Christopher Jencks and David Riesman in which they described black colleges collectively as "an academic disaster area." Monro, who had been inspired by Riesman's creative, student-centered teaching style at Harvard, was stung by the epithet, which he called "the cruelest kind of phrase-making." These so-called disaster areas were accomplishing unusual things, he argued, pointing to programs being developed at Miles for "the whole spread of students—remedial programs, reinforcement programs, enrichment programs, special curricula in black history, black culture, black problems." Proudly identifying with these efforts, he said: "We care about these youngsters. . . . This is one institution that belongs to the black community" (77).

So deep was Monro's commitment to black colleges that Richard Arrington, a Miles alumnus himself, claimed that his belief in their inherent value had been solidified by Monro. "Working with him gave me a deep reassurance that what I was doing was right," Arrington says today. "It wasn't just his leaving Harvard to come to Miles. It was how he got involved and the deep interest he had in students whose families had never had anyone go to college. . . . He felt that major opportunities came to them through the black colleges, and that they could meet needs other colleges couldn't or wouldn't" (personal interview, 22 July 2003).

Explaining the importance of institutional strength, Monro observed that the power structure in America was indifferent to weakness or need, which was why the early labor unions got nowhere decrying the exploitation of underpaid workers but saw results when they went on strike ("Escape" 437). "In this country, you've either got institutional strength or you've got nothing," he concluded ("Negro Colleges" 74). To those who feared that institutional strength would fuel the black power movement, Monro replied that the real danger was "continuing black powerlessness, tokenism, and oppression" ("Escape" 436). As another form of institutional strength, Monro pointed to graduates of black colleges who left home to earn advanced degrees, then returned to fill local leadership positions. In a 1968 interview he identified a trend in that direction and optimistically predicted, "In a few years, some really important people in town will be educated Negroes" (Hogan).

DARING TO DREAM

One of the most illustrious Miles alumni to bring his education back home was Richard Arrington, who became dean just as Monro was moving to Miles. Like

Pitts, Arrington came from humble beginnings. When he was six, his struggling family moved to Fairfield, where the steel mills offered more financial opportunity than sharecropping did (Franklin 15). His father became a steelworker for the Tennessee Coal, Iron and Railroad Company (20), and the family set about adjusting to life in a steel mill town. Arrington chose the vocational track in high school so that he could take a course in dry cleaning and get a job while he was still in school (33). He graduated cum laude despite his thirty- to forty-hour workweeks then applied to Miles so that he could live at home and keep his job (38).

By the time Arrington graduated, in 1955, Miles had expanded his horizons. "When I entered college I figured if I was lucky I'd get a bachelor's degree and a teaching job in public school. . . . Miles made me dare to dream of doing things I had never thought were possible" (qtd. in Kahn 64). His dreams sent him to the University of Detroit for a master's degree and the University of Oklahoma for his doctorate, then brought him back to Miles, where Pitts, cagily drawing on Arrington's gratitude to the college, asked him to become acting dean and director of the summer school (Arrington, interview). By 1967, when Monro arrived, Arrington was dean of Miles and chair of the Department of Natural Sciences (Franklin 46).

Arrington and Monro were kindred spirits as well as compatible colleagues. They shared a heritage rich in values, a commitment to hard work, a zest for challenge, a love of teaching, a belief in the importance of education, and loyalty to Miles as a special place. For the all-too-brief time that they were at Miles together, Arrington, Monro, and Pitts formed a creative, dynamic triumvirate, and Arrington's support was crucial to the success of the freshman program Monro had helped design.

GETTING WITH THE PROGRAM

As director of the Freshman Studies Program, Monro was responsible for hiring, training, placement, curriculum design, and assessment; in addition, he taught two sections of English and one section of Social Science ("Negro Colleges" 78). Despite the heavy workload, he described his demanding position as "perfect." He liked the fact that teaching was an integral part of his job and that he had a strong voice in curriculum development, whereas at Harvard, teaching had been tangential and he had had to fight for a role in shaping academic policy. He also valued the autonomy he enjoyed as program director.

But above all he valued his position for the leverage it provided in "giving the world a shove," because he considered the freshman curriculum nothing less than the key to equal opportunity in higher education. "Once they have their identity as freshmen, you can set them loose on other things," he claimed ("Doing"). Miles was an ideal testing ground for his theory because so many of its incoming students were underprepared products of the abysmal local schools. Alabama spent less than any other state on its public schools, and expenditure per pupil was even lower in its black schools. On standardized tests Miles freshmen routinely tested in the bottom 10 percent in mathematics, and half of them were reading at a ninth-grade level (Monro, "Teaching" 237). If anything, the test scores were somewhat inflated: English teacher Kim Townsend suspected that some students received scores at the sixth-grade level only because that was the bottom of the scale (personal interview, 13 Aug. 2003).

But Monro insisted that given a suitable course of study, from 90 to 95 percent of the country's high school graduates could "learn to think straight, to deal with reasonably complicated information, and to write out their thoughts in clear, comprehensible standard English prose" ("Teaching" 235). At Miles he aimed to slash the dropout rate in half, reducing it to 25 percent, and he saw the Freshman Studies Program as a giant step in that direction.

Freshman English

Vocabulary, grammar, reading comprehension, and writing were the cornerstones of the Freshman English course (Greenhouse 89), and although Monro never stopped tinkering with methodology, these four components remained the linchpins of his teaching for the rest of his career. He had stumbled onto the importance of vocabulary building while teaching the summer workshop. One day his students responded apathetically to an editorial about race riots in Detroit and Newark. Puzzled by their indifference, he began asking what some of the words meant—words such as *aggression, concession,* and *cooperation*—only to discover that they were unmoved by the editorial because they could not penetrate its language ("Doing"). In an effort to remedy the deficit, he had the students study vocabulary from *The Autobiography of Malcolm X,* which they were already reading. But as he watched them shuttle fruitlessly between the dictionary and the autobiography, he realized they needed a more efficient system, even though current educational theory dictated that vocabulary be studied in context. Other Freshman English teachers noticed the same phenomenon: one student looking up *vengeance* slammed the dictionary closed in disgust, complaining that it contained nothing but "more words" (*Crucible* 5).

Drawing on the inductive approach he had used to develop Harvard's financial aid formula, he began with a basic data bank: *The New Horizon Ladder Dictionary of the English Language,* which listed the five thousand most frequently used English words, arranged in order of frequency. A fifty-word vocabulary test containing ten words from each thousandth showed that the Miles freshmen were comfortable with words in the one thousand to three thousand range but had difficulty with those in the four thousand and five thousand range.

From then on, each week the freshmen memorized the definitions of thirty-five words drawn from the upper-frequency ranges. The only contextualization that occurred was class discussion. In this way, over the course of two semesters they grappled with a thousand words they were likely to encounter in their reading. Monro admitted: "I know very well how bad this all is. I will not try to defend what we are doing except to say that it seems to work pretty well. . . . Every way I know how to observe it, a large percentage of these words, hit thus head-on, is assimilated so that the words become operational" ("Teaching" 241).

For reading and writing skills Monro's methodology was unapologetically bottom-up. He once compared writing to playing the piano, pointing out that just as a musician had to practice scales before playing sonatas, writers had to master sentences, paragraphs, and brief essays before they could produce more mature texts ("Teaching" 241–42).[1] Writing instruction began at the sentence level: "We practice working ideas or information into short sentences, ten to fifteen words. If you can program yourself that way, and have it under control, you can write. Indeed, you will write better than most professors." After working with sentences, the class advanced to paragraphs, and only in the final two weeks of the first semester did they attempt short essays (241–44).

Some of the Freshman English teachers were skeptical about this approach, which looked suspiciously like the "kill-and-drill" pedagogy that had already numbed their students' imaginations. But the students found Monro's class exciting and liberating; according to one of them, "He teaches you how to grab ideas and how to formulate opinions—that is, how to think" (qtd. in Kahn 58). Richard Hannon, who had returned to school after a stint in the armed services, called the course "a thinking person's class" and noted that Monro took "an editor's approach" to his students' work, teaching both writing and analytic skills (personal interview, 14 Mar. 2008).

Monro took his students' essays with him wherever he went. When asked to describe his appearance, colleagues, friends, and relatives invariably mentioned the tall stack of student essays that accompanied him. Whether on vacation, on holiday break, or headed to a conference, commencement, or board meeting, as soon as he found a comfortable chair, he would tip it back on its hind legs, prop up his feet, pluck an essay from the top of the stack, and lose track of the outside world. "He thought that there was nothing more satisfying than grading student essays," recalls Freshman English teacher Jimmy Harper (personal interview, 6 Mar. 2008). He saw significant victories in humble places and was inspired by a particularly fruitful class on punctuation to conclude, "I sometimes think that people move into a new stage of expression all at once when they move into the semicolon" (qtd. in Greenhouse 89).

Freshman Social Science

The pilot version of Freshman Social Science played out while Monro was still at Harvard, but he was heavily involved in its creation. The course that it replaced, a traditional world history survey, could not have been better designed to exacerbate the difficulties Miles students brought with them from high school: they had to read long, complex textbooks in spite of poor reading skills; attend large lecture classes in spite of poor note-taking skills; and write long essays about remote topics in spite of problems with both writing and abstracting. In addition, program director Neil Friedman and many of the other social science teachers regretted that although the students were "cultivating their black consciousness" outside the classroom, there were no courses to encourage this trend. "Where are the courses in African and Afro-American literature, art, music, culture?" Friedman asked ("Miles College" 369). Determined to fill the void, many of the social science teachers devoted the final weeks of their courses to black history, arguing that although it might not seem an appropriate subject for white teachers to discuss, nobody else was stepping up to the plate.

Monro, who taught Freshman Social Science for several years, praised the controversial content for creating a classroom situation in which "we are always operating on the edge of annoyance and frustration, and because it is tough and tense, it is the best educational mix in the world" ("Escape" 436). With each passing semester the black history component gained more prominence, until eventually it morphed into the first semester of the course and laid the foundation for Miles's comprehensive Afro-American Studies Program.

Happy Campers

The common readings and assignments in the freshman courses were chosen consensually and were subject to revision or cancellation as their effectiveness— or lack of it—played out in the classroom. This trial-and-error method was time-consuming and sometimes contentious, but the trade-off was that the teachers were willing to work hard on the program because they considered it their own.

And work hard they did. Even with the restricted class size that outside funding made possible, each teacher had at least sixty students, many of whom required extra time and attention. There was a constant scramble to adjust materials based on day-to-day experience, and because few existing texts were suitable for the program, the faculty spent hours developing and duplicating appropriate readings and handouts (Friedman, "Miles" 17). Faculty meetings, which had to be shoehorned into an already crowded schedule, frequently took place on weekends or evenings. One marathon meeting of the social science faculty, which took place at Friedman's house, did not break up until two in the morning.

Freshman Studies teachers with the stamina to handle the work were rewarded with a good deal of independence. Abraham Woods, who taught social science, said, "There was individuality in teaching, but a common goal." Steve Whitman, who chafed under authority in general, appreciated Monro's democratic style, which involved getting everyone together "to work out a common path" rather than imposing curriculum from above (telephone interview, 28 July 2003). Richard Hannon, who taught social science after taking Monro's Freshman English course, said: "Anybody who worked for Dr. Monro was a happy camper. . . . Once he'd looked at your syllabus, you were ready to go" (interview). Even when he challenged a syllabus, Monro was open to persuasion, as Edith Estes learned when he suggested that her students might find *Huckleberry Finn* racist. She countered that when students analyzed the book, they would realize it was the opposite of racist. "We sometimes had to argue, because he was a Yankee and didn't understand some things," she quipped (Edith Estes MacMillan, telephone interview, 22 Mar. 2008).

But the campers were happy only if they were a good fit, and Monro spent considerable effort searching out teachers who would be comfortable with the experimental nature of the program. In general he favored applicants with lots of energy and few preconceived notions, rather than those with traditional credentials or years of experience. As a result, his hires became notorious for their unconventional résumés. When he interviewed Jimmy Harper for a position teaching English, Monro did not take exception to his degrees in history and religion but asked whether, as a white southerner, Harper would be comfortable teaching The Autobiography of Malcolm X (interview). Steve Whitman also taught Freshman English, although his doctorate from Yale was in epidemiology and biostatistics, and he had been hired to teach mathematics. "John was easy about things like that," Whitman recalled. "I think it was clear I knew how to read and liked it" (interview).

Monro brought one recruit with him from Harvard: Hubert Sapp, with whom he had worked to strengthen the Association of African and Afro-American Students (AAAAS). As he prepared to graduate from Harvard, Sapp faced the fact that law school no longer appealed to him, and he began casting about for an alternative. Recalling that he had enjoyed tutoring youngsters at a local community center, he thought he might try teaching. Monro urged him to come to Miles, where his degree in government would qualify him to teach Freshman Social Science, and where his wife, Jane, could teach music (personal interview, 30 July 2003). Jane Sapp was a "catch" for Miles in her own right. She had grown up in Augusta, Georgia, and was playing piano for two church groups by the time she was nine. After graduating cum laude with a music degree from Marymount College in Salina, Kansas, she successfully auditioned for the formerly all-white Augusta Chorale but was barred by her race from becoming a soloist (Gordon E4). When she arrived at Miles, she was already an accomplished singer, composer, and pianist.

Monro did not limit his search, however, to people he already knew. On the contrary, when he knocked on Jeff Zorn's door one late summer Saturday in 1968, Monro was a total stranger. Zorn had just completed his first summer of study at Harvard's Graduate School of Education and needed to earn some money before he resumed his studies. Monro had read his résumé at the placement office and thought he would be a good fit for the freshman program. Take your time deciding, Monro told Zorn, as long as you make up your mind by Monday (Zorn, "Monro at Miles" 1). In spite of the daunting job description—four classes, a forty-two hundred dollar annual salary, and long workdays on a bare-bones campus far from home—Zorn went to Miles and stayed for six years, lavishing attention on his students' writing and urging them to value education for its own sake as well as its marketplace value (e-mail, 1 Aug. 2003).

Swimming against the Mainstream

The Freshman Studies Program contradicted the conservative, teacher-centered pedagogy that prevailed at Miles and most other black colleges at the time. In a paper Zorn wrote for a graduate course at Harvard, he argued that this authoritarian approach reinforced the handicaps Miles freshmen brought with them from Birmingham's public schools. Because their writing skills were weak, multiple-choice items replaced essay questions on exams, and their writing skills deteriorated even further from lack of use. Because many were reading at a ninth-grade level, teachers chose oversimplified textbooks and spent precious classroom time explaining rather than analyzing or critiquing them ("Harvard Graduate" 5).

In dramatic contrast to the prevailing teaching style, the Freshman Studies Program acknowledged the importance of engaging student interest. Even Monro was startled by the eagerness with which the students, who had been "fed lies and eyewash so long," embraced provocative books such as Anthony Lewis's *Portrait of a Decade* and Martin Luther King Jr.'s *Why We Can't Wait*. He told a reporter, "Books that talk about something they feel fills a vacuum so fast" (qtd. in "Doing Something Relevant").

Rather than shrinking the course to "fit" the students' limitations, the freshman teachers capitalized on student strengths, particularly their "interest in the dramatic and the spoken word" (Bunting 5). In English this meant reading novels rich in drama and dialogue, such as *Huckleberry Finn* and *Of Mice and Men*; plays written in accessible language and clear chronological sequence; and powerful, concise short stories such as those of Shirley Jackson. In social science it meant role-playing, field research, skits, debates, discussions, and the use of audiovisual materials as well as texts (Friedman, "Miles College" 363).

Grammar instruction was crucial, but since memorizing rules had not worked during the first twelve years of schooling, the freshmen learned grammar "by practice, not principle," in the context of their own writing (Bunting 10). Richard Hannon, who credited the Freshman English course with sharpening his writing skills after years of neglect, recognized the superiority of the applied approach: "When you're . . . putting ideas into your own prose, it's quite easy to see what you're doing. But if you're just conjugating verbs, at what point do you translate that into comprehendible prose?" (interview).

In another student-centered move, the freshman teachers routinely assigned paperbacks, which were part of the familiar, reassuring world of newsstands and drugstores but rarely appeared on college campuses. Obviously, paperbacks were less expensive and easier to carry than textbooks—a significant advantage for students who spent hours riding buses to and from school, work, and home. Miles alumni recall that freshmen were easy to spot: they were the ones clutching paperbacks and poring over vocabulary lists as they crisscrossed the campus.

Building Bridges

Monro knew from his administrative years at Harvard that misunderstanding could sabotage even the noblest efforts, so he worked hard to narrow the gap between Freshman Studies and the rest of the curriculum. He explained the program whenever he was asked and often when he was not; he joined every committee to which he was invited; made presentations to other departments and to the faculty at large; and saw to it that freshman essays appeared frequently in the weekly publication *Miles Ahead*. He met regularly with faculty from other departments, both to demystify his program and to learn about theirs. His aggressive role in shaping educational policy at Harvard had exposed him to a wide variety of fields, and he was intrigued by interdisciplinary approaches to learning.

But in spite of his efforts, the program was frequently misunderstood. Some faculty believed that Monro did not teach grammar, a claim to which Richard Hannon strenuously objected: "That wasn't true. He just didn't teach it the way they did, and his way was better because he got results" (interview). Many of Monro's former colleagues informed me that he allowed his students to write in black English and did not correct grammar errors, a claim contradicted by every word that he wrote or spoke.

Overall, friends in high places probably did more to win acceptance of the program than Monro's attempts at outreach. Always a shrewd master of public relations, Pitts constantly thrust Monro and his program into the limelight. Pitts predicted that materials generated by the program would prove equally effective nationwide, and he pledged to publish them through the Miles College Press, an entity that existed only in his fertile imagination and his optimistic vision of the future (Pitts, "Memorandum").

Arrington, a gifted teacher himself, was another valuable ally. He knew what made the program special and what role it played in the mission of the college. He admired the hard work, collaborative curriculum building, and search for approaches and materials connected to the students' lives. Most important, he defended its experimental nature, which many faculty members viewed as a flaw. He suggested that the entire college could do worse than take the program as its model. Talking like the scientist that he was, he insisted: "Miles HAS to be an experiment—a laboratory school. If placement tests were our only guides, we should be guilty of shameful waste of valuable men and women" ("Montage").

FITTING IN

By the beginning of Monro's second year at Miles, he and Dottie had settled into a busy but comfortable routine. They joined First Congregational Christian Church, which, unlike the other Congregational churches in the area, was integrated, even though it had only a few white parishioners (First Congregational Church Group). It boasted a socially diverse membership, including academics from Miles and other nearby institutions; Angela Davis and her parents; civic leaders such as Odessa Woolfolk and Arthur D. Shores, the attorney whose house was bombed during Monro's memorable first visit to Birmingham. Both of them took advantage of the church's strong social action program, joining clubs and auxiliaries, teaching Sunday school, and attending meetings as well as Sunday services (Odessa Woolfolk, personal interview, 10 Mar. 2008). Dottie joined the women's Angola Guild, and John joined the layman's fellowship and a committee that the school superintendent had invited to attend board of education meetings. Eventually, he was made a deacon, a position that involved visiting the sick, distributing communion, helping select readings and hymns, and occasionally writing and delivering the homily.

UAB

Another community that John and Dottie joined was the University of Alabama in Birmingham (UAB), which had been designated a university in 1966 and would soon change its name to the University of Alabama *at* Birmingham.

Monro served on the twenty-seven-member Urban Council, a citizen group created by Joseph F. Volker, who was then executive vice president and became UAB's first president, to shape the university's community relations and outreach activities (McWilliams 199). At Monro's urging the council recommended that a Center for Urban Studies be created, following the lead of progressive universities such as the University of Chicago and the City University of New York (Edward S. LaMonte, e-mail, 28 May 2008).

In the winter of 1969, shortly before Volker announced the creation of the center, Ed LaMonte wrote to Monro, reporting that he had completed his course work at the University of Chicago. He was thinking about teaching at Roosevelt College while he wrote his dissertation and asked what Monro thought of the plan, given his familiarity with Chicago schools (McWilliams 200). Instead, Monro told Volker that LaMonte would be an ideal assistant director for the center, then told LaMonte that Volker wanted him to fly down for further discussion (letter to LaMonte). Sheepishly admitting that he was playing fast and loose with LaMonte's preexisting career plans, Monro offered a persuasive excuse: "I am so much impressed with the drive, and purposes, and fundamental intelligence I see at work at UAB. I have to think it would be a constructive and rewarding place to work, both personally and professionally." As usual, his matchmaking instincts were on target, and LaMonte was hired. A year later he was named the center's director (LaMonte, e-mail, 3 June 2008).

At UAB Monro became better acquainted with Odessa Woolfolk, who attended First Congregational and shared his skepticism about the value of advanced degrees. Woolfolk had graduated from Talladega, earned a master's degree in Urban Studies from Occidental College, and was beginning her doctoral studies at the University of Chicago when she heard about a project for needy families in Utica and obtained a one-year grant to work there. Getting the grant persuaded her that she already had the training she needed to succeed in her field and that a doctorate would be superfluous. Eventually, she succeeded LaMonte as director of UAB's Urban Studies Center (Kemp). Woolfolk approved of the supporting role Monro had carved out for himself at Miles: "He was not a flaming or philosophical liberal leading the charge," she said. "He was a very caring person who . . . felt his job was to take a group of students who had not had opportunities and to provide the opportunities" (personal interview, 10 Mar. 2008).[2]

Monro enjoyed working with Volker, who used his presidency to foster collaboration with Miles. He was especially supportive of its Upward Bound program, offering university recruitment resources; extending cafeteria and other undergraduate privileges to participants; providing buses, classrooms, and a lab for their use; and guaranteeing financial aid to participants admitted to the university (Volker). When Pitts asked for advice about creating health care services, Volker initiated a grant application that eventually funded a UAB-staffed dental clinic at Miles, which offered the country's first free comprehensive dental plan on a college campus ("New Dental Clinic").

Dottie too found a niche at the university, volunteering at the Educational Program for the Individual Child (EPIC) school, established by the Birmingham Board of Education as a training center and teaching laboratory for students minoring in early childhood education.

Meeting the Neighbors

The Monros were warmly welcomed into Birmingham's liberal white circles, whose members treated John like "a combination of the Music Man and the Miracle Worker," according to Gale Goldberg Robinson. "He was the heart and center of it all; it rippled out from him" (personal interview, 8 Feb. 2008). Among the white liberal community's most prominent members were Cecil and David Roberts, generous patrons of UAB's arts programs and charter members of the President's Council. John and Dottie, sometimes accompanied by the Arringtons, frequently had Sunday dinner with the Roberts, either at their home or at nearby Mountain Brook Country Club, and John usually joined David Roberts at the post-Thanksgiving Auburn-Alabama football game (Robin Roberts, personal interview, 3 Mar. 2008).

In 1956, when Cecil Roberts was named Birmingham's Woman of the Year, a *Life Magazine* photo showed her careening on a bicycle at breakneck speed along a quiet suburban street ("David Roberts"). The image accurately reflected her view of life as a wild ride to be relished regardless of the risks involved. She and Monro shared a knack for circumventing standard operating procedure that threatened to cramp their style. When the Town and Gown production of *Bye Bye Birdie* required a long wooden table as a prop for a scantily clad dancer, Cecil dispatched her son, Robin, and several of his friends to the Birmingham Public Library to commandeer a table she remembered seeing there. Once the musical closed, they returned the table, and nobody challenged them at either end, in spite of the fact that they had not explained what they were doing (R. Roberts, interview).

But it was their shared commitment to civil rights that truly cemented the friendship between the Monros and the Roberts. The prominence of the Roberts name, with its fortune based on coal mining, meant that the couple's actions were avidly covered by the media, and they used their visibility to promote change. They literally took the first step in integrating Birmingham's audiences when they escorted black civil rights leader John Nixon and his wife down the aisle of the Municipal Auditorium. Cecil was an active member of the Democratic Party, an outspoken supporter of voting rights for blacks ("Cecil J. Roberts"), and a Miles trustee and member of the executive committee for many years. When Monro became dissatisfied with the direction Miles was taking, Cecil's resignation from the board was motivated in large part by sympathy for him (R. Roberts, interview).

Joining John and Dottie in the Roberts's social milieu were Mervyn and Dorah Sterne and Charles and Bernadine Zukoski. Although his formal education had ended with the eighth grade, Mervyn Sterne's legendary fund-raising skills benefited Miles, UAB, Samford University, Birmingham-Southern College, and the United Way, among others, and UAB showed its gratitude by naming its library after him. The Zukoskis had hosted the controversial cookout for the Miles and PBH grade school tutors during the summer of 1964. Charles was president of the local Harvard Club and trust officer for First National Bank, where he unsuccessfully attempted to desegregate the elevators (Russakoff, "Remembering Birmingham"). Told that his controversial newspaper columns were offending some of the bank's most prominent customers, he took the pen name Button Gwinnett —after one of the signers of the Declaration of Independence—and continued writing until the bank let him go (Edward S. and Ruth LaMonte, interview).

The Monros also became friends with Irene and Abraham "Russ" Russakoff, both of whom were southern transplants. The son of Russian immigrant parents, Russ earned undergraduate and medical degrees from Tufts then moved to Alabama to head the state's tuberculosis control program (Gale Russakoff, e-mail, 8 Dec. 2008). In 1964 he tested the recently passed Civil Rights Act by putting one of his black patients in the same hospital room as a white patient; up to that point hospitals had paid lip service to the act by integrating floors but keeping rooms segregated (Russakoff, "Lessons").

Irene, who was born in Baltimore, centered her civil rights efforts around Miles, launching a drive to raise funds for a new library and recruiting her friends to write appeal letters to their friends—an early application of the direct-mail strategy. The campaign was a success, and the new library became an important factor in the college's reaccreditation bid. During a visit to Monro, Dale Russakoff once belittled her mother's civil rights contributions, suggesting that because she and her friends were not marching, they were accomplishing little. Monro corrected her in no uncertain terms, saying that their work was absolutely essential to the movement (telephone interview, 1 Dec. 2008).

Social Life at Miles

Social life at Miles was rich and varied. Its many organizations, particularly fraternities, sororities, and music groups, sponsored a plethora of events, and many academic meetings were quasi-social and included a reception, party, or meal. The first family entertained a good deal, and the young white teachers who were at Miles for a year or two spent much of their leisure time together, drawing the Monros, neighbors, colleagues, and students into their orbit. Arrington, Monro, and Pitts were a social as well as a professional unit, frequently going out together or along with their wives.

But in spite of his many acquaintances and the fact that he was widely admired, Monro did not acquire many close friends. Even Merle McClung "did not feel close to him as a friend might" (interview). The simple truth was that Monro was too absorbed in his work to cultivate friendship for its own sake. The best way to get close to him was to become involved in one of his causes, as his friendship with Betty Gates illustrates.

Gates, Monro's collaborator in creating and administering the Freshman English curriculum, was a complex person. She taught in both the English Department and the Freshman Studies Program, though they were frequently at loggerheads. She had a master's degree from Georgia State but was unfazed by Monro's cavalier approach to postgraduate credentials. She suffered from obesity, diabetes, and depression and struggled with a chronic drinking problem but was productive and effective in her job and extravagantly admired by the young teachers she mentored. Prill Ellis, writing to LaMonte at the beginning of the pilot year of Freshman English, found Gates inspiring: "She is eager to dig into the teaching, and is so intelligent and sensible as a director. A remarkable person, of many facets, wisdom, humor."

Gates and Monro were ideal partners. After helping design the Freshman English program, she directed it for the first two years, reminding her colleagues that Monro's leadership had been crucial in shaping the curriculum; she turned the program over to him when he arrived in 1967. They codirected the summer precollege English workshop for many years. Telling son-in-law Phil about a writing proficiency exam they had developed, Monro said that Gates would be a formidable ally in the fight for its acceptance (Dreyer, e-mail, 27 Sept. 2007). Monro cared so deeply about Gates's well-being that he cosigned a loan for her, and, when he was notified that she had filed a debtor's petition, he replied, "I wish . . . to assure you that I am prepared to meet my responsibility in the case, and to note that I have every confidence that Miss Gates will pay her debt, given time" (22 Oct. 1975, DP). Gates cared so deeply about Monro that she had to fight back tears when Pitts withdrew his support from Monro during a particularly confrontational faculty meeting (Townsend, interview).[3]

THE AFRO-AMERICAN STUDIES PROGRAM

The curricular reflections of black identity and black pride that Neil Friedman had vainly searched for in 1967—"Where are the courses in African and Afro-American literature, art, music, culture? Where is there a major in Afro-American studies?" (369)—began to take shape at Miles the following year, bolstered by encouragement from Arrington, behind-the-scenes support from Monro, and savvy leadership from Hubert Sapp, who was now Arrington's assistant as well as director of Freshman Social Science.

Arrington took the lead, asking the faculty to discuss the possibility of an Afro-American Studies minor during their October 1968 meeting ("First Faculty" 1). Following the meeting a Faculty Committee on Afro-American Studies was created and charged with drawing up a proposal. As committee chair, Sapp wrote the proposal, which identified twelve existing courses that dealt with the black experience, along with relevant activities, including theater productions, choral groups, a summer humanities workshop, offerings in the sophomore seminar-style tutorial program, and the library's Afro-American Materials Center Program for public schools (Sapp 3).

The proposal added an arts workshop and a community studies and action program to the minor the faculty had already discussed: now, in addition to taking designated courses, students minoring in Afro-American Studies would enroll in either the community program or the workshop (Sapp 5), and future faculty would be hired with an eye toward their ability to teach courses counting toward the minor (7). Faculty approval was so swift that the Afro-American Studies Program was incorporated into the 1969–70 catalog.

So that Sapp's prominence in the program would strengthen the reputation of Miles as a center of black institutional strength, Monro kept a low profile in on-campus discussion, but he willingly spoke elsewhere about black studies. In an interview with *Birmingham News* reporter Barbara Thomas, he said that black studies were just as important for white students, who needed to understand that "the white community has a bad record in the treatment of other races," as for black students, who needed to learn that "black people have made a tremendous contribution to America" (Thomas).

Its rich, multi-pronged program put Miles in the educational vanguard as less ambitious black studies programs and courses sprouted up—and filled up—on campuses across the country. The black history course at the University of Alabama was so popular with white students that black students sometimes found themselves shut out; 90 percent of the students in a similar course at UAB were white (Thomas).

The topic of black studies was so hot that in 1969 the American Council on Education chose "The Campus and the Racial Crisis" as the theme of its annual conference. There Monro served as respondent to a paper by W. Todd Furniss, director of the council's Commission on Academic Affairs. Furniss cautiously praised black studies programs but warned that black history courses should not replace or devalue conventional "academic" approaches to history. He recommended that colleges slow down desegregation until longitudinal studies revealed the consequences of what he called "non-curricular contacts" between the races.

Monro disagreed with Furniss's characterization of academic historians as detached and rational; instead, he accused them of turning a blind eye to the centrality of black history and letting racial tensions fester. Challenging their objectivity, he pointed out that in spite of W.E.B. Du Bois's stellar credentials—undergraduate and graduate degrees from Harvard, graduate studies at Friedrich Wilhelm University in Berlin, a dissertation on the African slave trade that initiated Harvard's Historical Series publications—Du Bois had not received a single offer from a white college in his initial job search. As for slowing down interracial noncurricular contacts, Monro replied that it would be folly to wait for longitudinal studies because integration itself was by definition "an unsystematic, long-range test—a very real test and not just a study—that will decide whether our society, 'or any other society so conceived and so dedicated,' can long endure" ("Comments").

OLD SCHOOL TIES

Monro was so busy at Miles that he had difficulty getting to the Phillips board meetings, so he resigned from several trustee committees, hoping to concentrate his energy where it would do the most good (letter to John Kemper). He did find time to serve on the board of Beaver Country Day School, in Brookline, Massachusetts, which he had joined at the behest of his former section man Don Nickerson, now Beaver's headmaster. Nickerson sought Monro's advice as the school went coeducational, created a financial aid program for minority students, and launched ambitious capital campaigns (e-mail, 13 Aug. 2010).

To keep himself from waxing nostalgic about his alma mater, Monro ruthlessly choked off Harvard media during his early years at Miles and did not even subscribe to the alumni magazine or the *Crimson* (Greenhouse 90). But he nurtured his personal ties with Harvard, particularly with his former administrative assistant, Nancy Deptula, who wrote chatty letters filled with Harvard gossip and personal news. Before joining Monro's staff, Deptula had been a research assistant at Harvard's Russian Research Center, and she possessed a formidable flair for languages. Monro had been proud of the brilliant woman who ran his office. When George Deptula came to pick his wife up from work, Monro would point to her and boast, "Look at her—she could work at any embassy in the world" (G. Deptula, personal interview, 2 Sept. 2003). He realized, of course, that she was overqualified for her position, and he asked her what she intended to do to develop her talents. She confessed that she would like to complete her undergraduate studies, which she had dropped to work as a secretary while her husband continued his graduate studies. From Miles, Monro heard about a new program at Wellesley and suggested she look into it. Originally called the Continuing Education Program and now known as the Davis Degree Program, it was founded to meet the needs of women "beyond traditional college age." With his encouragement Deptula enrolled in the program and flourished, winning the Deborah W. Diehl Prize for excellence in historical studies and the Mayh-ling Soong Chiang Scholarship for outstanding research paper (Deptula and Hess). Along the way she learned Chinese, French, and Russian.[4]

Another Harvard Transplant

Sometimes Harvard came to Monro in bodily form, as it did when Peter Gomes arrived at Tuskegee in 1969. Gomes had been studying at Harvard Divinity School when Monro left Harvard, but their paths had not crossed in Cambridge. As Gomes completed his studies, he came across a job listing for director of the Freshman Experimental Program at Tuskegee, remembered Monro's move to Miles, and decided to apply. He was offered and accepted the position (personal interview, 10 Mar. 2006).

When Monro and Gomes finally met, at a gathering of freshman program directors, Gomes startled Monro by addressing him as "Dean Monro." Accustomed to the drawled southern honorific, "Doctor MOHN-ro," Monro replied. "You must know me from somewhere else" (interview). Gomes explained his Harvard affiliation, and from then on, Monro took a special interest in the Tuskegee program. Serving on a curriculum review committee for the institute, he advised president Luther Foster Jr., "Whatever happens to you . . . don't lose Peter Gomes," and years later he maintained that Tuskegee's freshman program was one of the best he had ever encountered (qtd. in Aubry 26, 27).

The program that Gomes headed had resources Monro could only dream about. It enjoyed Title III funding, boasted seminar-style classes of six to eight students, and drew highly motivated students because it was an elective rather than a required course. Like Monro, Gomes included black writers in his reading list, but Gomes placed special emphasis on Booker T. Washington, who was held in low regard by many students on the campus he had founded. As part of an oral history assignment, Gomes invited Washington's daughter-in-law, Edith Washington Sheehy, to visit the class. Sheehy, who was in her eighties, talked about her life, particularly her relationship to her illustrious father-in-law, then took questions. Gomes later described the incident, illustrating the verve that made him a world-renowned preacher:

> One kid got up on his hind legs and said, "Your father-in-law was an Uncle Tom. Du Bois is my man." I thought, "I'm going to be fired, putting this lady into this set of circumstances." Then the room calmed down, and she said, "Dr. Du Bois was a great man. . . . He went to Fisk and to Harvard and he had a German degree and he is the most eloquent leader of our people, young man. You have much to

be proud of in Doctor Du Bois." She paused. "My father-in-law was born a slave in Malden, West Virginia, never knew who his daddy was. And all he has to show for his life is this school, in which you are a student." There was a deep intake of breath, and the students knew they were in the presence of something. I'll never forget it as long as I live (Interview).

THE REACCREDITATION YEAR

Throughout the fall semester of 1969, Miles's lack of accreditation remained a source of anxiety as well as a financial and public relations liability. Pitts optimistically predicted that the Southern Association of Colleges and Schools would vote for reaccreditation when they met on 3 December (Chisum 17), but just to be safe, he flew to Dallas to plead the case in person ("Band"). As he had hoped, the committee voted yes, and he reported the victory via telephone amplifier hook-up at Miles, where a crowd had gathered to wait for the news. Monro was a part of the jubilation, telling the crowd: "I remember a friend's saying ten years ago that even God himself couldn't save Miles. But look at us now" (qtd. in Kahn 46).

Pitts asked to be greeted at the airport, and more than a thousand of his jubilant fans obliged. As he emerged from the plane and waved to the crowd, the eighty-five-member college band, wearing purple-and-gold satin and standing on the terminal roof, performed a rousing rendition of the "Hallelujah Chorus" from Handel's *Messiah* (Kahn 46).

The December 1969 issue of the student publication the *Illuminator* was devoted entirely to the victory. The headline read: "Welcome home Mr. President. We've climbed the mountain—now the Jordan." Pitts described the "rapture" he had felt when he heard the students' "cries of joy" (1). The Rev. C. Howard Nevett incorporated Miles's victory into the sermon he preached on Transfiguration Sunday, stating that going to the airport to welcome Pitts had been a transfiguring experience for him (4–5). One student-athlete, in a refreshingly down-to-earth reaction, wrote: "I am really glad for Miles. I hope now we can get a gym" (7). Monro's statement showed that he was more interested in moving on than basking in success. "We have had our day of rejoicing," he wrote. "Let us now settle down, in our new strength, to the great tasks ahead" (1).

Neither he nor Pitts used the accreditation victory to request an increase in their meager salaries. Instead, Pitts, who after eight years as president still was not matching what he had been earning in Atlanta, refused to accept the pay raise the board had voted him, saying: "It would throw things out of balance along the line. I've got too many people with good offers elsewhere who stay here at heavy sacrifice" (qtd. in Egerton 112). Similarly, when Pitts added a thousand dollars to Monro's annual salary, Monro refused to sign his contract until the raise had been canceled and his original salary of ten thousand dollars had been restored (Greenhouse 91).

Once Miles made headlines with its reaccreditation, the college received media attention for minor events as well. After vice president Spiro Agnew claimed during a speech in Chicago that the college's open door policy weakened the "natural aristocracy" of intellectual achievement, a group of prominent Chicago residents, including alumni and supporters of the college, flew down to see how the open door students were faring (P. Moore 15). They sought out Pitts, whose reaction to Agnew's comment was unprintable. They also sought out Monro, who quipped, "I always feel safer when I find myself on the opposite side from Spiro and Martha [Mitchell]."

One unfortunate side effect of the reaccreditation was that it precipitated the departure of Dick Arrington. The loss of his protégé was a bitter blow to Pitts, but he had only himself to blame, because it was he who had encouraged Arrington to get involved in community affairs. In 1969 they had jointly organized a meeting of black leaders to discuss employment discrimination and police brutality. Arrington volunteered to write up the group's recommendations, and the report led to the formation of the biracial Community Affairs Committee (Franklin 61).

In the spring of 1970, six months after the accreditation victory, Arrington agreed to become executive director of the Alabama Center for Higher Education (ACHE), which had been founded in 1968 by Pitts and the presidents of seven other historically black colleges (Franklin 46). Arrington had refused several earlier invitations from ACHE, but now, with Miles reaccredited and on firmer ground, the time seemed right. Louis Dale, a Miles graduate and chair of the Division of Natural Sciences, agreed to serve as interim dean for the upcoming school year ("Miles Alumnus").

Arrington and his family remained in the Birmingham area, and he worked with Monro at every opportunity. Nevertheless, his resignation was a great professional loss for Monro, because there was no guarantee that the new dean would understand and support the Freshman Studies Program as wholeheartedly as Arrington had. The Sapps were also leaving, to pursue graduate degrees at the University of North Carolina at Chapel Hill, Jane in music and Hubert in political science (interview).

COMINGS AND GOINGS

Thanks to the revolving door nature of academic postings, Monro was partially compensated for the loss of former colleagues by the arrival of new faces on campus in the fall of 1970. One New England transplant was Dick King, who had followed Monro's advice and applied for a position at UAB as professor of educational research. The Kings had been neighbors in Winchester, and Toddy King and Dottie were friends.

King, a Williams College alumnus, had graduate degrees from Harvard in comparative literature and educational measurements, and he often followed in Monro's footsteps because of their common interests and concerns. In 1950 he had joined Monro as a financial aid officer at Harvard, helping to shape the formula that became the model for the College Scholarship Service (CSS) ("Richard G. King"). In 1954, while Monro was chairing the CSS, King became assistant director of the College Board, and in that capacity he took the CSS to task for not doing enough to guarantee that financial aid went to the neediest students (R. G. King, "Educational").

Like Monro, King had served in the Pacific during World War II and was proud of the fact. Monro relished this particular similarity, and when Phil, as an upperclassman at Harvard, reported that King had been extraordinarily helpful in offering academic advice, Monro replied, "Well, you know, he was a submariner in the Navy, and they are the best" (Dreyer, e-mail, 31 Mar. 2008). The Kings' presence in Birmingham widened John and Dottie's circle of friends and strengthened their ties to UAB.

The Townsends

Late in the summer of 1970 Robert "Kim" Townsend arrived with his young family and prepared to teach English at Miles for a year. At thirty-five Townsend was older than most of the other white faculty, and he was also far more experienced, having been awarded tenure at Amherst. Townsend wanted to do something significant with his sabbatical year, and in March 1970 Linda Greenhouse's *New*

York Times article reminded him of Monro's unusual career move and piqued his interest in the Freshman Studies Program at Miles. He wrote to Monro, who was impressed by his credentials: graduation from Deerfield Academy and Princeton; a Fulbright Fellowship at Cambridge, England; and a Harvard doctorate in English Literature. Monro set up an interview, Kim and his wife, Shane, flew down to meet him and Pitts, and Kim agreed to teach several courses in the English Department as long as he could also teach Freshman English (personal interview).

Coming to Miles required many adjustments for the Townsends. They traded their comfortable Amherst home for a tiny on-campus apartment, and Shane, a Smith graduate, dropped out of a supportive women's group and put aside her painting to handle the logistics of settling into a new home (S. Crabtree, personal interview, 8 July 2003). The transition was probably least traumatic for Roger, who was almost three, but Haig, eight, and Mary, ten, passed up a year at the progressive Common School and took their chances with the Alabama schools, which were still adjusting reluctantly to desegregation (S. Crabtree, e-mail, 17 Oct. 2008).

Kim's journal and Shane's diary, which she titled "My Year in the South," provide detailed descriptions of life at Miles as it appeared to temporary residents sympathetic to the college but strangers to its culture. As Shane had feared, the family struggled to squeeze into their small apartment, which was located in a two-story brick building on the dusty edge of the playing fields. The children, who had each had a room of their own in Massachusetts, shared a tiny bedroom, and there was no quiet place to study or work. With new understanding Shane commiserated with "all the overcrowded blacks with no place to get away from the confusion" (Crabtree, Diary).

The family was plagued by ceaseless health problems, their source almost surely the pollution generated by the nearby steel mills, which struck Shane as deceptively picturesque: "The air outside is heavy and tastes metallic. The sky always has clouds of pink and gray. You can see the smoke stacks and high red flames going into the sky." She began tracking the local newspaper's pollution report, which was given in number of micrograms of solid pollution particles per cubic meter of atmosphere sampled. One such report listed the downtown count as 397 (14 Nov. 1970). The U.S. Department of Health classified anything over 80 as having an adverse effect on health, and anything over 200 as critical. Because Miles was even closer to the Fairfield mills, the count was almost certainly higher there than downtown.

Roger proved especially susceptible to the poor air quality. On 30 September Shane kept him out of school to take him to the doctor's, and in the days that followed, he spent more time in the waiting room than the classroom. All three children came down with bronchitis, and Haig tested positive for allergic sensitivities, either to the virus or to the pollution (13 Nov. 1970). In December the allergist announced that Roger had asthma.

Monro did what he could to help the Townsends through their difficult year. Upon learning that their small, hot apartment was making Shane feel ill, he invited her to come over to the house and cool off during the day (Crabtree, personal interview). He also helped the family deal with a small but potent tragedy. In a decision that Shane regretted as soon as she saw how small their apartment was, they had brought along the two family cats. Because there was barely room for the family in the apartment, letting the cats out at night seemed like a good idea; it might even, the Townsends reasoned, turn them into "outdoor cats" (Crabtree, e-mail, 8 Mar. 2011). But one morning the children awoke to discover that one of them, Walter Cron-cat, had been mauled to death. After Monro explained that a pack of feral dogs roamed the area at night, the surviving cat, Betty, was let out only with an escort (Crabtree, Diary, 5 Nov. 1970).

Monro's efforts to help the family were motivated by both generosity and affection. He admired Shane, an intelligent, talented, well-educated woman, working hard to keep her family happy and healthy under trying circumstances but also eager to find meaningful projects of her own. Kim was a colleague with whom he could discuss pedagogy and academic politics, even if they did not see eye to eye on every issue; he often joined Monro and Betty Gates in a lonely alliance, defending the program against criticism from other departments.

The effect Miles had on the Townsends confirmed Monro's belief that time spent at black colleges would give whites "a clarity of vision about the realities of American life" that they could get nowhere else ("Escape" 434). Shane came to realize just how privileged her family's former lifestyle had been. Squeezed into tight quarters, she experienced the psychic consequences of insufficient living space: "There's no room for possessions. No room for anyone to have his own private place." Discovering that the children of a neighboring family shared a single bicycle, she reflected on the materialism of middle-class America: "Our kids all have their own things all geared to their own age and interests, fostering individuality, but also associating *things* with identity" (24 Sept. 1970).

Perhaps most important, Miles clarified Shane's thinking about her career. She had already decided that she wanted to go back to school to study either art, which had been her undergraduate major, or nursing. Before the end of the fall semester, she settled on nursing because, she explained, "I felt the [undergraduate] art training had made my education unbalanced. . . . I needed to be trained to be useful and I was interested in things physical, the body and how it worked" (e-mail, 18 Oct. 2007).

The family's many health problems may have intensified Shane's desire to understand how the body works and what to do when it stops working, but her view of education as a way of preparing for meaningful work in the real world—with self-actualization or learning for its own sake running a distant second—also bears a striking resemblance to the attitude most students brought with them to Miles.[5]

For Kim family difficulties were somewhat offset by the rewards of teaching at Miles. He admired the students and the impressive progress they made in spite of their poor preparation. He was struck by how much was at stake for them: education was their only chance for a better life, whereas at Amherst students who foundered academically could often fall back on family, prep school ties, alumni, class, and other support systems (Townsend, "Teaching" 15). Back home he widened his range of teaching, offering a course on civil rights literature. He also represented Amherst and was the only white member of the committee that developed a format for James Baldwin's Five College professorship (interview).[6]

As adults, Mary, Haig, and Roger have vivid memories of Miles: the stinging red ants that were the scourge of the campus; the violent death of Walter Cron-cat; confrontations at school, assorted injuries, falls, and accidents. Mary remembers going home with a black friend, Deirdre, whose mother whipped her brother when he attempted to join the girls, shouting at him, "Don't you ever talk to a white girl." Haig remembers the physical differences and similarities between himself and his black playmates: When he needed stitches after falling off a swing, he noticed, "White people bleed the same blood," but he recalls "shaking my head back and forth, showing the black kids that my hair moved differently from theirs" (e-mails to Crabtree, 15 Oct. 2007).[7]

PITTS MOVES ON

In December 1970, a year after the reaccreditation victory flooded Miles with jubilation, another announcement from Pitts swept the campus like an icy wind: effective 15 June 1971, he would leave Miles to become the first black president of Paine College, his alma mater. He had been mulling over the move for some time. In late 1969 he hinted to an interviewer that his usefulness to Miles was drawing to a close: "We need a young, vigorous, trained educator and administrator, and I'm none of those—I'm a preacher." But, he continued, "accreditation has to come before I go—nothing but death would make me leave before then" (qtd. in Egerton 114). Once the accreditation campaign had succeeded, he said that although choosing between the two colleges was as painful as choosing between a mother and a child, he felt compelled to return to Paine "in a time of crisis in black education" (Hicks).

Pitts was drawn to Paine for several reasons. First, there were his deep roots in Georgia: if he ever stopped working—which was doubtful—he intended to retire to a farm in Jones County, his birthplace (Conley, "Paine"). More specifically, there was his strong affection for his alma mater: he told friends that he loved every blade of grass on the Paine campus and that when the presidency opened up, "He felt that his mama was calling him home" (Clemon, personal interview, 7 Mar. 2008).

The move was also politically shrewd. For his entire adult life Pitts had wanted to be a CME bishop. When the Miles presidency became available, some of the bishops had urged him to take the position, with the understanding that they would support his run for bishop when the time came. He would soon be eligible to run, and now the bishops were conveying the same message regarding the Paine presidency (Clemon, interview).

Pitts was going to be a tough act to follow, given his formidable charisma and powers of persuasion. The Rev. Abraham Woods, a Miles alumnus and faculty member, said that Pitts "could sell an Eskimo a refrigerator" (personal interview, 21 July 2003). Mary Smith still marvels that Pitts persuaded her to leave Texas A&M, where she had taught for twenty years, and take a two thousand dollar pay cut to join the Division of Education at Miles. "He could make you do almost anything," she reminisced. "I used to tell him he was nothing but a con man" (personal interview, 7 Mar. 2008).

In addition to the charisma factor, the new president would be expected to get along, without going along, with the Birmingham business and educational community, a tricky balancing act that even Pitts's critics acknowledged had been one of his most impressive accomplishments. Based on the cordial relations he cultivated, Birmingham businessmen had raised $90,000 of the $450,000 cost of the science center, and he had persuaded prominent members of the white community to serve on the executive committee of the board of trustees

(Chisum 19). At a testimonial dinner in his honor the Friends of Miles presented Pitts with a portrait, a check for $2,000 for the college, and a plaque inscribed with a message written by Monro and calling Pitts "a God directed force in our midst" (Vann, "Testimonial Dinner" 1).

For Monro Pitts's departure was more than another painful parting—it was a seismic shift in his professional life as well. He would be losing both the inspiring figure who had lured him South and the champion who promoted, praised, and protected his program. This was an especially dangerous situation because Pitts's tendency to micromanage had resulted in a rickety administrative structure with no effective check on presidential power. Although the board of trustees technically had the final say on matters of substance, Pitts's authority was so total that during a two-week trip away, all college business ground to a halt until he returned (Zorn, "Harvard Graduate" 4). His successor would inherit that authority.

Hoping to maintain some continuity in leadership, Monro quietly sounded out many faculty members, then encouraged Arrington to apply for the presidency, assuring him of faculty support. Arrington agreed, and the faculty petitioned the board of trustees to interview him, even though he was a Baptist and all presidents so far had been CME members; in fact, all presidents so far had been CME ministers, except for Bell, Pitts's predecessor (Kahn 45). The board interviewed Arrington but passed him over for the Rev. W. Clyde Williams, a CME minister and church elder who had graduated from Paine.

If Arrington could not be president, Monro and many other faculty members felt the next best scenario would be for Arrington to return as dean and provide academic expertise as Williams grew into the presidency. In a note thanking Monro for his efforts but turning down the suggestion, Arrington merely said that his decision had been based on "many considerations" (21 Apr. 1971, DP), but he later explained that after talking to Williams, he concluded that Williams was not enthusiastic about Arrington's resuming the deanship (interview). Having exhausted the only options he considered worth pursuing, Monro resigned himself to working without the reassurance and clout of his two strongest allies.

A FALLING OUT

Monro's regret over Pitts's departure was complicated by a rift that opened between them just days before Pitts left for Augusta. The occasion was the final faculty-staff meeting of the school year, which took place on 1 and 2 June 1971.

Pitts was scheduled to introduce Clyde Williams at the meeting and wanted to ensure that he drew on the expertise of interim dean Louis Dale. This desire may explain why Pitts, Monro's longtime friend and booster, suddenly allied himself with Dale in a bitter controversy over student writing.

Dale had created a committee charged with developing a writing proficiency exam, and the Freshman English faculty were not represented on the committee, in spite of the fact that their students would be taking the test and would have to repeat the course if they did not receive a passing score. The examination was presented as the work of the committee, but it was widely known that Humanities Division chair Beatrice Royster was its prime mover, and the exam materials were housed in her office and in her secretary's keeping.

The first administration of the exam took place in May. The Freshman English teachers, who had been instructed to score their students' exams, met twice before the exam date, frantically trying to come to terms with the test. For the second meeting Kim Townsend requested copies of the exam from Royster and distributed them to faculty members who did not already have them. Because none of them had yet seen the answer key, he also went to Royster's office and got a copy from her secretary. The key only made things worse, since some teachers disagreed with several of the answers that the key listed as correct (Townsend, Journal). After the test was administered, both Townsend and Monro returned their students' exams to Dale without scoring them, explaining the serious reservations they had about the test.

That was where matters stood when the faculty-staff meeting convened. Dale asked Royster to provide some background information on the exam, but she said nothing about the most hotly contested issue: whether the test was a valid indicator of students' writing proficiency or mastery of the course content. Then Monro spoke, attempting to establish some common ground while clarifying his objections to the test. He agreed that the exam was important but said it was even more important to work together and find a satisfactory solution to the problem they faced: serious reservations among the Freshman English faculty about the exam and the uses to which it was being put (Townsend, Journal).

Betty Gates agreed with Monro, but nobody else said anything. Then Pitts announced that he suddenly realized there was a simple solution to the problem, which he was implementing immediately: he was lowering the passing score for the exam by five points—a move that satisfied nobody, although it reduced the number of students who would fail the exam. This clumsy attempt to cut the

Gordian knot illustrated Pitts's fatal tendency to micromanage. As the meeting crept on, he continued to blunder, trying by sheer force of will to maintain control over a future he would not be there to see. When Dale, following tradition, began listing faculty and where they would be the following year, he concluded by saying, "If I'm not Dean, I'll be at—," Pitts interrupted him, insisting, "Dean Dale will be returning to school next year" (Townsend, Journal).[8]

In his office the next day Monro told Townsend that he felt betrayed by Pitts and alienated from the faculty, and wondered whether he was doing the college more harm than good by staying on (Townsend, Journal). It is easy to understand why he was so upset. The issue discussed at the meeting was one that mattered profoundly to him: he was convinced that the exam was unfair to the students and undermined the Freshman English course. In addition, the flawed results generated by the test offended his respect for the persuasive power of carefully gathered and interpreted data, like the kind he had used to develop Harvard's financial aid formulas and the freshman vocabulary program at Miles. The bitter meeting itself—where he presented his opinion and waited in vain for others to agree—felt a lot like his lonely stand on the parietals controversy at Harvard. But he was most upset by Pitts's sudden, public withdrawal of support, which stood in stark contrast to the customary warmth of their relationship. More typical was a letter so effusive that it made Pitts sound like an ardent suitor. "Some days in my 'slough of despond,' I feel real courage to go on because of you," he had written the year before Monro moved to Miles (22 Dec. 1966, MCA).

Pitts must have realized he had let Monro down, because he enclosed a personal note with Monro's contract for the following year, stating that he "hoped and prayed" Monro would "return to Miles College where we have dreamed and labored and where we still have some unfinished business." The note and the contract were sent on 3 June, the day after the contentious meeting, and the contract contained the usual thirty-day deadline for signing and returning it.

Normally a stranger to procrastination, Monro waited almost a week before returning the contract—unsigned. In a cover letter he explained that he would not sign until he could talk to Williams and give him the opportunity to "change or cancel the present arrangement, if he thinks best, without the rupture implied in a thirty-day notice" (9 June 1971, MCA). Beneath the carefully chosen words was the implication that Monro no longer felt confident of the administration's support. Pitts wrote back at once, insisting that Williams was "as desirous as I am, if not more, of having you continue your work" and expressing Pitts's desire to talk to Monro "at length" about the matter that day or evening (12 June 1971, MCA). If the meeting took place, it did little to reconcile them. Monro was still feeling betrayed when a memorial book being inscribed for Pitts made the rounds on campus. Alongside a long, emotional poem from Betty Gates and extravagantly fond messages from people who barely knew Pitts, Monro signed his name and added no message at all (Townsend, interview). The impersonality of the abrupt entry spoke volumes about how deeply he had been hurt.[9]

There is room no longer for surprise. There is room
only for admiration.

—HONORARY DEGREE, Amherst, 1 June 1973

9
GOING IT ALONE
1971-1978

The summer of Pitts's departure, Monro went to Evanston to help Phil, Janet, and the children move to Atlanta, where Phil had accepted a position as assistant professor of psychology and educational studies at Emory (Dreyer, e-mail, 30 Jan. 2008). While Phil drove the U-Haul truck with seven-year-old Scott riding shotgun, Monro drove the tightly packed station wagon most of the way, accompanied by Janet, three-year-old Rebecca, and the family pets (Dreyer, e-mail, 27 May 2008). Everyone, especially Dottie, was happy about the move because Atlanta was an easy drive from Birmingham.

In South Freeport, Monro spent time on a task he had promised to complete for the Phillips trustees: a draft resolution honoring his friend Jack Kemper upon his retirement as headmaster. As Monro pointed out in the resolution, Kemper had attracted a stellar faculty and giving them a larger role in determining the fate of the school, updated and improved the physical plant, maintained a balance between crucial detail and overall vision, and advanced equal opportunity in education. Many of the curricular innovations he oversaw—such as Outward Bound, Washington internships, School Year Abroad, and a community service program in nearby Lawrence—nudged students beyond the parameters of their cozy campus (Allis 221). Now the lung cancer for which Kemper had undergone surgery the previous spring had recurred and become terminal. He died a few months after the board's October meeting. Meanwhile, a very different kind of leader was taking the helm at Miles.

* * *

PRESIDENT WILLIAMS

W. Clyde Williams, who fell far short of the "trained educator and administrator" Pitts had envisioned as his successor, was thirty-nine years old when he became president, having spent most of his working life in the church rather than in academe. For the previous two years he had served as general secretary of the Consultation on Church Union in Princeton, and for seven years he had been affiliated with the Interdenominational Theological Center, in Atlanta, where he earned a master of religious education degree in 1961 (Vann, "New"). He was on the Board of Directors of the National Committee of Black Churchmen, the Editorial Board of J. S. Polack Publishing Company, and the Church Commission on Scouting ("W. Clyde Williams"). The first priority in Williams's five-year plan for the college was a more visible affiliation with the church.

In August 1971 Williams replaced acting dean Louis Dale with Alandus C. Johnson, whom he knew from their undergraduate days at Paine. Johnson's qualifications for the deanship were skimpy, to say the least: although he was chair of the History and Philosophy Departments at Grambling College, in Louisiana, he lacked a graduate degree, and the depth of his scholarship was reflected in a conference paper he had recently presented on "Adding More Soul to Creoles" ("Dr. Alandus Johnson"). Substituting Johnson for Dale, who had years of teaching under his belt, administrative experience as a department chair, and was closing in on his doctorate at UAB, boded ill for Miles's future and was an early indicator that Williams would treat the presidency as a stepping-stone to his goal of becoming a CME bishop.

Williams further telegraphed his ecclesiastical ambitions by making sure that his first official presidential appearance occurred under church auspices. The occasion was the Birmingham Conference of the CME Church in August. Not so coincidentally, the conference leader was Chester A. Kirkendoll, whose dual roles as presiding bishop of Alabama and Florida and chairman of the Miles board of trustees made him a key figure in Williams's bid for a bishopric (G. Moore).

Monro could have responded to the change of command by leaving, but he was too invested in the college to walk away, and he was especially eager to put the finishing touches on the Freshman Studies Program, which he estimated would take two more years (Greenhouse 92). Besides, Williams deserved a chance and might, like Prince Hal, grow into the job. After all, Pitts too longed to be a bishop and had accepted the Paine presidency as a step along that path. In what seemed a positive sign of his interest in the curriculum, Williams created a commission for curriculum development, under the chairmanship of Wayman Shiver (Williams, *Annual Report*). Shiver, who had come to Miles in 1970 to direct the Services to Enhance Educational Potential program, had worked at the Consultative Center for School Desegregation in Oklahoma, taught high school, held several positions with the Georgia Teachers and Educators Association, and gone to Thailand as a Peace Corps volunteer. What he had never done was teach or work in a college or university, an omission that made him a puzzling choice to spearhead an examination of the curriculum ("Dr. Wayman Shiver").

In addition to its turnover in leadership, Miles was experiencing the general crisis in black education that Pitts had described when he left for Paine. In 1961 half of all black college students were attending black colleges; by 1971 the figure had shrunk to a third (Pitts, "Black College President"). Funding was also shrinking: in 1970 only 3 percent of the federal funds for higher education went to black colleges, and former U.S. education commissioner Earl J. McGrath estimated that at least five hundred million dollars would be needed over the next five years to put black colleges on an even financial keel (Hechinger, "Should I").

In an attempt to address the crisis, Monro wrote to McGeorge Bundy, who had left Harvard for a position at the Ford Foundation, and urged the foundation to arrange long-term loans for black colleges and other struggling educational institutions. Bundy promised to reevaluate the long-term loan idea despite its having been found impractical in the past. His assurance that "we will keep working on it" was cold comfort to Monro, who read between the lines and inferred that the foundation was preparing to shrink its support of higher education. As he suspected, in October 1971 the foundation announced that it would support only ten black colleges, and Miles was not among them (Delaney).[1]

All Monro could do was make sure that whatever money he brought in was spent where it would do the most good. Shortly after a Radcliffe alumna donated seventy thousand dollars to Miles, Monro's friend and former protégé Archie Epps visited and was shocked to find him working in a sweltering basement room. When Epps suggested that a sliver of the donation might have been spent on an air conditioner, Monro replied: "I gave it to the financial aid office. I'm doing fine" (Pasternack A1). To scotch suspicions that he was making a sacrifice, he claimed to love the heavy southern heat, which reminded him of the sultry Pacific climate he had become used to aboard the *Enterprise* (Dreyer, "Eulogy," Cambridge).

FROM CRISIS TO DILEMMA

Monro used every bully pulpit at his disposal to raise awareness of the black college crisis, but he realized that interest in the subject was waning. To rejuvenate the topic, when he went to the University of Michigan to accept an honorary degree in December 1971 he talked about "the Black College Dilemma," evoking Gunnar Myrdal's *An American Dilemma* and its contrast between America's theoretical embrace of equality and its all-too-real record of racism.[2]

One contemporary manifestation of the dilemma, Monro said in his speech, was a host of hard questions black colleges were having to ask themselves. Chief among them was whether they should consider themselves temporary responses to racism or permanent sources of black institutional strength. Monro's answer, of course, was that just as the automobile industry needed General Motors and automobile workers needed the United Auto Workers, the black community needed its colleges in order to survive in a society so "tough on unorganized, powerless people" ("Black College" 1). He confessed he was puzzled that whites consistently undervalued or ignored the safety valve function of black colleges. In spite of their recent falling out, he praised Pitts for defusing potential campus violence the day that Martin Luther King Jr. was assassinated, and he condemned a recent *New York Times* article for suggesting that integration might be rendering black colleges obsolete. "Why does the *Times* think we have riots in our great cities, and Black Panther shoot-outs with the police?" he asked. "It is idiotic, not to say suicidal, to talk of phasing out the few effective black institutions we now have" (7).

FIVE-YEAR ANNIVERSARY

As he began his fifth year at Miles, Monro left South Freeport earlier than usual to speak at UAB's summer commencement. He had addressed many such gatherings, but this one was especially gratifying, given his many connections to the university. His speech, peppered with pronouns of identification, left no doubt that he considered himself a part of the UAB community: "I feel, as I know you do, a deep sense of excitement and hope for what our university can accomplish for our city in the future ("University of Alabama" 3). With almost proprietary pride he described UAB as "the great institution now taking form between Sixth Avenue and the mountain" and contrasted its charter class of 136 extension students with the large competitive school it had become in just thirty-six years (4–5). He praised UAB for its "statesmanship and concern" regarding the black college crisis and presented an impressive list of the ways in which UAB was collaborating with Miles: by establishing the much-needed dental clinic, helping create new business programs, permitting cross-registration, jointly developing health care recruitment programs, and laying the foundation for sharing and exchanging faculty (11).

Throughout the school year Monro continued to excel in his role as cash cow. He helped obtain a $75,000 Danforth Foundation grant for faculty development programs ("Miles Receives"), and in January 1973 the Freshman Studies Program received a $120,000 federal grant to support a merger with some version of the College Educational Achievement Program (CEAP), a recently lapsed program that had provided financial aid, tutoring, remediation, and cultural enrichment for one hundred seriously underprepared students.

Home from Radcliffe for the winter break, Dale Russakoff interviewed Monro about his first five years in the South, then wrote an article about it for the *Crimson*. Dale, the daughter of Irene and Russ Russakoff and the godchild of activist banker-journalist Charles Zukoski, was initially surprised by Monro's modesty, especially in light of his reputation at Harvard, where the legend of his heroic sacrifice stubbornly refused to die. His on-the-job demeanor struck her as "very modest and humble; he was uncomfortable in the role of white knight." His simple wardrobe—slacks, blue button-down shirt, and tie—was appropriate for the hands-on nature of his position. "He dressed simply, like a worker in the vineyard," she recalls (telephone interview, 1 Dec. 2008). He also talked like a worker in the vineyard, describing his role as a purely supportive one: "A white man can work at a black college, provided that the black community runs it. There's no question about that here—the black community runs Miles. I only work for them" (qtd. in Russakoff, "Miles").

Knowing that his remarks would be read by former colleagues in Cambridge, he told Russakoff that Miles was doing a better job than Harvard in developing curriculum to meet the needs of its student body. He was particularly proud of a work-study program for business majors he had recently helped set up. By releasing students from classes for a semester to work in local businesses, the program provided both income and hands-on learning, diversified Miles's list of majors, strengthened an area that was becoming increasingly popular, and created a conduit for black institutional strength in the business community. Weighed against such advantages, the logistical nightmare of rearranging the students' schedules was a trifle. "When you've got a program that's as dead right as this one, you don't worry about it," he said dismissively (qtd. in Russakoff, "Miles").

GUEST APPEARANCES

Black History Week found Monro talking to students at Ramsay High School. He reminded his young listeners that history books were the work of human beings, prone to error and limited by their biases; that history was written by the winners; and that black history in particular was often misrepresented in order to soothe the winners' sensibilities. "If you are kidnapping tens of millions of men and women and bringing them into slavery for profit, it helps your conscience to think that you are rescuing all these savage people from a dark, barbarous continent, and making them over into God-fearing Christians," he dead-panned ("Look Hard" 2).

In the audience at Ramsay was Dick Arrington, now one of two black members of the city council. Since his election, racially motivated police brutality had diminished, a few black officers had been added to the force, and he had proposed that vacancies in city departments be filled in proportion to racial percentages of the population (Franklin 73, 94). When Stanford University awarded Monro an honorary degree and invited him to speak at the June 1973 commencement, he described Arrington's election as one of several encouraging signs that institutionalized racism in Birmingham was on the wane ("Stanford Commencement" 8).

All the Stanford commencement speakers noted the one-year anniversary of Watergate, but Monro devoted most of his speech to two other milestones: the tenth anniversary of the Year of Birmingham and the fifth anniversary of Martin Luther King's assassination ("Great Revolutionary Effort"). He proposed King as a role model for the graduates as they faced Watergate and other national problems. Like them, he pointed out, King had stood at a crossroads when he graduated. Like them, he could have chosen a life filled with comfort and professional advancement, but when he was asked to lead the Montgomery bus boycott, he rejected the security that was within his grasp and instead "took to the streets." Monro described the obstacles that had faced King in Birmingham, not to impress the seniors with King's heroism, but to draw a parallel between the seriousness of King's cause—what he called "the raw stuff of revolution"—and the seriousness of the task they faced: "to regain control from the men and interests who have stolen it away from us since World War II" ("Stanford Commencement" 3, 10).[3]

He urged the graduates to join him in "getting our backs into the struggle" to regain control, and as an example of positive action he pointed to a satellite campus program in Eutaw, about ninety miles from Birmingham, that he was impatient to begin. One excellent first step in turning the country around, he said, was for each of its four-year colleges to "find some forsaken corner" like Eutaw and set up a satellite campus there. Believing as he did that education was the first step toward social progress of any kind, he did not think it was far-fetched to propose satellite campuses as a way for citizens to reclaim control of their country. To persuade skeptics in the audience, however, he performed one of the nimble rhetorical maneuvers he was so good at. "Does all this seem a touch visionary?" he began, posing what he imagined might be his audience's main objection. Then, admitting that such an objection might be valid, he answered his own question. "Perhaps so," he said. "Let me just say that's how we feel at Miles College, down there in Birmingham," he continued, situating himself within the obviously admirable group of possible doubters. Then he concluded the exercise by inviting any holdouts to join him: "I would be an ungracious guest indeed to assume any less high hopes or vision for Stanford" (13).

Monro also received a degree from Amherst College, where he was accompanied by his mother and escorted by Kim Townsend, who had nominated him for the honor (Townsend, e-mail, 24 Sept. 2010). Responding to Amherst president John William Ward's invitation, Monro asked for a favor. "I am fairly allergic to 'homage' of any kind," he wrote, "so I would be most comfortable if that element in the proceedings can be kept low key, very low. I am old enough to know, as [former Harvard] President Eliot warned, not to inhale the junk, but the temptation is always there." Ward obliged with a warm but low-key tribute, singling out Monro's endurance for special admiration: "We at Amherst pay you public homage not because you moved, but because you stayed. . . . There is room no longer for surprise. There is room only for admiration" (honorary degree, 1 June 1973, DP).

Monro also spoke at the annual spring luncheon of Urban Gateways, an arts education program founded in 1961 to address the dearth of artistic exposure in inner-city schools. As usual, Monro had read up on the program in advance, and he praised it in particular for encouraging students to think of themselves as artists ("Urban Gateways" 1). Reflecting on the lessons he had gleaned from his research, Monro concluded that the arts deserved a far larger role in the college curriculum than they currently possessed, particularly for black students, whose "deep springs of creative energy—some somber, some lyrical, some thoughtful, some angry and explosive, some just plain joyous"—were often drowned out by the ubiquitous presence of the majority culture (14). To convey the pleasure, stimulation, and solace he drew from the arts, he used three examples: "From Picasso's *Guernica* I know the basic horror of our century. From Henry Thoreau, I learn the importance of confronting life and nature simply, and alone, and observantly. From Bach I know how the angels sing, or anyway how the angels wish they could sing" (6).

FRESHMAN STUDIES GOES ON THE ROAD

Late in July a project that Monro had been working on for more than a year bore fruit, and Miles received a $151,000 grant from the Fund for Independent Post-Secondary Education (FIPSE) to create a "portable freshman year experience" in Eutaw, just east of to the Mississippi border.

Greene County, with a fragile economy based on agriculture, had a population of about thirteen thousand, 85 percent of whom were black. The average per capita income was nine hundred dollars, and the county's economic problems were rooted in its dismal legacy of racism. Even after the Voting Rights Act of 1965, legal shenanigans kept Greene County blacks from voting until a Supreme Court decision in 1968 mandated a special election in the area. The first officials elected by black voters—the probate judge, school superintendent, and county board members—took office in 1970. When the black officials walked into their offices that year, the white staff walked out in protest, but more black officials were elected every year. Colleges, civil rights organizations, and northern institutions provided advice and sent volunteers to help get through the crisis, but the permanent solution—a critical mass of residents with the educational background to run things—was still lacking (Hubert Sapp, personal interview, 30 July 2003).

As in Birmingham, the root of the problem was the substandard public school system, which was predominantly black. In 1973 the county's public high schools enrolled three thousand students, only forty of whom were white, and the dropout rate was about 50 percent (Monro, "Stanford Commencement" 12).

Monro proposed the Portable Freshman Program as a small but important step toward filling this educational void. Under his plan a single year of intensive study would include the same courses as the Freshman Studies Program, plus a full remedial program. The leap to college, which up to now had been impossible for nine out of ten high school seniors in the county, would be offered, tuition free, in their own backyard. At the end of the year participants would receive help in applying for transfer to another college. Once the program got going, it would cost only a thousand dollars per student to run. Eutaw faculty members would belong to corresponding departments at Miles, and faculty from the main campus could teach at Eutaw if they wished.

Realizing that the best way to gain local support was to make the residents feel the program belonged to them, Monro asked the county school board and the county commission for help developing the program and then for permission to use the county buses, school cafeterias, and laboratories (Monro, "College" 59–60). Finally, he applied for the FIPSE grant and kept his fingers crossed.

When the grant came through, the remainder of the summer—which must have felt a lot like "that first wild summer" of Peace Corps training at Harvard—became a frantic scramble to assemble the program in time for the fall semester. Serendipitously, Hubert Sapp, who had just completed his course work at UNC, contacted Monro to request a letter of recommendation for a teaching position. Monro agreed but added that he wanted to talk about something that would really interest Sapp (interview). The "something," of course, was the Eutaw project, which was scheduled to begin right after Labor Day and required a director to build it from the ground up. Were the Sapps interested? Would they fly to Miles for an interview?

They were, and they did, although their enthusiasm was tested during their interview with dean Alandus Johnson, whose attitude toward the project was so "frank and cautionary" that it might have frightened them off under other circumstances. Instead, they decided to drive to Eutaw and at least see what they would be getting into.

It was daunting on every level. The county had purchased an antebellum mansion for the program, but once the Sapps got beyond the Tara-like pillars and balcony, the building revealed its checkered past. First used as a girls' academy, it had been converted into apartments and then allowed to go to seed ("Miles Eutaw"). They were assured, however, that the building would be converted into classrooms in time for the beginning of the semester. With a lot of hard work and absolutely no snags along the way, it looked just barely possible. They agreed to take the assignment then went back home to pack (interview).

When they arrived shortly before the Labor Day weekend, they wondered what had possessed them. The mansion now contained two rooms that were empty and reasonably clean; the others "looked exactly the way an apartment does when the tenants move out"—in other words, closer to a shambles than to a college building. There was no electricity above the ground floor, and when Sapp called to complain, a power company representative said its records indicated that the program had been scrapped (interview).

A serious scheduling problem also cropped up. One hundred students had applied for the program, which was the minimum that the FIPSE grant had specified, but because most of them had day jobs, only thirty could come during the day, when classes were being offered. Sapp faced a dilemma: if he revised the schedule to include evening courses, the program would not open on time and would include classes that had not been part of the original proposal. If he clung to the daytime schedule and opened on time, enrollment would plunge, jeopardizing the re-funding application that was due at the end of the first semester. He chose to postpone the opening for a week and add evening classes, gambling on the likelihood that if evening courses were already in place, they would be approved as part of the renewal proposal (interview).

Once the decision had been made, the Sapps and a skeleton crew attacked all the problems simultaneously: they got the electricity turned on, the building cleaned, applications processed, faculty notified of the postponement, and an emergency shopping list sent to the main campus. Desks and supplies arrived on Friday, with barely enough time to unpack them before classes started. It promised to be an interesting school year.

TRYING TO ADJUST

Monro was buoyed and exhilarated by the last-minute scramble to get the Eutaw campus operating. He gamely served on the program committee for Williams's inauguration, and when a *Newsweek* reporter asked how things were going after five years at Miles, he implied that earlier difficulties had been resolved: "I'm not young and I'm not black, and one time or another that has been an issue. But we've been through that and come out the other side." Less graciously, Williams told the reporter, "John Monro has seen the Ivy League, and now he sees where education really is" (qtd. in "Man from Harvard"), but later in the year he credited Monro as well as Pitts with having turned Miles around (Delaney).

The truce between Monro and Williams masked a deep divide in their ideas about what was best for Miles and its students. Determined to put his stamp on the college, Williams emphasized style over substance and the physical plant over academic growth. He took advantage of every opportunity to publicize his efforts, including a trip in November 1973 to Shea Stadium, where he presented an honorary degree to Willie Mays upon his retirement from professional baseball ("Willie Mays Receives Honorary Degree").[4] Despite the college's shaky finances, Williams launched a campaign to purchase the Birmingham-Southern campus from the United Methodist Church, which was asking nine million dollars (U. W. Clemon, personal interview, 7 Mar. 2008). Realistically speaking, there was no way Miles could afford such a purchase, even with the three million dollars Williams optimistically estimated he could raise ("Man from Harvard"). In the summer of 1974 he hired a consultant, launched a feasibility study, and prodded the Miles trustees and the United Methodist Church board to approve the purchase (Williams, "State"). But after raising only a million dollars and failing to meet two deadline extensions, the acquisition campaign collapsed (Wright and Reeves).

In academic matters Williams invariably went for high-profile projects rather than essential but unglamorous matters such as boosting faculty salaries, upgrading classrooms and labs, and strengthening programs. He spearheaded the creation of an evening law school, which he argued would reduce the dearth of practicing black lawyers in the state by offering classes at a time when aspiring black attorneys with day jobs would be able to attend ("Miles College Opens"). The opening of the law school in 1974 was accompanied by a good deal of hype, even though its lack of accreditation meant that graduates would not be able to take out-of-state bar exams ("Newly Founded Miles Law School"). Williams could now take credit for creating the college's first professional school. Firsts made headlines, and he was hoping they made bishops too.

TAKING A STAND ON NEUTRALITY

In July 1974 Monro attended the First Annual Edward T. Ladd Conference on Educational Policy, held at Emory University to honor one its most distinguished professors of education. Monro's paper, "The College as an Agent for Social Change," explored one of the hot-button issues of the day: should colleges and universities take a stand on contemporary social and ethical issues, or should they remain neutral? Monro took exception to Harvard's support of neutrality, which president Derek Bok had spelled out while defending the university's continued investment in South African corporations. Bok strictly limited the mission of colleges and universities to "the discovery and transmission of knowledge. . . . Their institutional goal is not to reform society in specific ways" (qtd. in Willie, "Black Colleges" 47).

Disagreeing with Bok, Monro allied himself with student activists who claimed that campus ROTC programs, as well as research funded by the Defense Department, put the lie to administrative claims of neutrality ("College" 51). Because neutrality was not only impossible but undesirable, he claimed, colleges needed to take stands on important social issues, and he knew just where they should start: with the dismantling of institutional racism, "the crippling idiocy of a great country" (53).

Monro praised Miles and other historically black colleges as more effective and willing agents of social change than Harvard and its ilk. While prestigious colleges employed admission procedures driven by standardized test scores, he said, open door colleges like Miles let a student prove his mettle in the only way that was 100 percent reliable: "Get him under skillful, responsive instruction and watch his mind work" ("College" 56). He pointed proudly to the discrepancy between low scores and successful performance at Miles: of the ninety-one Miles sophomores still enrolled after four semesters, half had tested at eighth-grade reading level when they arrived, and none had achieved scores high enough to get them into a state university, never mind a competitive college (55).

Monro made a sharp distinction between these success rates—which were due to careful curriculum design, advisement, and support services—and the high mortality rate among minority students at selective colleges, where they were admitted in the name of affirmative action and then left to flounder. He had seen the results of this "revolving door" policy too often to speak calmly about it; instead, he attacked it with near-biblical wrath: "To bring previously ignored college students to our campuses and then lose them in the shuffle is something more than a self-defeating process; it is a new slaughter of the innocents, hopeful innocents" ("College" 57). The implication was clear: if colleges and universities wanted to be agents of social change, they needed to start with internal reform. Describing the Eutaw program, Monro contrasted Miles's concern for the underprivileged with the indifference of "our great colleges and universities, who just do not care enough about poor people, or black people, or Chicano people. . . . If you are looking for reasons why our country needs black colleges, I suggest you start with the question: who else cares?" (60).

MILES ALUMNUS, STATE SENATOR

Back in Birmingham, local politics took a positive turn when Miles graduate U. W. Clemon '65 and another black candidate won seats in the State Senate, which had not had a black member since Reconstruction (Egerton 120). Like Arrington, Clemon came from a large sharecropping family drawn to Birmingham by job opportunities at the steel mills. When his father proved incapable of holding onto his wages long enough to pay for food and shelter, Clemon's mother moved with her children to cheaper and more primitive lodgings each time the landlord demanded the back rent. Clemon traced his political awakening to the Montgomery bus boycott, which took place when he was thirteen; as he saw it, the lawyers and judges, not the police, had upheld the law and kept the peace (121). His respect for law enforcement officials was further eroded by his confrontation with public safety commissioner Bull Connor at a city commission meeting. When Clemon began reading a petition requesting that blacks be added to the police force, Connor told him to "shut up and sit down" because he was not a resident of Birmingham, and as the meeting adjourned, Connor ordered one of his subordinates to "get some police and get these niggers out of here" (qtd. in Egerton 123).

At Columbia Law School Clemon graduated third in a class of two hundred, and of the seven black students from the South he was the only one to hang up his shingle in his hometown (Egerton 124). He met Monro during the summer of 1964, when Pitts sent him to pick up Monro at the airport. Once he began his practice in Birmingham, he and Monro would get together to talk about classes, cases, politics, and Miles. When it was time for Clemon to write his first brief, he submitted it to Monro for his suggestions. In 1969 Clemon filed the lawsuit against Paul "Bear" Bryant that brought desegregation into the locker room of the UAB football team. The police brutality cases he took on eventually prompted a black citizens' group to protest, and its stand in turn led to a grand jury investigation (125). It is easy to see why Monro once told an audience,

"One U. W. Clemon is enough to justify the existence of Miles College" (qtd. in Egerton 120).[5]

PIAGET AND PURDUE AT MILES

The most interesting development on campus during this period, at least from Monro's perspective, was a two-day visit from Floyd Nordland, a biology professor from Purdue University. Nordland was dissertation advisor to Bernice Coar-Cobb, assistant professor of biology at Miles, who was doing her doctoral research on Jean Piaget's theory of cognitive development as it applied to the teaching of science. Monro was intrigued by the project, having been introduced to Piaget's work by son-in-law Phil, who had written a graduate school paper applying Piaget's framework to *Hamlet* (Dreyer, e-mail, 27 Mar. 2008).

Piaget had described four stages of cognitive development, but only the third and fourth were relevant to Coar-Cobb's research. In the third, concrete stage, usually reached sometime between first grade and early adolescence, a person can think logically but only about concrete or observable phenomena; in the fourth, formal operational stage, usually reached sometime during adolescence, a person can reason, hypothesize, deduce, and otherwise think logically about abstract, non-observable phenomena (*Learning and Teaching*).

Piaget's work interested Monro because it explained why so many of his obviously intelligent freshman students had difficulty working with abstractions: they were still at the concrete stage but were being asked to perform formal operational tasks without the benefit of a step-by-step procedure. The Audio-Tutorial Center that Coar-Cobb set up provided just that kind of procedure, and her data showed that even students who were still in the concrete stage could complete the course work if they were given additional time and the support supplied by the lab.

Eric Fancher '78 was one of the project's most impressive success stories. Using the center's facilities, he finished the course a week early and passed with flying colors, all without setting foot in a classroom. Monro arranged for Coar-Cobb and Fancher to visit Harvard and explain the Audio-Tutorial Center to faculty and students, and he visited Purdue himself, encouraging faculty members to consider teaching at Miles, at least briefly (Bernice Coar-Cobb Sterling, personal interview, 13 Mar. 2008).[6]

A YEAR OF CELEBRATION AND LOSS

For the country at large 1976 was an extravagant two hundredth birthday party. In addition, the College Board turned seventy-five, and so did Francis W. Parker, the Chicago high school Monro had admired for so long. He was invited to all the parties and got many presents; he also marked the occasions in personal ways, writing and delivering a bicentennially appropriate sermon at First Congregational on "The Pursuit of Happiness."

The celebration Monro enjoyed most was the Parker School's anniversary, which became a delightful double feature for him in his capacity as that year's Sarah Greenebaum Distinguished Visitor. Named after a revered alumna and teacher who had spent fifty-five years at the school, the award went each year to a "cutting edge educator," who was invited to visit the school for several days, addressing the faculty, sitting in on classes, and talking informally with members of the community (Grunsfeld 295). Monro visited in February then returned in October to speak at the anniversary dinner. In his remarks he described the "remarkable effect" his half-dozen visits to Parker had had on him as an educator, beginning when he was a young administrator recruiting for Harvard. "By some magic . . . I always come away from these encounters deeply refreshed and heartened and reassured about the state of education and the future of mankind," he mused ("Francis W. Parker Anniversary" 1).

The year of public festivities also brought a personal loss. On 11 February 1976, after a brief illness, Frances Monro died at the age of eighty-nine. She had enjoyed her independence up until close to her death, selling the family home and purchasing a smaller house in North Andover, renting a room to boarder Lewis Brown for five years, buying a new car every other year, and driving solo each winter to visit Sutton and Sue in Pennsylvania, Claxton and Vicki in Texas, and sometimes John and Dottie in Birmingham. As her health declined and she reluctantly discontinued her winter travels, her sons hired live-in help so that she could stay in her own home. When that was no longer enough, she moved to Valley Manor Nursing and Convalescent Center in Coopersburg, Pennsylvania, which was close enough to Sutton and Sue's farm so that they could visit often ("Mrs. Frances F. Monro"). She died soon after the move and was buried at her husband's side in the family plot adjoining Andover's Christ Church ("Frances Monro").

A BLACK COLLEGE CONFERENCE—AT HARVARD

Two months after his mother's funeral, Monro returned to New England for a conference about black colleges and their contribution to American education. For a year now he had been a member of the Harvard Board of Overseers, working on committees responsible for the Department of Afro-American Studies, Harvard and Radcliffe Colleges, the Department of Geology, and University Extension, the last of which he chaired ("Dr. John Monro"). The conference, which was supported by a grant from the National Institute of Mental Health, had been organized by Harvard sociologist Charles V. Willie, who traced his interest in black colleges to Monro's move to Miles (Willie, Prologue ix). They had met while Willie was visiting his brother, Louis, in Birmingham, and Willie had asked Monro to bring some Miles students to visit Willie's graduate school class and talk about their experiences. During the visit Willie mentioned some preliminary ideas for the conference, and Monro agreed to help plan it and to present a paper (telephone interview, 12 July 2003).

There were more than a few raised eyebrows over the strange pairing of Harvard and black colleges, particularly in light of the 1967 Jencks-Riesman article and its accusation that black colleges were "academic disaster areas." Willie had been stunned when several black college presidents declined to attend on the grounds that the gathering might project the same negative image as the Jencks-Riesman article had. One president wrote: "Those of us who work in the historically black colleges feel that we have been studied enough, too often by persons who know least about these institutions. . . . The reports and writings flowing from these studies have been too often hyper and unfairly critical of our institutions, showing little sensitivity and even less understanding" (qtd. in Willie and MacLeish 146). The black college presidents who did attend were invited, along with Riesman and several other Harvard faculty members, to a luncheon arranged by Harvard president Bok, and afterward Riesman told reporters that he had "rethought [his] original position" (Pressley).

Monro, one of only two white speakers, described the Freshman English course at Miles, proposing it as one way to replace copycat Ivy League–style courses with an approach better suited to the needs and interests of black college students. But before getting into the details of the course, he promulgated "Monro's First Law": "Faculty is what matters. If you have a good faculty, they will develop a good program. No matter how good the program, a poor faculty will butcher it" ("Teaching" 236). It was not surprising that Monro emphasized the importance of faculty, given that he lavished so much time and energy recruiting teachers. What was surprising was the dramatic language he used to convey their importance.

Monro's use of *butcher* showed how seriously he took the faculty's ability to create or to destroy, as well as how attached he was to the Freshman Studies Program, which he described elsewhere as having been developed "bit by bloody bit," as if it were a living thing ("Teaching" 238). In addition, the word contained a grim prophecy. The curriculum committee that Williams had created on his arrival at Miles was now proposing that the Freshman Studies Program be incorporated into the overall curriculum. Monro saw this move as nothing less than dismemberment, with the program being carved up and apportioned to individual departments. Such radical surgery, he was sure, would kill the patient.

THE DISMEMBERMENT BEGINS

As Monro's word choice implied, the Freshman Studies Program was in peril. A combination of curriculum revision and campus-wide reorganization had begun to obscure the unique characteristics of the first-year program. Monro's title had already been changed from director of the Freshman Studies Program to dean of Freshman (General) Studies ("Miles College Undergoing Major Reorganization"). Under the new system Monro no longer hired his own faculty, and curriculum decisions were subject to departmental approval, eroding the nimbleness that had been one of the program's greatest assets. Worst of all from Monro's point of view, Freshman English would now be taught by members of the English Department, almost all of whom had expertise in literature rather than writing or the unique needs of first-year students.

Just in time to supervise the absorption of Freshman Writing into the English Department, Beatrice Royster returned from leave and resumed her position as chair of the Division of Humanities. With an undergraduate degree from Alabama State, a master's degree from Howard, a doctorate from Emory, and a book contract for her dissertation, "The Ironic Vision of Four Black Women Novelists," she was one of the college's most accomplished faculty scholars ("Dr. B. H. Royster").

Like Monro, Royster was a dedicated teacher and a productive, conscientious citizen of Miles and the local community. She directed a program, funded by the National Defense Education Act, for public high school English teachers; coordinated the Interdisciplinary Program in Humanities at Miles; and was a member of the American Association of University Women ("Dr. B. H. Royster"). But their huge capacity for service and their love of teaching was just about all that Royster and Monro had in common. Over the years they came down on opposite sides of virtually every campus controversy, and Royster had championed the writing proficiency exam that Monro and the Freshman English faculty so strenuously objected to in 1971. Royster, with her hard-won academic credentials, had great respect for the specialized postgraduate degrees that Monro was frequently willing to waive when hiring teachers for the freshman program. She believed that mastering the Western classics was the only way graduates of black colleges could win respect and that asking anything less of them perpetrated "the soft bigotry of low expectations" (T. Friedman). Monro, on the other hand, believed that in black colleges the classics of black culture should take precedence over the traditional canon and that privileging the canon over black literature was both wrongheaded and racist. As Humanities Division chair, Royster believed that all writing courses should be administered through the English Department; as shaper and director of the Freshman Studies Program, Monro believed that the special nature of the freshman year required its own unit and a faculty with no departmental allegiances.

Another development that threatened to undermine Monro's position was growing resentment toward the thriving Eutaw campus, which was succeeding beyond everyone's expectations, including his. The program had been re-funded, sophomore courses had been added to the catalog, and students from five counties were enrolled in what was now a two-year program (Sapp, interview). An adult literacy program offered training for 400 people, and a placement center helped rural women find nontraditional jobs ("Miles-Eutaw"). Most of the roughly 30 day students who completed the initial one-year program were doing well in the colleges to which they had transferred (Sapp, interview). By spring 1975 the program had 120 students, and it was praised in the *Los Angeles Times* as filling an educational vacuum ("Miles College–Eutaw Project").

Most impressive of all, the Greene County program was a major factor in Miles's successful application for a $2 million federal grant, by far the largest in its history. Of that, $140,000 went directly to Eutaw, with another $660,000 earmarked for financial aid, $470,000 for curriculum development, and $800,000 for programs such as Teacher Corps, a Teacher Training Institute, the Birmingham Dropout Prevention Program, Upward Bound, Talent Search programs, and the Volunteers in Service to America program (VISTA) ("Awards and Contributions"). When Shiver and the business manager ordered Sapp to rate the program quantitatively in terms of its value and success rate, he calculated that the fiscal value of the program exceeded by at least $200,000 the funding it was currently receiving from FIPSE (Sapp, interview). Once again, a brainchild of Monro was benefiting Miles and keeping black colleges in the public eye. But at the same time the success of the satellite campus cast an unflattering light on the failed Birmingham-Southern campaign, and Monro was increasingly aware of the administration's coolness toward both him and his most recent victory.

A Willing Ear at UAB

Even after the full implications of the restructuring had sunk in, Monro's loyalty prevented him from complaining to anyone at Miles. He did confide to Dick Arrington that he was no longer getting the support he had been able to count on in the past (Arrington, interview, 22 July 2003), and he also discussed his problems with Bob French, assistant to the president at UAB.

As the university's coordinator for the Greater Birmingham Inter-College Council on Higher Education, French was always on the lookout for ways to link local colleges and universities, and he had immediately recognized that Monro would be invaluable in UAB's pursuit of a national reputation. Monro frequently attended meetings of the UAB Institutional Planning Group, which French chaired, and they sometimes bumped into each other at Miles, where French taught management principles and business policy for four years. In 1977 French had to discontinue his teaching to work full-time with S. Richardson Hill as he took over the UAB presidency from Joseph Volker (French, letter to Patnaik).

Sometime that winter Monro told French about his dissatisfaction with Miles. Hoping to replace Monro's motley assortment of UAB affiliations with an official position, French reported to Hill that Monro was quietly "negotiating to phase out his administrative responsibilities" at Miles. "We should give some thought at this point as to how we want to use the services of John Monro," he urged, referring to "his very good contacts in Washington (HEW [Department of Health, Education, and Welfare]), at Harvard and Andover, and in New York and New England." "As you know," he reminded Hill, "he commands enormous respect in national educational circles" (French, memo to Hill, 19 Feb. 1977.) Hill was interested but cautious, scrawling across the top of the memo, "Bob—I agree with you—I would like to sit down with you and [University College vice president] George Campbell and discuss first." There the matter rested for a full year.

In the meantime Monro continued to identify with the black college community and demonstrate his loyalty to Miles. At a seminar sponsored by the College Board and the Educational Testing Service, he described the next decade as "critical" in the continuing struggle to "break the shackles of institutional racism" ("Case for Special Attention" 10). The statement was obviously a rallying cry, a plea for his listeners to mark the milestone by joining the struggle. It was also a hint that, as he closed in on a decade of service at Miles, he was thinking about where he could make the biggest difference during that critical decade. It was beginning to look more and more like Miles was not that place.

In the fall of 1977 Monro's title was changed once again, to coordinator of Freshman English—another serious demotion (Maeroff). Now that English Department faculty members were teaching Freshman English and the other freshman courses had been shunted off to appropriate departments, he was a ruler without a kingdom. He taught two sections of Freshman English, but for all practical purposes the Freshman Studies Program had ceased to exist.

Monro had never deluded himself about the permanence of academic postings, especially his own. In 1970, estimating that the freshman program needed three more years to reach its full potential, he had said he would be happy to continue teaching at Miles at that point. But, he had added, "I don't know what the state of black-white relationships will be in three years, and anybody's out of his mind to predict where a college administrator will be in one year or five" (qtd. in Greenhouse 92).

Nevertheless, there was enough handwriting on the wall to suggest that in another year he would be even more powerless than he was now. He and Dottie began to consider their options, taking into account the fact that he could soon begin drawing on his Harvard retirement funds. If they returned to New England, they could slip back into the social and family circles that had surrounded them before they went South; they could catch up with their daughter Ann, who had attended Katherine Gibbs Secretarial School, moved into the family home in Winchester, and taken a job at Harvard as administrative assistant to Mike Shinagel, Monro's former section man and now dean of Continuing Education and University Extension. Moving to California would put them closer to Phil, Janet, and the family, who had relocated in 1976, when Phil became an associate professor of education and psychology at Claremont Graduate School. Moving to a college with a more supportive administration and a more compatible curriculum would mean building a new life from scratch, whereas if Monro could find meaningful work in Birmingham, they could continue the life they had worked so hard to create.

The last possibility, the least disruptive of the lot, spurred Monro to confide again in Bob French, who had repeatedly urged Hill to meet with Monro and discuss a position for him at UAB. Hill remained unresponsive, however, and nothing came of French's efforts. It is not clear that Monro and UAB would have been a good match. On one hand, his warm commencement address and enthusiastic endorsement of the university to Ed LaMonte and Dick King proved that he held the university in high regard. But he sometimes expressed doubt that UAB was fully committed to underprepared and nontraditional students (Arrington, interview), even though LaMonte reminded him that UAB already enrolled more black students than Miles did, and that the Division of Special Studies had been created in part to support precisely the type of student he was concerned about (interview, 28 Mar. 2008). In addition, his lack of a graduate degree was a serious stumbling block at UAB, which as a relatively new player had to take traditional credentials very seriously.[7]

On 21 January 1978 Monro gave Williams written notice that he was leaving at the end of the school year (French, memo to Hill), and on 6 March he publicly announced that he was leaving Miles to join the English Department at Tougaloo as Lawrence Durgin Professor of English. Striking the gracious posture he had perfected at Harvard, he insisted that he was motivated by a desire for new experiences rather than dissatisfaction with his current situation. He told *New York Times* reporter Gene Maeroff: "After 11 years here, I'm just looking for a new perspective. It's another black college, and I'm interested in what the black colleges are doing." He refused to criticize Miles, saying, "I didn't come down here to hurt Miles College, and the last thing I would do is say something that might damage the institution," adding that he remained satisfied with his decision to leave Harvard: "I was never so right. . . . This has been a marvelous experience and I've done exactly what I set out to do in teaching and in developing curriculum" (qtd. in Maeroff). But once the three-hour interview was under way, Monro revealed the main source of his discontent. "Freshman English in the hands of English teachers is ludicrous," he scoffed. "English teachers are interested in literature and they each have little slices of specialization, like 'Romantic poets from 1789 to 1820.'" He was even more frank when explaining his motivation to friends.

In a letter to Kim Townsend he wrote: "As you will guess, given reasons are not the same as real reasons, and the hard truth is [Miles] is being badly managed and the Church Board just refuses to pay heed. So I am trying to run up a signal before time runs out" (25 May 1978).

Send-Off

Monro's final days at Miles were marred only by Beatrice Royster's response to his remarks in the *Times*. Her vehicle was a column by Miles alumna Doris Rutledge in the *Birmingham World*, one of Birmingham's black newspapers. Rutledge, who had taken Monro's Freshman English class and majored in English, greatly admired Royster, whom she credited with inspiring her poetry collection, *The Weeping Poet* (Jackson). In a lengthy statement that took up most of Rutledge's column, Royster called Monro's move to Miles "a farce" and "a hoax on black education" and said that he had come to the college not out of idealism but because he lacked the credentials to teach elsewhere. She accused him of paternalism, stating, "He has moved with smug authority through Southern Black colleges as if he were the linguistic savior of their students" (qtd. in Rutledge).[8]

From all other quarters Monro was showered with honors and ceremonies. At commencement Williams presented him with a Recognition Award for his "excellent contribution to the development of the Eutaw Campus and to education" and a Distinguished Service Award, calling him a man "of noble spirit and humanitarian principals and trailblazer in education" (Honorary Degree, DP). He also received an award for Distinguished Leadership in Education from Booker T. Washington Business College, a commendation for community service from the city of Birmingham, and honorary degrees from the College of Wooster and from Oak Grove.

Monro accepted the awards with good grace, ignored Royster's accusations, and concentrated on making the move as painless as possible for Dottie. He did not reveal the emotional toll his resignation had taken until months later and then only obliquely. In a note apologizing that his complicated teaching schedule at Tougaloo prevented him from attending the fall trustees' meeting at Phillips, Monro wrote, "It has been a tough year" (20 Oct. 1978, PAA).

Isn't that the definition of home? Not where you
are from, but where you are wanted?

—ABRAHAM VERGHESE, *Cutting for Stone*

10
THIS LOOKS LIKE THE PLACE
1978-1984

As Monro became more uncomfortable at Miles, he was drawn to Tougaloo for
a multitude of reasons. The first was its leadership role in the civil rights movement, which can be understood only in the context of Mississippi's history of
racism. If it is true that the greatest potential for improvement occurs where
there is the deepest trouble, Mississippi was the ideal place to be during the crucial decade Monro had predicted. The state's record as a bastion of racism was
long and relentless. Its constitutional convention of 1890 was convened specifically to wipe out the Negro vote, which it did by establishing the most restrictive
voting requirements in the South (Dittmer 6).

When the *Brown vs. Board of Education of Topeka* ruling was announced on
17 May 1954, the *Jackson Daily News* labeled the date "Black Monday" (Katagiri xxviii), and the court decision spawned a government agency devoted to
preventing or at least delaying desegregation. The Mississippi State Sovereignty
Commission was established by the state legislature in 1956, "to protect the sovereignty of the state of Mississippi, and her sister states from federal encroach-
ment" (Dittmer 60), but the commission's records, made public in 1988, revealed
that it was "the most active pro-segregation and pro–states' rights governmental
agency throughout the South" (Katagiri xiii). It opposed the Civil Rights Act of
1964 and the Voting Rights Act of 1965, and by the time of its dissolution in 1977
it had collected information on eighty-seven thousand "suspects" (240).

Fierce resistance to school desegregation continued in Mississippi for at least
a decade after *Brown*. As late as 1964, only twenty-six of the state's fifty-eight
thousand black students were enrolled in historically white public schools (Dittmer 170). In March 1964, when a district court ordered area schools to submit

desegregation plans in time for fall implementation, the Ku Klux Klan—dormant in the state since the 1930s—came roaring back with a vengeance. That year KKK membership approached five thousand (217), and there were thirty-five shooting incidents, sixty-five bombings or burnings, eighty beatings of activists, and at least six murders (251), including those of civil rights workers James E. Chaney, Andrew Goodman, and Michael "Mickey" Schwerner.

On the morning of 21 June 1964 three young Freedom Summer volunteers set off from Meridian, Mississippi, to check out Neshoba County's Mt. Zion Methodist Church, whose congregation had offered it for use as a school and community center. Chaney and Schwerner had worked together before, and Goodman, from Queens College, had been recruited by Schwerner to help register black voters (Dittmer 247). Local sheriffs and police chiefs already had a description of Schwerner's car, courtesy of the sovereignty commission (251).

As they began their trip back to Meridian, the three men were arrested on the outskirts of town, jailed, then released at about ten-thirty that night. Ten miles out of town they were stopped again by Neshoba deputy sheriff Cecil Price and handed over to a mob (Dittmer 247). Then they disappeared. Unofficial search parties were hastily assembled, the FBI sent agents to lead the search, and Congress of Racial Equality (CORE) workers pitched in, going out after dark to avoid encounters with Klansmen (249). On 4 August, following a tip from a paid informant, a bulldozer uncovered the three bodies under an earthen dam on a remote farm. Goodman and Schwerner had been shot once, Chaney three times. The pathologist who conducted Chaney's autopsy reported, "I have never witnessed bones so severely shattered, except in tremendously high-speed accidents such as airline crashes." The official conclusion was that the bulldozer had mutilated Chaney's body (283). He was buried near Meridian, and memorial services for Goodman and Schwerner were held in New York. The Schwerners' request that their son be buried near Chaney was denied because at that time Mississippi cemeteries were still segregated (284).

TOUGALOO'S ROLE IN THE CIVIL RIGHTS STRUGGLE

Tougaloo, which was known as the "bed of the movement," played a pivotal role in civil rights activism from the beginning (Brocks-Shedd). In 1948 Tougaloo alumna Gladys Noel Bates filed a suit against the Jackson school board, claiming that she and other black teachers were paid less than white teachers with comparable qualifications; at the time the average annual salary for white teachers in the state was $1,861; for black teachers it was $711 (Dittmer 35). Tougaloo was the site of an early chapter of the NAACP and the locus of a challenge to segregationist Theodore G. Bilbo's Senate seat. The campus provided a safe haven for Freedom Riders and other interracial groups, and its presence was a major factor in CORE's decision to launch its efforts in the state with a Madison County voter registration drive in 1963 (186–87). Tougaloo administrators helped launch the Work-Study Project, which gave college credit to black students while they participated in the movement. The college also hosted the Literacy Project, which taught reading and writing to those who lacked a formal education. The Mississippi Council on Human Relations held its meetings on campus, and the state chapter of the American Civil Liberties Union (ACLU) was established there in 1969 (Campbell and Rogers 225). At the peak of the civil rights struggle, when many black colleges were expelling students who took part in demonstrations, Tougaloo was accepting their transfer applications (Dittmer 198–99).

An early activist with connections to Tougaloo was sociology professor Ernst Borinski, affectionately nicknamed "Bobo." When he fled Nazi Germany in the 1930s, he was a practicing judge and attorney; once he got to the United States, he earned a master's degree in sociology from the University of Chicago, then accepted a position at Tougaloo in 1947 (Lowe 32). In the basement of Beard Hall he established a subterranean kingdom, known to its denizens as the Social Science Laboratory, and in 1952 he launched a speakers' series whose roster came to include Martin Luther King Jr., James Baldwin, John Kenneth Galbraith, David Riesman, diplomat and Nobel Prize winner Ralph Bunche, journalist Hodding Carter, Medgar Evers, broadcast journalist Pauline Frederick, socialist and political scientist Michael Harrington, defense lawyer and civil rights activist William Kunstler, economist Otto Nathan, *Ramparts* editor Robert Scheer, and folksinger Pete Seeger. The informal speakers' program evolved into a series of bimonthly Social Science Forums and received funding from the Field Foundation (Cunnigen 405).

Borinski was also active at nearby Millsaps College, where he visited classes, taught conversational German on an informal basis, and encouraged faculty and students to build on the ties that had existed between the two colleges since the 1940s (Dittmer 61). Under his leadership the Intercollegiate Fellowship was created, bringing together students from other local colleges as well as Tougaloo and Millsaps. He claimed that his experience with Nazism helped him develop strategies for dealing with Mississippi racism, explaining, "Coming out of the Jewish situation in Germany, I had no difficulties understanding oppression" (qtd. in Lowe 33).

The Jackson Read-In

In 1961, a year after students in Greensboro, North Carolina, initiated the lunch counter phase of civil rights demonstrations, similar events blossomed throughout the South, many of them hastily thrown together and doomed to failure. Tougaloo's version, which was well organized and carefully planned, took the form of a "read-in" at Jackson's segregated Municipal Library in the center of town. First, the students, members of Tougaloo's NAACP youth council, drew up a list of books unavailable at Carter, the "colored branch" of the library. On 27 March nine students went to Carter and asked for the books. Then they went to the main branch, consulted the card catalog, took books from the shelves, and began reading them. Ordered to go to Carter, they refused and were arrested for breaching the peace. The following day a small group of Jackson State students marched toward the jail where the "Tougaloo Nine" were being held, and when they refused to disperse, the police used clubs, tear gas, and dogs to get the job done (Dittmer 87–88)—the first time in Mississippi that police dogs were loosed on demonstrators and two years before the police dogs in Birmingham made national headlines (Campbell 198).

Then, on 28 May 1963, three Tougaloo students staged a lunch counter sit-in at Woolworth's, arriving early and taking their seats at the near-empty counter. As lunchtime approached and additional supporters from Tougaloo showed up— including sociology professor John Salter; chaplain Edwin King; president Adam Daniel "Dan" Beittel; and many students and faculty—things quickly turned nasty. One of the original three students was punched and dragged off his stool by a former policeman; others were kicked, beaten, and festooned with lunch counter condiments. Entreated by Beittel to disperse the crowd, the police refused, saying they could do so only if the manager asked for help. The manager never called the police, but when the crowd began hurling merchandise, he closed the store (Dittmer 162).

Tougaloo activists frequently joined forces with Medgar Evers in his capacity as local field secretary for the NAACP. He attended the trial of the Tougaloo Nine and participated in protests alongside Tougaloo students and faculty, most notably John Salter (Vollers 81). Evers and Salter were arrested together while picketing on 1 June 1963 and named in an injunction banning them from picketing, demonstrating, or encouraging others to do so (113, 117). When Evers was shot and killed in his driveway shortly after midnight on 12 June 1963, Tougaloo's new president, George Owens, knocked on Salter's door in the middle of the night to break the news so that he would not first hear of it from the media (130). In honor of the battles Tougaloo and Evers fought together, his widow, Myrlie, has donated his papers and the family home to the college (327).

Given Tougaloo's high profile in the civil rights struggle, it could have been predicted that the sovereignty commission would make the college one of its prime targets. During the sit-in period lieutenant governor Carroll Gartin called Tougaloo a "cancerous growth" and a haven for "queers, quirks, political agitators and possibly some communists," and lawmakers asked the commission for advice about how to shut down the college (qtd. in Katagiri 153). A bill to close the college for having violated an obscure clause in its charter died in committee when out-of-state educational institutions protested. Frustrated by its failure to destroy the entire college, the commission zeroed in on President Beittel, who became both a lightning rod and a scapegoat in its campaign against Tougaloo.

Pressured Out of the Presidency

When Dan Beittel agreed to become president of Tougaloo, he was chaplain and professor of religion at tranquil Beloit College in Wisconsin—a point in his career that closely resembled Monro's situation when he left Harvard. At the age of fifty-nine Beittel had already been a college professor, a college dean, and president of a black college, Talladega. Both he and his wife were looking forward to his sabbatical in the Middle East, followed by retirement four years later. He agreed to scrap the sabbatical and come to Tougaloo only after the trustees promised that he could remain in office until he turned seventy and that after he turned sixty-five he could decide a year at a time whether he wished to remain there (Campbell 196).

Beittel was an unapologetic supporter of civil rights. He visited the Tougaloo Nine when they were in jail and arranged bail for them, saying that he respected their willingness "to pay the price for what they believe to be right" (qtd. in Campbell 198–99). Asked why they had not used the Tougaloo library to do their research, he replied with a poker face that he did not think books were the real issue (198). In March 1964 commission director Erle E. Johnston Jr. notified the governor that Beittel and chaplain Ed King were suspected of being "veteran supporters of communist causes and communist enterprises" (Katagiri 154). Johnson claimed that if Beittel and King stepped down, the commission would persuade the legislature to abandon the "punitive action" it was considering against Tougaloo. On 21 April Johnston and a Jackson attorney flew to New York and met with several of Tougaloo's trustees. Six days later the board of trustees announced Beittel's retirement, effective 1 September (Katagiri 155–56).

In actuality the commission's drive to oust Beittel was redundant, because three months earlier the trustees had decided that he had to go. While the commission was turning its guns on Beittel, the trustees were finalizing a partnership with Brown University, and they were eager to remove any obstacles to its implementation. With that plan as the subtext, the board met in executive session in New York on 16 January 1964 to discuss a single subject, which the minutes obscurely referred to as "Dr. Beittel's health problem as revealed by Mrs. Beittel."[1]

During the session, trustee Lawrence Durgin reported that foundation representatives had told him they were "concerned and hesitant about giving money to institutions with presidents who may not carry through with the program." Everyone in attendance knew that the "program" was the Brown-Tougaloo partnership and that it was Ford Foundation funding that hung in the balance. The board voted to tell Beittel that a younger man was needed to lead the college (Executive Session Minutes). Immediately after the executive session, three of the trustees met with Beittel, and he reluctantly agreed to step down. With unseemly haste the selection committee swung into action and drew up a list of likely candidates, including Monro. Beittel had just turned sixty-four the previous month.

The announcement of Beittel's retirement raised eyebrows as well as questions. Three clergymen from the Board of Directors of the Mississippi Council on Human Relations asked the trustees to reverse their decision, saying that Beittel's resignation had been greeted in the local press as a victory for the "enemies of Tougaloo" and would "seriously endanger" recent civil rights advances (Campbell 216).

After agreeing to step down, Beittel turned intransigent and refused to state that he was leaving voluntarily. In a letter to Brown president Barnaby Keeney, Beittel reported that he had been told by someone at the office of the United

Church of Christ that his ouster had been "at the urgent request of Brown University" (5 Apr. 1964, BTE).[2] Keeney vigorously denied that he or anyone else from Brown had been involved in Beittel's ouster, but additional correspondence tells a different story. On 9 March Keeney had written to Beittel, scolding him for joining with other black colleges in a bid for Ford Foundation funding that Keeney saw as overlapping the Brown-Tougaloo partnership. Then he fired off a note to Larry Durgin stating: "The Chairman of the Board should write Frank Bowles [director of the Ford Foundation's Education Division Program] as soon as possible that efforts are being made to secure a new president. They will not do much, if anything, until they have this assurance" (9 Mar. 1964, BTE).

Three days after Beittel's retirement was announced, Keeney received a chummy handwritten note from Bowles: "Dear Barney, The [Ford Foundation] Fund Board, Monday afternoon, approved $240,000 for Tougaloo, without strings. To be administered by Presidents of Brown and Tougaloo or their duly authorized deputy. Have fun. Larry" (30 Apr. 1964, BTE).

THE LURE OF TOUGALOO

At least as important to Monro as Tougaloo's history of civil rights engagement was his personal familiarity with the college, which had begun in earnest with the search for Beittel's successor. Since 1966 Monro had been a hands-on trustee, not just attending board meetings but also visiting the college on his own, attending celebrations, and donning academic regalia for the Founders' Day procession. He helped plan the events surrounding George Owens's inauguration, organized and chaired one of the inauguration panels, and was a featured speaker at the centennial festivities (Campbell 234).

One of Tougaloo's strongest attractions for Monro was his easy working relationship with Owens. Monro always did his best work in situations in which he saw eye to eye with the administration, and the last few years had been a painful reminder of how frustrating it was to swim against the current. It was surely no coincidence that in 1975 Owens was asked to join the Harvard Overseers' Committee on University Extension, which Monro chaired.

Both men believed in the importance of black colleges as sources of institutional strength, and Owens even suggested that "the people who believe and nurture the theory that black colleges are on the wane may have a grand design to weaken us" (qtd. in Campbell 235). Like Monro, Owens's idealism was tempered by pragmatism, especially in the civil rights arena, where he preferred to work within the system, a strategy he defended as a way to build institutional strength: "Blacks have never had a foothold where decisions are made. . . . There are those who want to change society. Well, I do too. But you can't change it until you get inside it" (qtd. in Posner 2).

At the same time Owens honored Tougaloo's tradition of civil rights activism. On 25 June 1966 he opened the campus to participants in the March against Fear, who had been attacked earlier that day in Canton, Mississippi (Campbell 299). Two years later he risked local disapproval in the aftermath of Martin Luther King Jr.'s assassination. Because memorial observances were banned in Madison County public schools but permitted in Jackson, a group of Madison County high school students set off on foot for Jackson, only to be blocked by patrolmen near Tougaloo. Owens said he would be responsible for their behavior, invited them to attend the memorial service at Woodworth Chapel, and sent them home on a college bus when the weather turned stormy (231).

The Curriculum

During his visits as a trustee, Monro learned a lot about the curriculum, and he liked what he saw. He was especially attracted to the Basic Studies Program, which resembled the late lamented Freshman Studies Program at Miles but was more ambitious and better organized. Program director Naomi Townsend had masterminded its creation in 1977 and obtained funding through the Title III Advanced Institutional Development Program. First-year students took courses in English, Mathematics, Reading, Speech, Logic, Study Skills, and Library Skills, moving to the next level only when they had mastered the material thoroughly (Shores 32). If they did not pass a course or examination, they were given an "NG" (No Grade) rather than a failing grade and encouraged to repeat the course or work with a tutor until they could pass the test. This competency-based system balanced rigor with the personal attention that Monro's critics at Miles had interpreted as paternalistic coddling.

The wide range of majors at Tougaloo encouraged students to consider many career options besides the old mainstays, preaching and teaching. Those who did go into education were urged to become leaders and policy setters: as early as 1917, a third of Tougaloo's graduates became principals, head teachers, or matrons (Campbell 123). The business program included an innovative alliance with General Foods, which provided management opportunities and training. In the co-op component of the alliance, students spent a semester working full-time at General Foods, much like the business program Monro had helped create at Miles (Cooper).

Tougaloo was supportive of graduate study, encouraging the kind of black leadership Monro considered a key to institutional strength. In 1969 43 percent of the graduating class went on to graduate schools or equivalent postgraduate programs (Robinson). Seniors were directed toward summer programs at Columbia, Harvard, or Yale, where they could learn what to expect at graduate school (Sharpe). At one point Tougaloo sent more students to Harvard's Health Careers Summer Program than any other college did ("Tougaloo's Special Programs"), and in 1973 it had more Danforth Scholars than any other southern black college ("Lady Encore"). By 1975 the forty Tougaloo graduates studying medicine outnumbered the black doctors practicing in Mississippi (Shore 23), and 10 percent of the class of 1978 went on to medical school (Shores 31).

Partnerships

One important factor in Tougaloo's enviable graduate school placement record was its strong ties to prestigious colleges and universities. Tufts Medical School had created an early, informal partnership with Tougaloo by way of the Delta Health Center. Founded in 1968, Delta was the country's first community health center located in a preponderantly black, rural region (Morgan 17), and its director, Dr. H. Jackson Geiger of Tufts, encouraged Tougaloo's science and health services majors to study medicine at Tufts. The opportunity was especially attractive because as late as 1975 Mississippi's single medical school, at the University of Mississippi, was still refusing to accept black applicants (20).

Tougaloo's most enduring connection to a prestigious institution was the Brown-Tougaloo Exchange Partnership, which became the gold standard for collaborations between Ivy League institutions and historically black colleges. Monro fostered it, praised it, and deeply regretted that Harvard was not doing something like it. The alliance was formalized in May 1964—the tenth anniversary of *Brown vs. Board of Education*—but its origins reached back at least as far as 1961. At that time Larry Durgin, a Tougaloo trustee and pastor of Central Congregational Church in Providence, Rhode Island, was worried about the financial crisis the college was facing. On a weekend fishing trip hosted by Barnaby Keeney, who worshipped at Central Congregational, Durgin unburdened himself, and the two men began exploring possible solutions (Shore 19). Representatives of Tougaloo and Brown visited each other's campuses, and a proposal funded by the Ford Foundation initially called for Brown to help Tougaloo with an ambitious academic development program. As the story of Beittel's ouster reveals, Keeney's leverage helped get the project funded in the amount of $363,000, $245,000 of which was from the Ford Foundation's Fund for the Advancement of Education (20).

In 1965 the partnership became a national model when many of its details were incorporated into Title III of the Higher Education Act (Shore 22). The timing was perfect: now Brown could help Tougaloo adapt to the mainstream career opportunities that affirmative action was opening up to its graduates (21). Student exchanges, which began that fall, were a natural outgrowth of the academic development plan, and students who traveled in either direction were enthusiastic about the experience. In 1970, at the height of the Black Pride movement, the student exchange component was discontinued, but somehow the partnership survived that difficult period, student exchanges resumed and new points of convergence appeared in 1972, when Brown began granting medical degrees. Through an early identification system two Tougaloo sophomores each year were guaranteed a slot in Brown's medical degree program, contingent upon continued academic success during their junior and senior years. In return Tougaloo alumnus Dr. Robert Smith '57 created a clerkship program for Brown medical students at the Mississippi Family Health Care Center, where he served as director (23).

The Challenges

But Tougaloo also faced many problems, which only made the place more attractive to Monro, because it meant there was important work to be done. For starters the college was struggling to improve its relations with the community, in spite of the fact that Tougaloo had been a good neighbor and made important contributions to the area. Beittel had instituted a precollege summer program for local high school graduates who needed additional preparation before entering college. In 1966 Tougaloo became one of the first Upward Bound sites, and it also ran several Head Start programs, the Madison County Project, and a Supplementary Training Program for Choctaw Indians (Campbell 222). Recently governor William Waller had appointed Tougaloo graduates to several state commissions, reversing an unwritten whites-only policy that dated back to Reconstruction. But town-gown rapport came slowly, hobbled by lingering resentment of Tougaloo's tradition of activism. In 1968 a local newspaper, dubbing Tougaloo "Cancer College," printed a cartoon of a black student and a white teacher (named "Lefty Liberal") stirring a pot adorned with a hammer and sickle and a label reading "Tougaloo" (Posner 1).

Tougaloo was also feeling the effects of a statewide crisis in public education. In a classic vicious cycle, court-mandated desegregation triggered massive white flight to private schools, further accelerating the deterioration of the public schools. Monro had been only half-joking when in 1970 he told visitors to Miles that Alabama had passed Mississippi—on the way down—in the meager amount each state expended per pupil (Moore 15). In 1976–77 Mississippi's allocation per high school student was forty-sixth in the country (Shore 23). Moreover, Mississippi was one of the few states offering no financial aid to students at private colleges (Posner 4). Monro minced no words in describing the situation: "The whole education system [in Mississippi]—from grade school all the way to college—is doing a lousy job for poor and minority people" (qtd. in Shores 31).

The financial pinch was especially severe at Tougaloo, which drew little funding from the local community. The United Church of Christ contribution, about $1 million in 1976–77, covered less than a fourth of the operating budget, and alumni donations covered only another 1 percent. The endowment, which had doubled since 1972, was still a meager $326,000. It was easy to see how the college had accumulated an operating deficit of $800,000.

But the brunt of the state's dire educational and fiscal condition was borne by the Tougaloo students. At least 25 percent of the incoming class were severely underprepared and were reading at a seventh-grade level. In 1976, 90 percent had needed some kind of financial aid, and 75 percent were from families with annual incomes of less than $7,500 (Posner 4). Edith Estes McMillan, who served as Freshman English coordinator after Monro left Miles, suspected that he went to Tougaloo primarily because "the Mississippi students were even worse off than the Alabama students" (personal interview, 22 Mar. 2008). She was probably right. Tougaloo looked like a place where Monro's energy, connections, and skills could be put to good use as the struggle for equal rights continued and the role of black colleges became increasingly complex.

STARTING OVER

Relocating to Mississippi kept John and Dottie occupied for most of the summer, finding a new home, a new church, and new doctors. They purchased a simple bungalow-style house at 1858 Hamilton Boulevard, part of a quiet development about five miles from Tougaloo. The short commute meant that Monro could be at the beck and call of students and colleagues, and the large backyard provided a broad canvas for his gardening activities as well as a haven for birds, squirrels, and other wildlife. The remaining details of their new life were shaped by Dottie's failing health.

For much of her life Dottie experienced debilitating migraines, a problem she may have inherited from her mother. She also suffered from congestive heart disease, and the simple task of getting enough oxygen frequently left her exhausted. Much as she anticipated spending Christmas with the Dreyers in California, the trip took a greater toll on her every year, and she spent much of her time on the couch, quietly observing the festivities. The traditional Thanksgiving visit to the LaMontes, which had begun when the Dreyers moved to California, was arranged to accommodate appointments with Dottie's doctors in Birmingham. An old friend in South Freeport noticed a dramatic decline in Dottie's energy level from one summer to the next (Dreyer, interview, 9 Feb. 2005). Monro estimated that her health had begun to decline even further at about the time they left Birmingham (letter to Merrifield, 1996), and in 1979 she spent two weeks in the hospital (1 May 1979, PAA).

It is unclear whether the move to Mississippi had a direct impact on Dottie's health, but she certainly had difficulty summoning the strength to create a new life from scratch. Jackson was a far quieter place than Birmingham, and she knew few of the friends John had made during his visits to Tougaloo as a trustee. Because she no longer had the stamina to participate in parish life, John attended Sunday services on campus at Woodworth Chapel, and Dottie joined him when she felt up to it. He solicitously supervised her daily routine and prepared her lunch each morning, either returning to join her at midday or calling to make sure she ate it (Rose Parkman Davis Marshall, personal interview, 8 Mar. 2009).

Full-Time Teacher

Although he arrived with an impressive-sounding title—the Lawrence Durgin Professor of English—Monro's workload was more suited to a Clydesdale than to a thoroughbred. He taught three sections of Freshman English and specifically asked to be given developmental sections, which were designed for students with the most pressing writing problems and required them to meet with their professor outside of class at least two hours a week (Autrey). His official office hours were from 10:00 a.m. to 4:00 p.m., but he frequently came in on weekends, and appointments spilled over into the evening so often that he stocked his office with sandwich makings so he could dine at his desk (Autrey). Nonetheless, he professed to be invigorated by the demands of his job, telling a reporter: "I'm constantly refreshed by what I find. I look at it as a great way to wind down" (qtd. in Shores 25).

Early on, Monro identified the Writing Center as a project that was ripe for his hands-on approach. Originally created to provide the tutorial support required by the terms of the Basic Studies grant, the Writing Center eventually expanded its mission to serve the entire college population, and Monro was happy to help staff it. When he arrived, the Writing Center was housed in a cramped, decrepit trailer that had to be vacated when the Catholic chaplain was celebrating Mass (Shore 30). Its remote location on the edge of the campus signaled that it was anything but an integral part of academic life. There was barely room for a tiny office for John Burrows, the English professor who directed the center, and Monro had to commute from his office in Coleman Hall, a long, muddy slog on a rainy day. In his exploratory rambles around campus, he discovered that a large open area in the basement of Galloway Hall, one of the men's dormitories, was currently being used for storage, and he realized that with modest renovations it would be ideal for the Writing Center. In a stroke of perfect timing, just as Monro was getting interested in the Galloway space Boston dairy magnate Gilbert H. Hood sent him a fifteen hundred dollar check and gave him full discretion in spending it (Hood). Monro used the donation to begin the renovations, clipping Hood's letter to the architect's plans as a reminder that the improvements were not draining money from the operating budget. The building, which dated back to 1930, had its problems: it was showing its age, there were complaints about noise and dirt, and unsavory odors emanated from the bathrooms. But the new space, once renovations were complete, was larger, more centrally located, and better suited for the center's mission than the trailer had been (Lawrence Sledge, telephone interview, 19 June 2008).

Monro's relocated office put him in close proximity to English professor Ken Autrey, who had been teaching middle school before coming to Miles and was eager to succeed in his first full-time college position. Autrey found Monro a willing and generous mentor, albeit one who turned "doggedly persuasive" when arguing for his favorite educational theories. On the days that Monro was not lunching at his desk or at home with Dottie, he joined Autrey in the cafeteria, where his self-imposed one-dollar budget paid for rice and beans washed down with iced tea.[3] When he learned about Monro's brief career as a journalist, Autrey realized that it accounted for the "journalistic snap" in Monro's writing style, as well as his habit of exhaustive data-gathering, which was driven by the journalist's respect for hard evidence (Autrey).

Another Summer Workshop

To keep busy in July, which Monro had spent on the precollege workshop when he was at Miles, he joined Tougaloo's five-week Summer Science Program. Funded by a U.S. Public Health Service grant, the program was a powerful recruiting tool, especially given Tougaloo's ties with the medical schools at Tufts and Brown (Shore 23). Its participants, gifted high school students who were interested in health care careers, studied biology, chemistry, math, and communication skills. Monro taught the communication component and required the students to keep journals and produce an essay a week. When the course was over, he assembled, duplicated, and distributed an anthology of the best work, believing that student writers needed to see themselves in print at least as badly as professional writers did (Marshall, interview).

The program's founder, chemistry professor Richard McGinnis, realized that scientists needed to be competent writers, and was impressed by Monro's attention to analysis and critical reasoning, particularly in assignments that required drawing logical conclusions from data tables. "It's very important to see that there's a connection between numbers and concepts and social issues," McGinnis stated (personal interview, 8 Mar. 2010).

As soon as the science program ended, Monro moved on to a self-imposed data-gathering project. First he analyzed and evaluated the 178 essays written for the final exam in Freshman English, then he painstakingly classified and counted the errors, illustrating them with examples from the strongest papers. After analyzing the data, he recommended that the Freshman English faculty spend more time on the most frequent errors (memo to Naomi Townsend, 17 July 1981, TCA), and by the following year all freshmen were taking an in-house grammar test based on his findings (Monro, "Tougaloo Experience" 7). He was gratified that his work had borne fruit so quickly and that his colleagues respected both his efforts and his expertise. The students did too: for the first but not the last time, he was elected Teacher of the Year, along with English professor Jerry Ward.

WIDENING SOCIAL CIRCLES

As the first busy school year ended, Dottie's health stabilized, at least temporarily, and both she and Monro began to feel at home and develop a quiet social life. They were invited to join a stimulating discussion group that had been formed fifty years earlier, when a group of doctors arrived to create a medical center at the University of Mississippi. The doctors started the group in an effort to widen their social circle and learn more about their new home (Brooks), and membership gradually expanded to include attorneys, lawyers, journalists, and academics (James Park, telephone interview, 24 Mar. 2010). Dottie rarely attended the meetings, but when the group gathered, Monro enjoyed swapping war stories with journalist Bill Minor, who had been an assistant gunnery officer on the destroyer USS *Stephen Potter*. Minor frequently incorporated aspects of the group's discussions into his widely syndicated column, "Eyes on Mississippi" (telephone interview, 19 and 20 Mar. 2010).

Colleague and Close Friend

At the end of the school year John Burrows left Tougaloo for a position at Florida International University. Enjoying his first stint as a teacher with no administrative duties, Monro was reluctant to replace Burrows as Writing Center director, so Rose Parkman Davis, a Tougaloo graduate who had been working in the center part-time, agreed to take the position. Davis quickly became a highly effective director as well as one of Monro's closest and most faithful friends.

She had been sixteen, and still Rose Parkman, in the summer of 1964, when her mother brought her and her sister, Joyce, to Tougaloo from their home in Prentiss, a small town about seventy miles south of Jackson. Paying their tuition with checks from the cotton mill, her mother warned her to stay out of the civil rights fray: "Don't be up there demonstrating, because if your name gets in the paper, they won't take our cotton at the gin and the bank will call your dad's loan in, and there'll be repercussions you don't even understand." But Rose did understand: in 1961 a student from her parish had participated in the Jackson read-in, and when the *Jackson Clarion-Ledger* named him as one of the Tougaloo Nine, the white mail carrier wakened his parents in the middle of the night so that they could get him out of town before it was too late (Marshall, interview).

Ignoring her mother's warning, Rose joined the civil rights struggle. She took part in the lunch counter sit-ins and was sorry she had been spending the semester at Brown when the Jackson State demonstrations took place. As she pursued her studies and worked in the college library, she was vaguely aware of a lanky, gray-haired trustee who appeared on campus even when the board was not meeting, who wore funny-colored robes for commencement and Founders' Day, and who stopped students to ask about their lives, their studies, and their dreams.

If Monro had stopped her during her senior year, Rose would have said that she dreamed of studying library science at Syracuse University but could not afford to. Instead, she enrolled in the English master's program at Illinois Institute of Technology, where she could get a full scholarship. In 1972 she married Tougaloo sociology professor Walter Davis, and they moved to Cambridge so that he could earn his doctorate at Harvard. In 1978 they returned to Jackson, and Walter rejoined the Sociology Department. Naomi Townsend, with whom Rose had studied as an undergraduate, offered her a part-time job in the Writing Center, and Rose accepted (interview).

In the Writing Center she met Monro, whom she had known only by reputation up to that point. Maybe the fact that she was young enough to be his daughter had something to do with the easy manner they fell into. She poked fun at his garish "hot pink" commencement regalia, which he insisted was proper Harvard crimson. He called her "Girl" and teased her about her friendship with Ernst Borinski, reporting that her "boyfriend" had come to see her while she was gone. When she became Writing Center director, he took to calling her "Boss" (Walter Davis, telephone interview, 25 June 2009).

Soon after Davis arrived, she began teaching with Monro in the Summer Science Program: Davis ran the classes, and Monro chimed in occasionally in addition to handling the writing assignments. They continued the arrangement every summer that they were both free, and once the program participants began to graduate, the two of them would get together to track the students' progress; indulging in a bit of Monday morning quarterbacking, Monro would gloat that he had known all along that this or that student would excel (Marshall, interview).

Like many successful collaborators, both Monro and Davis claimed to have gotten more than they gave. Davis distilled the numerous things that Monro taught her into a single idea: "I learned from him that in college the students came first, and everything else was secondary." For Monro, Davis represented one of two approaches to teaching that he had identified while developing his own pedagogy. On one hand there was the judgmental teacher, whom Monro ventriloquized as saying: "Here's the stuff, kid, I know it and I'm going to tell you what I know about it. Your job is to get it. Then I'm going to test you on whether you got it or not. Now don't bother me." The other type was the helpful teacher, epitomized by Davis, whose approach was to "take the individual seriously for where he is and what he's trying to do and then set up a situation where the teachers . . . are prepared to be helpful but not soft" (qtd. in Brooks 5).

Monro and Davis agreed that "helpful but not soft" was a crucial distinction to make. Davis knew it was important to establish a personal relationship with students but to observe boundaries: "I don't have any 18-year-old friends," she warned students who looked like they might be expecting her to cut them some slack. Monro knew it too, and he included both roles when he described the special demands of teaching freshmen: "The good [first-year] teacher will be at once professional, dealing with the materials at hand, and personal, letting students know that someone on the campus knows them, respects them, likes them as individuals, and is ready to encourage or goad, support, correct, or hold up objectives, as the situation requires" ("Current and Emerging" 166).

The rapport that existed between Davis and Monro eventually expanded to include Dottie and the Davis family circle. One year, when Rose learned that the Monros had no plans for Easter, she invited them over for the holiday. After that they were frequent guests for Sunday dinners as well as holidays and family occasions. If Dottie was tired, John came alone or dropped in briefly while she stayed in the car. She enjoyed the visits she felt well enough to join, especially at Eastertime, when the azaleas that grew in profusion in the Davis backyard were at their peak. She would sit on the patio and look on while John joined the egg hunt, cheating wildly as he guided the children, Lumbe and Jelani, to the more cleverly concealed eggs (Marshall, interview).

Another New England Couple

The Monros also enjoyed a combined professional-social relationship with Larry and Eunice Durgin, who had recently moved to campus when Durgin stepped down as a trustee to become vice president of development. While serving as pastor at Central Congregational Church in Providence, he had helped shape the Brown-Tougaloo partnership before moving to Broadway United Church of Christ, on the edge of Hell's Kitchen in New York (Waggoner). Durgin embraced the Broadway church board's decision, in 1969, to become a "church without walls," sell their building, and use the proceeds to continue their social service programs (Worth Durgin, e-mail, 27 Oct. 2009).

He was especially committed to the struggle for racial equality. Raised in Asia, where his father was working for the YMCA, Durgin traced his identification with minorities to a playground episode during which the other children, all Japanese, could not believe his fair hair was real and tried to pull it out (L. Durgin 6). One of his first official acts at Broadway United had been to appoint a black assistant minister. A visitation project, which bused family members to prisons during visiting hours, was conducted in partnership with a neighboring black church, and Broadway United was the departure point for the United Church of Christ delegation to the March on Washington (W. Durgin, e-mail, 27 Oct. 2009).

At Tougaloo Durgin was the namesake of the honorary professorship that gave Monro his official title. Originally intended for the Department of Religion and Philosophy, the professorship migrated to the English Department when Durgin asked that Monro, whose work at Miles he admired, come to Tougaloo as the Lawrence Durgin Professor of English ("College Receives $100,000"). Durgin considered Tougaloo's Basic Studies Program both a national model for "doable, duplicable" remedial education and a new way of envisioning academic potential. He intended to exploit the program as a powerful selling point in his development campaign, and he wanted Monro to join him in making pitches to potential donors (W. Durgin, e-mail, 27 Oct. 2009). Sadly, only a fragment of Durgin's ambitious plan was realized. After less than a year at Tougaloo he died on 11 August 1981 from complications following lung surgery (Waggoner).

MONEY AND PRESTIGE

Monro repeatedly tweaked his old New England ties to add luster to Tougaloo's reputation and donations to its coffers. Perhaps most notably, he talked Jerry Piel into become a Tougaloo trustee ("New Members"). Piel, who had graduated from Harvard two years after Monro and served with him on the Harvard board of overseers and the Phillips board of trustees, had bought and resuscitated *Scientific American,* transforming it from a near-moribund publication to a popular periodical with a circulation of over a million (Saxon). Accepting the trusteeship, Piel wrote, "I could not refuse a call to duty that originated with John Monro." His board membership added significantly to Tougaloo's stature in scientific circles.

Most often, however, Monro drew on his Ivy League connections to address the ongoing financial crisis at Tougaloo. The college was now almost $1.5 million in debt, and it was estimated that $15 million was needed to achieve true financial ease. At one point, when enrollment fell twenty or thirty students short of the break-even figure, the pupil-teacher ratio was increased, a desperate move that put Tougaloo's academic reputation at risk (Shore 22).

In 1980 Monro received a $2,000 donation from Gilbert Hood, whose first donation had helped pay for the Writing Center renovations in Galloway. This time Monro handed the check over to Owens, suggesting that it be used to install a public address system in the chapel and rebind library periodicals. Hood sent $2,500 in 1982 and $5,000 in 1984. In June 1984 Elizabeth K. Darlington wrote to Monro from Massachusetts asking how she and her husband could maximize the usefulness of their contribution to a historically black college. Monro promptly suggested that they underwrite scholarships, since financial aid that fell short by as little as $500 might prevent a student from coming to Tougaloo. The Darlingtons followed his advice and contributed $25,000 two years in a row (letter, 27 Aug. 1984).

In January 1981 Monro, Larry Durgin, and George Owens wrote to Chicago attorney Kenneth Montgomery soliciting a donation for the Writing Center, explaining that its existence would be threatened if federal funding for the Basic Studies Program were not renewed. After talking to Monro, Montgomery sent $10,000 to fund the Writing Center; in spite of the earmark, Monro forwarded the check to Owens, asking only that $800 go to Rose Davis while the two of them updated instructional materials over the summer (22 Apr. 1984).

Financial worries and personal losses notwithstanding, Monro was enjoying his work tremendously, and he continued to contradict suggestions that coming to Miles and Tougaloo had been a sacrifice. He said as much to the graduates of Saint Bonaventure's, where the honorary degree he received praised "his achievements as a scholar and teacher of the underprivileged—and one who, at considerable personal sacrifice, has provided leadership for change in society and education" (DP). He took exception to the wording of the degree, stating: "There has been no sacrifice, nothing like it. The past seventeen years . . . have easily been the richest, most rewarding, most eye-opening years of my life" ("Saint Bonaventure" 2).

The satisfaction Monro drew from his work is amply demonstrated in the file he kept for Peter Nwachukwu, a student whose low writing test scores placed him in the developmental section of the Freshman English course Monro taught. He noted that Nwachukwu had graduated from high school in Nigeria in 1975 but had been unable to get into a university there. Together they designed a sophisticated writing project that capitalized on Nwachukwu's identity as a young black African male: a cultural appraisal of Alan Paton's novel *Cry the Beloved Country*. Two weeks later Nwachukwu submitted a working draft, and Monro suggested some improvements. In mid-December Monro arranged to have the final draft typed. They continued to work together during the spring, and by April Nwachukwu had submitted several pieces for publication, was thinking about sending one to the op-ed section of the *New York Times*, and had begun writing fiction. Closing out the file, Monro described Nwachukwu as "a truly gifted and energetic man" ("Nwachukwu").

THE COLLEGE BOARD REVISITED

The previous summer Monro had been drawn back into the orbit of the College Board for a project that occupied him throughout the 1980–81 school year and beyond. When George H. Hanford became College Board president, he called on Monro to help deal with the claim that the board's standardized tests were shortchanging minority students. Hanford '41 and Monro '34 were connected in more ways than most Harvard alumni. It was Hanford's father, dean A. Chester Hanford, who had advised Monro to take a leave of absence when his commitment to the *Harvard Journal* wreaked havoc on his studies. While Monro was Harvard's counselor for veterans, George Hanford was an assistant dean at Harvard Business School. When Hanford became assistant treasurer for the College Board in 1955, Monro was chairing the College Scholarship Service Committee.

For years critics of the board claimed that its standardized tests, particularly the college admissions Scholastic Aptitude Test (SAT), were culturally biased. Monro himself implied as much in 1959, when he observed that "the tests we now use often have a cultural bias, favoring the right student from the right side" (qtd. in Hanford, *Minority* 5). As College Board president, Hanford met the accusation head-on, creating an Advisory Panel on Minority Concerns. Monro's experience at Miles and Tougaloo, as well as his directorship of the 1959 College Board colloquium, made him a natural for the panel. When he agreed to serve, he became, in Hanford's words, "the only honky" in the group (personal interview, 13 Jan. 2006).

At the panel's first meeting, in June 1980, the members resolved to "find a balance between the demands for quality and equality in education" (Hanford, *Minority* 19). That tricky balance involved the second major problem Hanford faced at the beginning of his presidency: the significance and the cause of falling test scores. In 1975 a front-page article by *New York Times* education reporter Gene Maeroff noted that SAT scores had been declining steadily since 1963 (Hanford, *Life* 51). A blue-ribbon panel created to investigate the situation concluded that a decline in the quality of high school education was responsible for the low scores (57–58). The panel also discovered, to general astonishment, that national standards for college preparation had last been examined in the 1930s (62). Hanford directed the panel to begin by determining what knowledge and skills high school graduates should possess when they entered college and what kind of curriculum would help them meet that goal (63), and the minority affairs panel on which Monro served became an important part of the process.

During their fall meeting Monro proposed that drawing conclusions from data—which required making connections between ideas—was one of the skills high school students needed to master. To illustrate his point he shared an assignment he had been using ever since his first summer at Miles: after examining and discussing a graph or table of statistics, students would write a short essay making an inference and supporting it with details from the chart or table ("Teaching" 244). His suggestion became part of the committee's recommendations, and the College Board publication that emerged after four years of drafting, arguing, and revising listed Reasoning—"the ability to draw reasonable conclusions from information found in various sources, whether written, spoken, or displayed in tables and graphs, and to defend one's conclusion rationally"—as one of six basic academic competencies students should possess by the time they entered college (*Academic Preparation* 9–10). Today Hanford insists that Monro's identification of "the fourth R" was as significant a contribution to higher education as the groundbreaking financial aid formulas he had developed in the 1950s (interview).

A TWO-YEAR REPRIEVE

As the fall 1981 semester began, the Basic Studies faculty breathed a collective sigh of relief when the program was extended for another two years. Suddenly the program became everybody's darling. Academic vice president Van S. Allen noted that freshman-sophomore attrition had dwindled since the program went into effect, although attrition was higher than ever among juniors and seniors. He urged faculty teaching upperclassmen to take a lesson from the Basic Studies teachers and consider adapting some of their strategies (Basic Studies Minutes, 7 Sept. 1981).[4]

Basking in the reflected glory of the Basic Studies Program, the Writing Center was evolving from a marginalized fix-it shop to an integral part of the college. More upperclassmen found their way to the center, and student tutors honed their skills in twice-weekly training sessions, attended a writing center conference at UAB (Writing Center Report, 8 Feb. 1982), and produced a manual called *Tutoring Is Terrific*, funded by a grant from the Minority Achievement Program of the American Association of Colleges. At the end of the school year Rose Davis left Tougaloo temporarily to care for her mother in the aftermath of a severe stroke (e-mail, 18 Sept. 2006). Monro reluctantly agreed to take over as Writing Center director in the fall, even though it violated his self-imposed ban on administrative duties. But once he had bitten the bullet, he threw himself into the job with his usual gusto and focused in particular on persuading faculty outside the Basic Studies Program that the Writing Center was an asset they and their students would be foolish not to exploit. By the following year the entire English Department was requiring students to visit the Writing Center at least once a semester.

Faculty members who used the Writing Center often extended their work with Monro into other areas. An especially productive relationship developed when Walter Davis, Rose's husband, began sending senior sociology majors to the Writing Center for an assignment many of them were struggling with (Minutes, 17 Jan. 1983). Davis '67 was the kind of Tougaloo graduate Monro admired most: after leaving the South to acquire advanced academic credentials—in this case a master's and a doctorate in sociology from Harvard—he had brought them back home. Some of Davis's colleagues felt that he should have left his "Harvard expectations" in Cambridge, but Monro admired his rigor, especially his requirement that all sociology majors complete a primary research project in their senior year. Monro volunteered to serve as an outside reader for the projects, and he attended the students' oral defenses as well. When the seniors came to the Writing Center for help, his familiarity with the assignment made it easier for him to offer advice.

As they worked together on the research project, Davis and Monro forged a truly symbiotic relationship. From their partnership Davis gained better work from his students and validation of his high standards, whereas Monro profited in multiple ways from their collaboration. His successful work with the seminar students proved the value of the Writing Center for upperclassmen. Talking to Davis and reading his students' projects sparked an enduring interest in the social sciences. And perhaps best of all, data that Davis gathered supported the value of Freshman English, which Monro was always looking for ways to document: by examining his students' academic records, Davis discovered that the students with the most serious writing problems were those who had somehow avoided taking Freshman English.

FINAL PARTING

The satisfactions Monro reaped from his work in the classroom and the Writing Center were small consolation when, after a five-year period of increasing frailty and failing health, Dottie died on 28 March 1984. A few days earlier she had asked to go for a drive so that she could admire her favorite spring flowers, which were just beginning to bloom (W. Davis, telephone interview). That morning she had complained that she was having trouble breathing. John took her to the emergency room, where she was admitted, and she died before he could reach the room to which she had been sent. The official cause of death was congestive heart failure (Dreyer, e-mail, 15 Apr. 2010).

Monro grieved deeply, but his coping mechanism was to immerse himself even more thoroughly in his work. Early on the day of Dottie's death he called Rose Davis, who had returned to the Writing Center since her mother's recovery. He conveyed the sad news then asked her to tell the three students with whom he had appointments that day that he would meet them the following day instead. She protested, saying that nobody would expect to see him for some time—half-seriously, she reminded him that in black communities the mourning period was sometimes as long as four years—but he insisted he would be back the next day, and he was (Marshall, interview). When Phil arrived ten days later,

Monro was still numb from the shock, although he was going through the motions of normal life (Dreyer, e-mail).

Because Dottie had been on campus so rarely, Monro's colleagues were uncertain about an appropriate way to note her passing. Reluctant to disturb Monro in his grief, they asked Rose Davis for advice, and she consulted Monro about what he thought Dottie would like. The following day he handed her a one hundred dollar bill and said that with it he wished to create the Dottie Monro Memorial Fund, which she should use to cover expenses she and Walter incurred while helping students, particularly in their capacity as advisors to Tougaloo Out-of-State Students. Faculty members added to the fund, which eventually reached six hundred dollars (Marshall, interview).

In Birmingham, Cecil and David Roberts donated fifty thousand dollars to create the Dottie Monro Presidential Minority Scholarship at UAB. The trustees' resolution that put the scholarship into effect referred to the Monros' marriage as a partnership, describing how Dottie's "loving support and remarkable adaptability allowed the two of them to pursue this pioneering work" at Miles (Board of Trustees Minutes, 26 June 1992, 429, UABA). Today the scholarship, valued at twenty-five hundred dollars per year, is awarded to African American first-year students.

Anyone who knew Monro, no matter how remotely, realized how difficult Dottie's death was for him. Lumbe Davis, young as she was, noticed that Monro's bouts of forgetfulness became more frequent after Dottie died (interview), and when Monro returned to Miles and Dottie's friend Emma Sloan asked about her, he replied quietly, "Emma, I've lost my best friend" (telephone interview, 10 July 2008).

In August, as Dottie had requested, there was a memorial service at the church in South Freeport, with Monro presiding. Her body was cremated, and the ashes were scattered in Maine. When the service was over and the guests had gone, Monro remained in the cottage where he and Dottie had so often taken temporary refuge from the ups and downs of academe. Now, stripped of her supportive presence, he faced yet another upheaval: George Owens had stepped down from the presidency at the end of the school year, and nobody know quite what to expect from his successor ("Owens to Retire").

This person sometimes stays in the background but
brings others into the marvelous light.

—*Eaglet* Staff, 1988

11
WEATHERING CHANGES
1984-1995

On 1 June 1984 J. Herman Blake became president of Tougaloo, stepping down
as provost of Oakes College to do so. It is easy to see why the search committee
found him attractive. He was a scholar in his own right, with undergraduate and
graduate degrees in sociology (Campbell 269). In 1978 *Change* had named him
one of America's emerging leaders in higher education, and he had served on the
national task force that produced the 1984 report *Involvement in Learning: Realizing the Potential of Higher Education* (Dreyfuss 13). He was also Tougaloo's first
president to have no ties whatsoever to the American Missionary Association or
its affiliates (Campbell 269).

A closer look at his previous position explains even more clearly why Blake
seemed tailor-made for Tougaloo. He had played a crucial role in shaping the
mission of Oakes, which was created in the aftermath of Martin Luther King Jr.'s
assassination, when it was suggested that the University of California at Santa
Cruz establish a black college. Blake, Santa Cruz's only black faculty member
at the time, proposed an ethnic studies college instead. With faculty approval
he and a colleague set about planning Oakes, building in a strong natural sciences component to give graduates expanded professional options, an aggressive program to recruit talented minority faculty, a larger-than-usual counseling
staff, and a panoply of support services to help first-generation students adjust
to college. In offering Blake the presidency, the Tougaloo trustees hoped to tap
into Oakes's sterling reputation as well as its "unique blend of compassion and
innovative academic programs" (Dreyfuss 13).

Monro too had high hopes for the new president. In a letter to Ken Autrey,
who had left Tougaloo to earn a doctorate in composition at the University of

South Carolina, Monro described Blake as "an energetic intelligent guy with just the background of training and experience we need here now" and compared him favorably to Owens: "New York and California instead of deep south hangin' moss Mississippi; Berkeley and Santa Cruz instead of Tougaloo, Miles, and Fisk; good solid academic experience and attitude instead of business office" (22 Sept. 1984). He expected Blake to "turn the place around," and he could hardly wait.

NEW PROGRAMS AND NEW DUTIES

Although he regretted the impending demise of the Basic Studies Department, which had not been extended a second time, Monro was an early convert to Blake's proposal for its replacement: an interdisciplinary first-year course along the lines of an Oakes program called "Values and Change." Underlying the course was the belief that students became engaged in learning when they could see that it was connected to their lives (Monro, "Literacy" 14), a point that Monro had repeatedly made at Miles and that had emerged from the 1984 national task force report.

In February Blake created a task force to plan the course, assuring the fiscally skittish faculty that he would find a way to pay for it (Blake, memo, 8 Feb. 1985, TCA). Monro agreed to participate, and during a brainstorming session he came up with the title "Invitation to Learning," which stuck. He was unable to teach it during its first iteration, but he attended the plenary lectures and took copious notes, and he especially liked the concept of a "floating seminar" of faculty members united by their commitment to the freshman curriculum and operating outside departmental boundaries (Monro, "Literacy" 15).

Despite Monro's enthusiasm for the direction the college was taking, his demanding job was beginning to take a toll. During the fall semester he was teaching eighty students, more than twice the normal number in Developmental English. Because of the overload, he asked to be replaced as Writing Center director, but by late September he was still holding down the fort, and the tutors who might have assisted him were being loaned to another faculty member with an overload. After receiving a reduced course load for the following year, he confessed that he was relieved, especially because he feared that his loss of stamina and dwindling "patience with non-performers" had been taking a toll on his students (letter to Autrey, 7 June 1985). The students, however, continued to admire and respect him and once again voted him Teacher of the Year.

No sooner had Monro received his course reduction than he agreed to chair the Academic Standing Committee, an assignment that swelled his workload back to unmanageable proportions. At the end of each semester the committee had to deliberate over approximately two hundred students who were on probation, examine their records, determine an appropriate course of action for each one, decide which students should be suspended, draw up a docket, record their decisions, compose and deliver letters to the students, prepare departmental lists, and handle student appeals. Remarkably, Monro managed to make the chairmanship even more labor-intensive than it already was. Whereas previous chairs had relied solely on numerical criteria in the committee's deliberations, he spent his winter break analyzing the probationary students' essays, poring over their grades, teasing out implications for improved teaching strategies, and devising new reasons to grant student appeals. As Richard McGinnis observed, "Nobody before or after ever put anything like that amount of time into assessing student progress and caring about the students as individuals" (interview, 8 Mar. 2010).

Initially, the termination of the Basic Studies Department was not as traumatic as Monro had feared. Many of the program's virtues survived in Invitation to Learning. Freshman English remained largely unchanged when its faculty migrated to the English Department, and a recently funded literacy project was disseminating many of the freshman program's goals and approaches throughout the curriculum. Monro's transition was also eased by the fact that he had already worked on committees and in the Writing Center with English Department chair Jerry Ward. A Tougaloo graduate with a master's degree from the Illinois Institute of Technology and a doctorate from the University of Virginia, Ward had become department chair in 1979 and was establishing a scholarly reputation in African American literature, with special emphasis on Richard Wright. More than once he and Monro were jointly named Teacher of the Year, and for several years they shared an honorary professorship, with Monro listed as the Lawrence Durgin Professor of Language and Ward the Lawrence Durgin Professor of Literature. Their most recent collaboration had been an ambitious literacy project funded by the Ford Foundation.[1]

FILLING THE VOID

Outside the classroom and the committee room, friends and colleagues provided company in the aftermath of Dottie's death. After philosophy professor Dick

Johnson and his wife, Margaret Wodetzki, invited Monro to spend an evening with them, he became a regular Friday night guest at their home (letter to Autrey, 7 June 1985). Rose Davis frequently dropped by his house, where she would bang on the door to attract his attention after he had removed his uncomfortable hearing aids. She pestered him—in vain—to install a system that would flash a light when the doorbell or the phone rang (Marshall, interview, 8 Mar. 2009).

Wisely, during his first few years alone, Monro locked up the empty house and traveled at every opportunity. He continued to spend Thanksgiving with the LaMontes in Birmingham, visiting U. W. Clemon and Dick Arrington, who in 1979 had been elected the city's first black mayor. He flew to California for Christmas and spent several weeks in South Freeport during August. He attended the thirtieth anniversary celebration of the College Scholarship Service, where he received a distinguished service award and was introduced by Donald "Skip" Routh, Yale's financial aid director, as "a man whose commitment to equal educational opportunity is so intense and pervasive that it has made a seamless garment of his life and work" (29 Oct. 1984).

He also attended an unusual College Board colloquium, "Measures in the College Admissions Process," in Wakefield, Massachusetts. Arranged by George Hanford shortly before he stepped down as president of the College Board, the colloquium reflected his fearless pursuit of transparency. In essence the colloquium was an open debate about the strengths and weaknesses of the board's standardized tests, particularly the Scholastic Aptitude Test. It was a messy, no-holds-barred affair, and Monro ate it up. "Everybody was discussing this, challenging the speaker or asking questions," all in full view of "some of the toughest reporters in the country," he gleefully recalled (Aubry 40). He acted as a respondent, urging the College Board to state more clearly what skills its tests were measuring so that the high school curricula could be designed around them (56).

RAPID TURNOVER AT THE TOP

The honeymoon phase of Blake's presidency was short-lived; by the fall of 1985 it was clear that hostility toward him was growing, and word was beginning to spread beyond the campus. A *Newsweek* article in November 1985 described the institutional temperament as "colicky," and in the same article history professor William L. Wood challenged Tougaloo's claim that it boasted a "family atmosphere," observing, "I've never seen a family dislike each other so" (qtd. in Schwartz and Burgower). Blake's opponents criticized his personal fund-raising efforts as ineffectual, although a number of the staff that he brought with him from Oakes established an impressive grant-writing record. Another complaint, especially from long-serving faculty, was that Blake was not sufficiently respectful of the college's traditions. For instance, he insisted on calling the main administrative building "College House," ignoring its time-honored label the "Mansion." The venerable edifice had been lovingly begun by plantation owner John W. Boddie as a wedding gift for his fiancée and then finished haphazardly when the engagement fell through. Under American Missionary Association ownership it was converted to classrooms and a residence for the principal (Campbell 10–11), and Tougaloo old-timers felt that Blake's generic label effaced the mansion's colorful history.

Blake's most outspoken critic and the staunchest defender of college tradition was music professor and humanities chair Ben Bailey. Since his arrival at Tougaloo in 1965, Bailey had become an indefatigable teacher and a record-setting fund-raiser. A widely respected authority on black music, he championed the choir and wrote several books about music at the college (Campbell 271). He turned his vacations and summers into busman's holidays, directing highly regarded faculty workshops on campus and a National Writing Project program (Autrey, e-mail, 10 Mar. 2011), and he freely dug into his own pocket to pay for materials or activities he thought the students should have.

In April 1986 Bailey resigned as humanities chair, claiming that he could no longer work with Blake (Johnson, Richard), and shortly before the end of the semester the faculty passed a resolution of no confidence in the president and his administration (Campbell 272). The following January the faculty council passed another no-confidence vote, and when the trustees met in February, Blake submitted his resignation before they could vote on renewal of his contract (274). Throughout the wrangling Monro remained aloof, although his refusal to join the debate could be construed as disenchantment, given his original enthusiasm for Blake. On the other hand, he continued to support Blake's initiatives, served tirelessly on his committees, and used his own connections and speaking engagements to praise the direction Tougaloo was taking. Today Blake remembers Monro as "a very supportive, encouraging gentleman," except for his concern that Blake's white staff members were diluting the image of Tougaloo as a center of black institutional strength (telephone interview, 30 Mar. 2009).

Administrative turmoil aside, it was a good time for Monro and his favorite projects. Under Ben Bailey's aggressive leadership the Writing Task Force, on which Monro served, was becoming increasingly successful in placing writing at the center of the curriculum. The previous year it had proposed a formal Writing across the Curriculum program; now it was recommending a college-wide senior research requirement. The task force supervised all freshman and sophomore courses, and it approved a noncredit workshop Monro was offering to students having difficulty passing the writing proficiency exam. Once again, the students voted him Teacher of the Year (Award, 23 Apr. 1986, DP).

However, the Academic Standing Committee gave him far less joy, and on 5 February he asked to be replaced as its chair (memo, 5 Feb. 1987, TCA). English Department chair John Teeuwissen, eager to keep Monro as a teacher, supported his request, calling him "the best teacher of underprepared writing students I have ever seen" and estimating that at least two full-time faculty members would be needed to cover his duties should he decide to leave (memo, 12 Apr. 1987, TCA). When no replacement could be found, Monro agreed to continue as chair, provided that a dean assume the administrative work (memo, 14 Jan. 1988, TCA), and newly arrived academic dean Bettye Parker Smith agreed to the arrangement.

THE STEWARD AND THE SEARCH

The 1987 fall semester was relatively tranquil for the faculty. Reverend Charlie Baldwin, whose role as coordinator of the Brown-Tougaloo partnership brought him to campus frequently, had agreed to serve as interim president when Blake resigned. He had a great fondness for the college—as Richard McGinnis observed, "His pulpit was at Brown, but his heart was at Tougaloo" (interview)—and his light hand was much appreciated by the faculty, to whom he deferred in academic matters.

On 7 November Monro was guest of honor at a surprise party presided over by Lucius Pitts Jr. and Walter Davis. The Birmingham delegation included Ed LaMonte, Dick Arrington, Miles academic dean Charlotte Carter, and J. L. Meyers, pastor of John and Dottie's former parish. Anthony Owens '85, who had taken Monro's Freshman English class, traveled from Baton Rouge, where he was studying for a master's degree in counselor education, and thanked Monro for encouraging him to pursue his dream of becoming a college administrator (telephone interview, 17 Mar. 2010). John Teeuwissen created a whimsical poem for the occasion:

> We'll give thanks to John Usher Monro
> As we harvest the seeds that he'll sow.
> He turns Fs into Cs
> And Ds into Bs
> Even As—for his students all grow.

The mastermind behind the celebration was Bernice Coar-Cobb, Monro's friend and former colleague at Miles, who was now Tougaloo's acting academic dean and had inferred from a conversation with Monro that his retirement was imminent. Perhaps he had been musing about retirement in the abstract or grousing about his impossible workload, but he never mentioned the subject to her again, and he continued to work for another decade (Sterling, interview, 13 Mar. 2008).

In another tribute to Monro's years of service, the seniors dedicated their yearbook, *The Eaglet*, to him. With typical undergraduate fervor and a nod to Bette Midler, they wrote: "This person sometimes stays in the background but brings others into the marvelous light. . . . His contributions to education— as an administrator, teacher, dean, trustee, advisor, counselor and friend—are truly immeasurable and without precedent in American Higher Education. This yearbook dedication is our way of saying 'THANKS,' Dr. John U Monro. . . . We will continue to soar as EAGLETS—because you are truly the wind beneath our wings."

NEW LEADERSHIP AT TOUGALOO

On 1 February 1988 Adib Akmal Shakir took office as president, and Baldwin, breathing a sigh of relief, returned to Brown. Shakir was a graduate of Morehouse College in Atlanta, with a doctorate in psychology from Florida State University and a keen interest in learning styles, a subject that Monro had recently begun to explore. After teaching psychology at Bethune-Cookman College in Daytona, Shakir had become vice president of academic affairs (Campbell 276). His combination of academic and administrative experience, his familiarity with black colleges in the South, and his youth—he was still in his thirties—all counted in his favor at Tougaloo.

Shortly after taking office, Shakir proposed a curriculum review and a stringent cost-cutting campaign that identified Invitation to Learning as one of its first targets. Although the innovative course had many critics, Monro was one of its staunchest supporters, and the details of an outside evaluation suggest why he believed it had merit. When Antoine A. Garibaldi, chair of the Department of Education at Xavier University, and Patricia Murrell, who headed the Center for Study of Higher Education at Memphis State, came to Tougaloo to evaluate the course, students testified that they had "grown academically," particularly in terms of writing and study skills and understanding points of view that differed from their own (*External Evaluation Report*). Few outcomes were dearer to Monro's heart than these.

Monro used his position on the Academic Standing Committee to argue for keeping the course. Drawing on his years as intermediary between the Harvard student body and the administration, he represented the committee in conversations with the Invitation to Learning faculty, urging them to strike a compromise with the departments and save the course (ACS Minutes). But neither side would budge, and no funding for the course was included in the budget when it arrived in the president's office. With his eye on the bottom line, Shakir signed the budget, and the course was dropped from the catalog. It was the third exciting freshman program that Monro, despite his best efforts, had been unable to preserve.

Ever the team player, Monro helped develop the next freshman program, attending a summer faculty workshop that Shakir convened for that purpose. Because Monro had not taught the Invitation to Learning course, he was not paid for his attendance, but as usual, financial remuneration was low on his list of priorities. In fact, in 1986 he requested that his six thousand–dollar annual salary be reduced to a dollar, and it remained at that level until he retired ("Tougaloo College Honors").

Mission: Involvement, the course that emerged from the workshop, looked a lot like Invitation to Learning. It included a plenary lecture, smaller section meetings, and films. It also included an extracurricular component, with activities in dormitories and other nontraditional settings, and service projects such as tutoring and working with the handicapped (*Proposal*). But it had far less intellectual content than Invitation to Learning, and—a fact that concerned Monro a good deal—did little to address incoming students' deficiencies in reading, writing, and critical thinking.

As disappointed as he was with the new course, in public Monro was supportive of Shakir, introducing him at the first assembly of the school year as "a young man in a hurry," with the requisite "energy, concentration, managerial ability, and drive" to once again make Tougaloo a model of black institutional strength ("Introduction"). On another occasion, he invited the Shakirs to attend the local discussion group of which he was now a veteran member, pointing out that their presence would permit the group's members to meet the first family and "learn more first hand about Tougaloo" (letter, 23 Aug. 1989, DP). But privately he was skeptical about the direction the college seemed headed in, and he was also uncertain about what his role should be.

TEACHING SOLO AND IN TANDEM

Monro remained as bent on improving his teaching as though it were his first time in the classroom. At the end of the fall semester he rigorously analyzed his student evaluations, insisting that in spite of his students' praise, he deserved nothing higher than a B. He was especially dissatisfied that five students had received Fs or Incompletes, finding it cold comfort that students were placed in his class precisely because they had the most severe writing problems. In a memo to Jerry Ward he concluded, "I think I must become more intrusive, insistent, and plain mean about getting people who need it into conference" (25 Jan. 1989, TCA).[2] Monro was always his own harshest critic, but it is highly probable that his effectiveness in the classroom had begun to diminish. His hearing was declining steadily, and he now struggled to remember students' names—a serious problem, given the emphasis he placed on getting to know students personally. These handicaps could be overcome in a one-on-one setting, but in a crowded classroom they were an embarrassing impediment.

The students did not seem to notice his discomfort or find him deficient. More than 70 percent of those in his fall English class enrolled in his spring semester class as well, and at the end of the school year he received the 1988–89 Ariel M. Lovelace Service Award, named after the school's beloved choir director. According to Bob Honeysucker '65, who replaced Lovelace as choir director, "Pops" Lovelace was "the personification of *in loco parentis*, the kind of father every kid wished he had. He could pat you on the back, but he knew when to push you to get the most out of you" (personal interview, 27 July 2009). Both the award and the description were tailor-made for Monro.

As it became more difficult to measure up to his self-imposed high standards, Monro was drawn to collaborations with faculty members from other departments. One offer he could not refuse came from mathematics professor John Garner, who was teaching Introductory Algebra and asked Monro to lend a hand. While Monro thought of himself as a "volunteer Teacher's Aide" (letter to Streeter), Garner considered him a full partner. He described how together they had decided to arrange the course around the theme of problem solving and to use word problems as their primary strategy, developing the problems collaboratively (e-mail, 11 Jan. 2003). Students were encouraged to see either Garner or Monro for help, but most of them sought out Monro in the Writing Center. If the writing problems stemmed from a student's inability to grasp the abstract concepts that abound in algebra, Monro would resurrect the strategies he had developed for Freshman English students stuck in Piaget's concrete stage of cognitive development (Barbara Rotundo, personal interview, 3 Oct. 2004).

Monro loved being part of the algebra course. Sitting in on the classes freed him from the group give-and-take that his hearing and memory loss were turning into torture. His role as writing coach allowed him to get to know the students and help them while their writing was still in flux, and his sessions with them confirmed his belief that writing about a subject was the best way to understand it.

In March 1989 Monro notified Bettye Parker Smith that after working nonstop for three years, he was "simply tired out, and not doing anything as well as I want to. So the time has come to back off" (20 Mar. 1989, DP). He explained that he would like to continue his Writing Center work, his collaboration with Garner, and the nonadministrative aspects of the Academic Standing Committee, but he humbly added, "If the college wants me gone, retired, and out of sight, I will certainly understand, and take my leave grateful for the eleven wonderful years I have had here." He urged that the Durgin chair be bestowed in its entirety to Jerry Ward, who "should have had it from the start."

Ward, as acting cochair of the English Department, supported Monro's request, arguing that the department would be able to serve its students better if Monro spent more time in the Writing Center (20 Mar. 1989, DP). In spite of their frequent disagreements over curricular matters, humanities chair Ben

Bailey also supported Monro, insisting that he stay on under the terms he had requested. "I, for one, certainly don't want to see you gone from Tougaloo. You are a part of us, and we are a part of you," he wrote (21 Mar. 1989, DP). Parker Smith approved Monro's new job description, and he faced summer activities with one less problem on his mind.

That summer Monro attended a workshop on learning styles, chaired by political science professor Steve Rozman and funded by a Bush Foundation faculty development grant. Monro's growing dissatisfaction with his teaching gave him a vested interest in the topic, and he was especially impressed by Valora Washington, dean of arts and sciences at Antioch, who described faculty development activities she had been conducting on her campus. Recent research, which had shown that learning styles were shaped by background, which in turn was shaped by race, reinforced Monro's belief that black colleges should stop imitating Ivy League programs and develop their own curricula.

He was still excited about the workshop when he spoke to College Board archivist John Aubry, who was documenting the board's early efforts to expand opportunities for minority students. They spent a hot July day together, touring the campus, having lunch in the cafeteria, and dining at a nearby restaurant, then Monro put Aubry up for the night, apologizing for the threadbare towels but explaining that he was "too old" to buy new ones (personal interview, 22 Mar. 2006).

After answering Aubry's questions about the College Board, Monro moved on to Washington's work at Antioch, saying it was the kind of institutional support that was required to adapt pedagogy to different learning styles. As he saw it, one key aspect of Washington's program was its black leadership. "You have to get some significant black person in a position of authority with support from the president who starts making things happen like this," he stated (Aubry 23). In dramatic contrast to Antioch, Monro claimed, Harvard's efforts to hire black faculty and administrators had been little more than lip service during his years on the board of overseers: "Departments just weren't going to do it. And the president wasn't going to make them. And the dean wasn't going to make them. . . . They talk a good game but they don't really do it" (26). He considered his appointment of Archie Epps "the best thing [he] did as dean" but regretted that Epps, who was now dean of students, was still one of only a handful of black leaders at Harvard (25).[3] Comparing Tougaloo to Harvard, Monro was guardedly optimistic about the possibility of change, stating at one point, "I'm hopeful about this little college, Tougaloo, because it's small. I can talk to the people. Ultimately I can have some sense of making some headway with it" (34). But a few minutes later he admitted that his recent attempts at curricular reform had not succeeded in "turning many people around" (36).[4]

GRAPPLING WITH PROBLEMS

From the outside Tougaloo seemed to be thriving under Shakir's leadership. In 1988 the college had been included in *U.S. News and World Report's* list of "America's Best Colleges" (10 Oct. 1988). Mission: Involvement, now funded in part by the Lilly Endowment, was being hailed as a trend-setting threshold program (McDonald). The deficit had been significantly trimmed, and for the first time in recent memory the faculty had gotten a raise (Sharon Streeter, personal interview, 5 Mar. 2010).

But as his comments to Aubry suggest, after suspending judgment for several years, Monro was becoming disenchanted with the administration. He indicated just that when Ben Bailey requested faculty input on a self-study he was preparing for the Southern Association of Colleges and Schools (SACS). Monro responded, "In the absence of purpose, leadership, and supervision from President and Dean, there has been nothing like the on-going, college-wide, centrally supervised effort" that would be needed to satisfying the SACS mandate that "instruction must be appropriate to the capabilities of the students" (5 Oct. 1989, MSA, box 8).

Monro was especially frustrated by recent developments on the Academic Standing Committee, which he still cochaired with Bettye Parker Smith. In November 1988 Parker Smith had proposed a procedural change he simply could not condone: to prevent clerical staff from working several days over the winter break, she wanted to notify some students of their suspension before they had completed their final exams. Monro resigned the cochairmanship in protest, calling the proposed arrangement "inconceivable" and objecting that it eroded the significance both of final exams and of teachers' end-of-semester evaluations (memo, 8 Dec. 1988, MSA, box 10). To handle the immediate crisis, Monro suggested that "some senior person" assemble a suspension list as soon as final grades had been submitted. He estimated that it would take four or five days and volunteered for the job, expressing confidence that during the spring semester they could surely work out a more satisfactory procedure. The faculty ignored his objections, however, and approved Parker Smith's proposal. A year later he was still smarting from the incident, calling it "a stunning and unforgettable lesson in what I might expect professionally and personally from a Dean I had worked so hard for" (letter to Ben Bailey).

In spite of such aggravations, for long stretches Monro was able to follow Candide's advice and cultivate his garden, focusing on his work with colleagues and students. He went to the Writing Center early and stayed late. He attended faculty meetings and workshops as well as English Department meetings, even though such events were now optional for him. At his request he was appointed to the Commission on Writing, which replaced the Writing Task Force and had recently proposed that each department develop or designate at least one writing-intensive course.

The writing-intensive requirement inspired mathematics professor Nimh Fahmy to jump in with both feet and make all of his courses writing intensive (telephone interview, 3 Sept. 2002). Fahmy, who had joined the faculty in 1986, was intrigued by the idea of using writing to help his students learn mathematics, and in 1989 he asked Monro to help him bring more writing into his calculus class. Students were required to keep a journal and write three two-page papers a semester. Monro developed the word problems for the course, read the students' drafts, met with those who needed extra help, and graded the writing component, while Fahmy graded the math component of the assignments. The course soon became the poster child for the commission's writing-intensive campaign, with Ben Bailey praising it for "demonstrating very dramatically that students can write themselves into understanding mathematics" (13 Mar. 1995, TCA).

During the spring of 1990 Monro shared Writing Center duties with Barbara Rotundo, who came to Tougaloo from the State University of New York at Albany (UAlbany), where she had taught in the English Department for a quarter-century. She and Monro hit it off quickly because they shared some important beliefs about teaching writing. Rotundo was so convinced of the value of one-on-one conferences that at UAlbany she had established one of the country's first writing centers. Like Monro, she respected grammar instruction and believed in shaping the curriculum to fit a specific student body: at UAlbany she custom-designed a punctuation course for education majors. She also believed in the importance of the freshman curriculum. At Tougaloo, although she could have taught nineteenth-century American literature or one of her other specialties, she was happy to teach Freshman English and help Monro in the Writing Center. Monro and Rotundo made sure that one of them was on duty during the Writing Center's official open hours, but students often dropped in at other times as well, fully aware that it was virtually Monro's second home. Watching Monro in action, listening to his end of long-distance phone calls, and patching together the details of his life, Rotundo recognized him as a mover and a shaker, stating, "He could influence people; not the *Wall Street Journal* types, but the *New York Times* types" (personal interview, 3 Oct. 2004).

That summer Monro skipped the Summer Science Program, instead joining John Garner to teach the Mississippi Secondary School Mathematics Summer Institute. Taking their cue from the algebra course they had collaborated on, they led the high school math teachers through a rich assortment of materials exploring math and writing as problem-solving activities that had many similarities. They analyzed and created word problems and explored Piaget's theory of cognitive development, including the findings of UAB physics professor Robert Bauman. They kept journals, shared their work with each other, read papers written by Monro's Freshman English students, and analyzed sections of the College Board publications to which Monro had made significant contributions. The participants found the material so stimulating that they continued to meet during the school year, and Garner and Monro enjoyed the institute so much that they taught it in 1991 and again in 1994 (Mississippi Secondary).

GROWING DISCONTENT—AGAIN

Two years into his presidency Shakir was drawing mixed reviews from the faculty. Monro and those who shared his dissatisfaction with the administration were insulted when Bettye Parker Smith appointed a new faculty member to chair the faculty senate, which had traditionally elected its own chair. Additional hackles were raised by Shakir's aggressive pursuit of an Afrocentric curriculum (Campbell 280). Faculty who protested that there was no such thing as Afrocentric science, math, or psychology were told by him that they had been "miseducated in the Eurocentric tradition" (Asoka Srinivasan, telephone interview, 16 Mar. 2010). One guest speaker sponsored by Shakir referred to the "aliens" teaching on campus, and it took the stunned white faculty several moments to figure out that he was referring to them (Steve Rozman, personal interview, 8 Mar. 2010). Monro considered Afrocentrism an intellectually dubious ideology and feared it would supplant the rich African American texts that had been at the heart of his teaching for so many years.

Monro's dissatisfaction was apparent in his response to a questionnaire about morale and governance that Ben Bailey asked the faculty to fill out. Monro refused to place his level of morale along the spectrum Bailey had proposed, preferring, like the dedicated wordsmith he was, to give a verbal description. It was not a pretty picture: because of "the virtual disenfranchisement of devoted senior faculty from participation in the academic decision-making process," he foresaw a vicious cycle of faculty defection, failure to find suitable replacements, and an inevitable tailspin into academic decline. He quoted Alfred Whitehead, "A great school dies, and it is ten years before anybody knows it," then concluded, "I think we are approaching such a down turn" (21 Feb. 1991, TCA).

An early example of the faculty flight Monro had foreseen took place in the winter–spring semester of 1990, when Larry Barclay, who had been appointed by Blake, resigned as dean of students. Although he was not a faculty member, Barclay had expanded his job description to include participation in academic matters, much as Monro had done with his Harvard deanship; and he was married to Regina Turner, a dynamic member of the English Department. Committed to combining academics with student life, Barclay attended the freshman lectures, on the lookout for promising links to activities outside the classroom. Monro tried to help, suggesting in a memo to Parker Smith that Barclay be given a Writing Center office and become part of an accelerated program to recruit the neediest student applicants (23 Aug. 1989, TCA). Instead, Barclay was assigned an office in a remote corner of the campus, in spite of the fact that his success as dean of students depended on the students' ability to find him (Regina Turner, telephone interview, 22 Mar. 2010).

Turner, who stayed on at Tougaloo for another year, had been given an office in Galloway and gotten to know Monro quite well. Upon her arrival in the summer of 1985 she had joined the Invitation to Learning workshop already in progress and noticed that Monro was inconspicuously influencing the proceedings. "He had a unique way of leading without leading," she recalls. "It was his ideas and his energy, but if someone came in and looked at the group dynamic, they wouldn't name him as the leader. That's the way he wanted it" (telephone interview).

Turner came to regard Monro as her mentor, relying on him to temper the extremes she went to when she was enthusiastic about a project. He unfailingly supported her efforts, taking an almost parental pride in "Misconception," a play that her Invitation to Learning students wrote, produced, and staged. In a letter of recommendation he called her "one of the best and most effective colleagues and teachers I have known over forty years of university and college work," and her departure was one more item in his long list of grievances against the administration (letter to Grant Miller).

THE SENIOR RESEARCH PROJECT

Monro devoted most of his time and energy during the 1990–91 school year to the senior research requirement the faculty had adopted. There was a good deal of confusion—not to mention panic—as the seniors wrestled with the new requirement, for which no guidelines or procedures were yet in place. After developing triage materials and methods to help them cope, Monro proposed that the Commission on Writing create a guide to the research assignment for the next senior class, and he offered to do the job himself over the summer.

Monro asked to be relieved of his teaching duties for spring semester, realizing that the seniors' anxiety level would increase as their deadline loomed. He also requested emeritus status so that he could coach them through the final stages, continue working with Garner, and see students in the Writing Center (22 Nov. 1990, TCA). Together he and the English Department adjusted their relationship to reflect his new role. It was decided that students in his noncredit workshop would be distributed among four teachers and meet with them twice a week—an indication of how labor-intensive the one-on-one sessions were and proof that Teeuwissen had not been far off when he predicted in 1987 that at least two people would be needed to replace Monro (minutes, 18 Jan. 1991, TCA).

Keeping his promise to create the research guide consumed most of Monro's summer. The first edition included a recommended schedule for breaking the assignment into manageable steps, beginning in October and running through the spring deadline. Realizing that few seniors had written a research paper before, he provided copious directions, right down to how many hours of work each step demanded and what kind of notes worked best at each stage. He also included an abstract of each paper submitted for the 1990–91 school year and four strong papers, printed in their entirety, for the incoming seniors to use as models (*Tougaloo College Research*).

Preparing the handbook as he conceived it was a huge job, since he had to read the seventy-odd papers in order to write the abstracts and select the models. After working seven days a week for almost three months, he ended up with a succinct handbook that could be used for writing of all kinds, even though the specifics were drawn from research-based writing (letter to Merrifield 1992). The costs of the first edition were covered by the Commission on Writing, and Monro paid for subsequent editions out of his own pocket (memo to Mabel Henderson, Aug. 1995, DP). In a cover message distributed along with the handbook, Bailey thanked Monro for completing "this monumental task" as well as for "his deep interest in cultivating good writing" (July 1991). Jerry Ward, who also served on the commission, called the manual "a labor of love" (e-mail, 22 July 2003).

LOOKING BACKWARD AND FORWARD

The 1992–93 school year was bookended by two lengthy interviews that set Monro musing on his past and attempting to reconcile it with the current state of the college. In November he talked to Rupert Wilkinson, an emeritus professor from the University of Sussex, in conjunction with his forthcoming book, *Aiding Students, Buying Students: Financial Aid in America*. Wilkinson, who knew Monro only from Harvard-era photographs, barely recognized the man who picked him up at the Jackson airport wearing a blue jersey and a black knit hat and looking like "an ordinary, fairly poor Southern white" (telephone interview, 9 Jan. 2006). Monro was happy to talk about his involvement in financial aid issues, but he made no secret of where his interests lay. As Wilkinson wrote in the notes he jotted down after the interview: "The most powerful interest he admits to is teaching writing. . . . He took quiet pride in being able to improve someone's writing, and does the same for math up to what he calls 'simple algebra'" ("Some Thoughts").

The "simple algebra," of course, referred to Monro's continuing collaboration with John Garner, which soon thrust him into a controversy that was anything but simple. Monro was not shy about standing up for his friends, and he threw all his powers of persuasion into a defense of Garner when two students accused him of sexual harassment and he was suspended from his teaching duties.

Long before the accusation, Garner had earned the nickname "Beautiful John" for his habit of greeting students with the words "Hello, Beautiful," accompanied by a hug. His behavior met with mixed reactions. Some students found it weird, others found it insulting, and still others said it cheered them up. Garner explained that he restricted his effusive behavior to students and members of his church, all of whom understood that it was not a sexual advance but a caring gesture, nothing more than his personal translation of Stokely Carmichael's "Black is beautiful" into "Everyone is beautiful" (Esters). In a letter to Parker Smith, Monro agreed that students had every right to decide for themselves, "in simple dignity," when and with whom to behave informally, but he asked that Garner's dismissal be reviewed, given that his only mistake had been a failure to register a shift in student attitudes (18 Jan. 1993, DP). The trustees ordered Garner and the administration to work out a settlement, and negotiations dragged on until 1998, when it was agreed that Garner would retire (e-mail, 11 Feb. 2009).

REFLECTING ON TOUGALOO AND HARVARD

In June Monro spent the better part of two days talking to Jessica Brooks, a recent Brown graduate who was assembling information for the thirtieth anniversary of the Brown-Tougaloo partnership. During her exchange semester at Tougaloo in 1991, she had seen Monro—one of the "old white guys" who had come South during the civil rights era and then stayed on—as he walked to and from the Writing Center. She noticed that he wore a jacket and tie, as both a gesture of respect toward his Writing Center "clients" and a throwback to his Ivy League days (personal interview, 20 July 2009).

When Brooks met Monro two years later, he was wearing two large, conspicuous hearing aids and often asked her to repeat herself. He was a bit unsteady on his feet, and he hunched over slightly when he sat, but he still had energy to spare, and he took her project much more seriously than most of her interviewees. Nor did he act like a man with one foot out the door; on the contrary, he had plenty of ideas about the future of Tougaloo, which he thought should include a cooperative program and an extension school. His interest in extension schools was keener than ever, and he said he would be willing to teach in one, where students would be older and therefore less likely to be embarrassed by his deafness and memory loss ("Brooks" 5). Unearthing a catalog from the Harvard Extension School, he pored over it with total absorption, finding something to admire on almost every page and praising Mike Shinagel, its current dean and his former section man, as one of the most gifted young administrators he had ever come across.[5]

Talking to Brooks, Monro sounded a bit more optimistic than usual about his alma mater's drive toward diversity. He had recently received a Lifetime Achievement Award for "Outstanding Contributions to American Education" from the Harvard Foundation, created in 1981 "to improve intercultural understanding . . . and to recognize the contributions of both national and international figures whose work and deeds have served to improve the quality of our collective life" (Harvard Foundation Website). At the awards ceremony foundation director S. Allen Counter described Monro as "the best of what Harvard is all about" ("Awards Honor" 2–3). In addition, the keynote speaker at Miles's commencement that year was psychology professor Alvin Poussaint, a notable addition, along with Counter, to the growing nucleus of black leaders at Harvard.[6]

Monro apologized to Brooks for the chaotic state of his office and said his house was almost as bad because he was trying to consolidate his belongings and spare his family the burden of a massive cleanup "when it comes." But he was clearly loath to move out and relinquish his ties to the college. "I mean, I can leave," he told her, "[but] I don't want to leave this place" (qtd. in Brooks 5, 9).

His reluctance to leave was partly selfish: in spite of his unhappiness with the leadership, he simply loved the college. An equally strong motivation was the belief that his Writing Center work was a particularly effective kind of teaching— the kind that could spell the difference between success and failure for students struggling to overcome severe academic deficiencies. He said as much when Dean Whitla, a former Harvard colleague, came to Tougaloo on a site visit for the Bush Foundation. Leading him to the Writing Center, Monro said proudly, "This is where the best teaching goes on: they sit there and write, then they bring it in and I correct it here, and they go back out and re-write it" (qtd. in Whitla, personal interview, 9 Feb. 2006).

Monro needed every bit of his boundless enthusiasm for teaching, since he was now working almost exclusively with students who had failed the writing proficiency exam, were struggling with the senior research requirement, or had been sent by a professor who found their work unsatisfactory. Most were reluctant participants, and Monro sometimes lost heart, at least when he was writing up his reports in private and could express his feelings honestly. Implying that it was a delightful exception to the rule, he described one session with a responsive student: "What a relief it is to work with a student who follows suggestions and makes progress" (1 Mar. 1995, TCA).

But even when working with passive students, it did not take much to nudge him out of grumpiness. During their first meeting one student acted "bored and uninterested" when Monro suggested ways to study for the vocabulary test she had previously failed. Irked, he wrote in his report: "I will not mention it again or discuss it further . . . . looking ahead, if there is no change in her feelings, I will not intrude further into her program for the spring" (14 Feb. 1995, TCA). But the next day, when she needed library materials but had lost her library card, Monro could not resist coming to her rescue: he told her to ask the librarian for a temporary card and promised that if that failed, he would get the materials for her (15 Feb. 1995, TCA). At the end of the semester he triumphantly reported that she had passed the vocabulary test and would graduate with her class (10 May 1995, TCA).

Time and again Monro's personal knowledge of students gave him insight into their academic difficulties. Noting that a student sent to the Writing Center to revise an unsatisfactory paper had just returned to college after an absence of nine years, he attacked her problem with such fervor that he appeared to forget who was the student and who the teacher. First, he gave himself homework: "Over the weekend I will study the paper and read the stories being considered" (3 Feb. 1995, TCA). Then he reported dutifully on the completion of his assignment: "I have read the stories and am prepared to discuss them" (5 Mar. 1995, TCA).

The students reciprocated Monro's personal interest, as Phil Dreyer observed when he came for a visit and they went to the local Kmart. Returning from a search down the aisles, Phil found Monro surrounded by a gaggle of Tougaloo students who worked at the store, all clamoring to find out how he was and how they could help him with his shopping (e-mail, 5 June 2002).

But despite Monro's availability and enthusiasm, attendance figures were declining in the Writing Center. In comparison to its heyday, when a cadre of tutors with strong writing skills generated excitement and a spirit of camaraderie, the center was now a one-man operation. Things got worse when, at the beginning of the 1993–94 academic year, the center moved from its dingy but well-established location in Galloway to Berkshire Cottage, the first major building to be constructed on campus in twenty years. The following fall the English Department unanimously voted to name the Writing Center in Monro's honor, and on 11 November a plaque on the door identified the modest room as the John Monro Writing Parlor (minutes, 19 Sept. 1995, MSA, box 8). It was a nice compliment, but the name underscored an unpleasant truth: the location that Monro had turned into an important resource was being branded as his pet project and drifting to the margins of the curriculum, where it had been when he arrived.

TWO PERSONAL LOSSES

By the spring of 1995 Monro had lost both his brothers. In 1991 Claxton had died suddenly from blood clots following surgery for prostate cancer. Since his retirement in 1981, he and Vicki had been living in Austin, Texas, and he had remained active in retirement, officiating at a funeral two weeks earlier and counseling an engaged couple the night before he died (Mary MacGregor, e-mail, 1 Apr. 2006). John and Sutton attended the memorial service and stayed with Claxton's widow, Vicki, for several days.

The brothers had not been particularly good at keeping in touch with each other, especially after Claxton moved to Texas—he frequently told his children that he and his brothers were all "too busy to get together." But John's image and reputation were often on Claxton's mind, and his daughter Mary, to whom he confided a week before his death that he "hadn't done enough and wasn't finished with [his] work," believes that he underestimated his own accomplishments because he felt that John had achieved more (MacGregor, e-mail). In actuality Claxton was highly respected in church circles, and his book, *Witnessing Laymen Make Living Churches*, had been well received. In the history of Calvary Episcopal Church he is praised as "a great speaker, a crusader and organizer" (qtd. in MacGregor).

In March 1995 Sutton died from a recurrence of prostate cancer. During his illness he was tended by his second wife, Judy Brook, who had become a family friend after meeting Sutton during her doctoral work at Lehigh, and had helped care for his first wife, Sue, as she succumbed to Alzheimer's. Sutton's death ended a complex sibling relationship. As a boy, Sutton had idolized John, a leader at camp, a whiz at prep school, and a legend in the *Crimson* offices, where as a special treat he sometimes let Sutton help with the newspaper layout (Brook, personal interview, 11 Nov. 2010). The adulation had lasted into adulthood: when Sutton briefly considered teaching in Afghanistan, he identified John's move to the South as a source of inspiration (P. Monro, e-mail, 29 Nov. 2010), and late in life he still spoke of John "almost reverentially" (Brook, e-mail, 29 Nov. 2010).

What Sutton may not have grasped was that the admiration cut both ways. John respected the fact that in spite of his early academic difficulties, Sutton had become an accomplished researcher and teacher. Even as a new arrival at Lehigh, he had made significant improvements in the industrial engineering curriculum, adding courses in probability and statistics, which he knew the importance of from his work at Bell Labs; then, although he did not have a doctorate, he had been promoted to full professor in 1964 (*Memorial Resolution*). John also warmly praised Sutton's decision to follow his bliss, buy a farm, and create a lifestyle that successfully balanced family and professional commitments—a balance that John realized he perhaps had never achieved (Dreyer, e-mail, 29 Nov. 2010).[7]

It is a lucky thing to feel some hope.

—JOHN U. MONRO

12
FINAL POSTINGS
1995-2002

Sutton's death heightened Monro's awareness of his own declining powers, although he had suspected for some time that his memory lapses were due to Alzheimer's. In fact, the disease may have been the "it" he mentioned when he told Jessica Brooks that he was cleaning out his office and his home so that "when it comes," his family would not face a huge cleanup task. He tried to prepare Janet and Phil, giving them articles about the condition and saying that he thought he was in its early stages (Dreyer, interview, 9 Feb. 2005).

Monro struggled against the inevitable, exercising his mind vigorously in an attempt to contain or reverse the condition. He played memory games, picking a time in his life and then describing friends, teachers, and books from that period as well as what he had done before and after school (Dreyer, interview). On his Friday night visits with Margaret and Dick Johnson, he told stories about his childhood and his life at Harvard and in the navy. He tested his musical memory too, playing piano versions of hymns and songs from his past, sometimes consulting a collection of favorites that Phil and Janet had put together for him (Johnson, interview). He also took realistic measures to keep from inconveniencing others. Wherever he went, he carried a packet of file cards filled with words he might need (Dreyer, interview). To navigate long-familiar routes, he drew painstakingly detailed maps that reminded him, for instance, whether to turn left or right upon exiting an elevator (Fahmy, interview).

In the fall of 1995 Jelani Davis arrived at Tougaloo for the start of the school year, hurried to Monro's office to say hello, and was crestfallen when his old friend did not recognize him. Several weeks later Jelani was driving near the college and saw a long line of cars crawling along County Line Road. He soon realized that the cause of the backup was Monro, driving his red Toyota Tercel at a snail's pace, oblivious to the logjam behind him. When Monro passed the turn to his house and pulled over in confusion, Jelani drove up alongside, then guided Monro home while the other frustrated drivers sped by (Marshall, interview).

As the semester progressed, more and more faculty members told Joseph Lee, who had succeeded Shakir as president in 1995, that Monro's memory lapses were becoming worrisome. Clarence Hunter, who ran the college archives and often joined Monro for lunch, observed that he was nodding off in the Writing Center more frequently than in the past (personal interview, 3 Mar. 2010). Ruth Johnson and Dilla Buckner, former colleagues from the English Department, noticed he was losing weight, concluded he was forgetting to eat, and began bringing meals he could reheat for dinner (Johnson, telephone interview, 15 Mar. 2010). Even so, nobody tried to talk him into retiring because, as Jerry Ward remarked, it was hard to persuade "that old Yankee to do anything he didn't want to" (personal interview, 12 Nov. 2010).

Later that semester Sarah Beard, who had recently joined the English Department, was assigned to join Monro in running the Writing Center—a diplomatic way of dealing with the fact that he could no longer work alone ("Writing Center Expands"). By November he did not feel confident enough to drive to Birmingham for Thanksgiving, so Ed LaMonte came and fetched him. At the holiday dinner table, everybody had to shout because he had forgotten his hearing aid, but he was quite lucid, and both Ed and Ruth remember that year's visit as particularly enjoyable (personal interview, 13 Mar. 2008). It turned out to be their final holiday together.

In early December, shortly before his eighty-third birthday, Monro's suspicions were confirmed when his doctor officially diagnosed him with Alzheimer's disease. Although it was not a surprise, it was a heavy blow, and he skipped his customary Christmas trip to California, telling Janet and Phil he needed time at home to adjust to the news. Nonetheless, he clung tenaciously to his duties at Tougaloo, insisting that if he could not drive he would bike to work, and he continued to attend Sunday services on campus until the excursion became too much for him (Rev. Larry Johnson, telephone interview, 25 June 2009).

At the end of the 1996 spring semester Monro reluctantly retired, but he flatly refused to move to one of the assisted living facilities near Claremont, telling Phil and Janet, "I don't want to go and sit around with a bunch of old people waiting to die." Since Dottie's death he had grown used to living on his own, and he had frequent visitors, including former colleagues Nimr Fahmy, John Garner, and history professor Jim Brown. In addition to their Friday night dinner dates, the Johnsons took him to the supermarket to make sure he was eating regularly (interview). In a letter to Phillips head Barbara Landis Chase, Monro reported with quiet optimism that he was blessed with a good doctor, "and it is a lucky thing to feel some hope" (26 Feb. 1997, PAA).

He continued to live at home until swelling in his legs turned out to be phlebitis. During an office visit on 10 September 1997 his doctor discovered a clot and immediately admitted him to Baptist Hospital. Trying to explain his condition to Phil and Janet over the phone but unable to summon the name of his condition or his symptoms, he finally resorted to visuals: "You know how your legs are supposed to be twins? Well, mine aren't. One is bigger than the other one" (qtd. in Dreyer, interview, 9 Feb. 2005).

By 19 September he was sufficiently recovered to be discharged, but because he could no longer live alone, Phil and Janet had him transferred to Ridgeland Court, a nearby convalescent home. Even plucked from his native habitat and in the advanced stages of the disease, Monro remained remarkably and sometimes comically himself, perhaps because he required few medications. When Phil and Janet came to see him, he gave them the equivalent of a campus tour, pointing out the nonexistent labs, library, and dorm rooms (Dreyer, e-mail, 17 Mar. 2009). During the Johnsons' many visits he walked them through the facilities, inviting admiration of the now-familiar artwork as though they were seeing it for the first time. Finally, in early July a spot opened up at Hillcrest Homes, a ten-minute drive from Phil and Janet's home in Claremont.

Getting Monro to California required elaborate preparations because he could not be left on his own. Phil flew to Jackson, rented a car, picked Monro up, and drove to the airport, where the Johnsons kept him company while Dreyer returned the car, then said good-bye as their friend boarded the plane. Monro and Dreyer missed a connecting flight and hit a snag at security because Monro had lost his driver's license and did not have an ID with a photograph. Dreyer, anticipating the problem, had brought along E. J. Kahn's 1971 *New Yorker* article about Monro, which included a pen-and-ink sketch of him. Although the security measures of the time were far more casual than they would eventually become, the security officer balked until Dreyer threatened to board the plane and leave Monro for the guard to deal with. From then on things went smoothly, and after lunch with Janet at a pleasant restaurant and a short intake interview at Hillcrest, Monro was admitted (Dreyer, e-mail, 26 Apr. 2010).

CLEANING OUT THE HOUSE

Once he was settled, Phil and Janet returned to Mississippi and began emptying the house so that it could be sold. They had to return several times before the job was done, and during their first attempt they worked in the dim light of a menorah they had discovered in a closet after a storm knocked out the electricity (interview). Papers were everywhere—a blizzard of papers, from the Y camp, Phillips, Harvard, the College Board, UAB, Miles, Tougaloo, professional organizations, family, friends, charities, supplicants, and strangers. All kinds of papers: letters, memos, class handouts, poems, grammar exercises, scrapbooks, newspaper and magazine clippings, photographs, concert and theater programs, yearbooks, souvenirs, official military documents, and the crossword puzzles Monro loved. Tossed in among the papers were his honorary degrees, which he had not bothered to hang or frame. Although others may have been lost, the survivors of his cavalier treatment are from Amherst, Brandeis, Carleton, Columbia, Harvard, Holy Cross, Manhattanville, Miles, Oak Hill, Oglethorpe, Saint Bonaventure, Stanford, Tougaloo, the University of Michigan, Wesleyan, and Wooster.

The house also bulged with books, which spilled out into the garage, where they were piled up so high that they threatened to topple over onto the car (Marshall, interview). Many were secondhand and mildewed from the southern damp.[1] There were books about education, philosophy, writing, civil rights, history, black studies, and women's studies. There were small collections of books about his heroes, Abraham Lincoln and Don Quixote. More than half the books stacked next to the bed were about religion, and near the top of the pile was Peter Gomes's *The Good Book: Reading the Bible with Heart and Mind* (Dreyer, "Eulogy," Cambridge).[2] The Dreyers kept some of the books, including Ed LaMonte's *Politics and Welfare in Birmingham, 1900–1975*, which LaMonte had inscribed, "To John Monro—with more gratitude, respect, and affection than I can ever express." They gave other books to neighbors, and a minister who lived nearby was happy to have the ones about religion. The vast majority—about five thousand volumes—went to the Jackson Public Library (Dreyer, e-mail).

FINAL ADDRESS

At South Woods, the Hillcrest facility for "the cognitively impaired" who were still fairly sound physically, Monro had a private room and was free to roam the attractive gardens and grounds and to play the living room piano when he could remember how.[3] He still exhibited flashes of his old sharpness. Once he surprised an activities director who was struggling to spark a discussion about a list of the century's one hundred greatest authors that the *Los Angeles Times* had recently published. There was dead silence until Monro objected that women were woefully underrepresented and that he could think of at least twenty women whose omission was an embarrassment (Dreyer, e-mail).

His condition began to deteriorate after he fell and broke his hip while standing on a chair to adjust a Christmas tree ornament. He was never completely mobile again and had to be moved to Wood, the facility for patients who required nursing care. It was older and far less attractive than South Woods; the rooms were semiprivate, and there was little stimulation other than the TV, with the volume turned up to a deafening pitch (Dreyer, e-mail). Monro was frustrated and confused by his wheelchair because he did not understand why it was necessary or what he was doing in it. At first he resisted it with surprising strength, and when Janet, who visited daily, tried to wheel him around the grounds, he would plant his feet to keep the chair still, then attempt to stand and escape its confines. Eventually he accepted its presence and learned to move by padding along with his feet on the ground. He slept a lot, and during his waking hours he sat in bed or in the wheelchair, going out into the hall or keeping the nurses company. He was a polite, pleasant patient, and in return the nurses, who were fond of him, gamely adapted to his version of reality, giving him their papers so that he could "organize" them in professorial fashion. One day a staff member told Janet, "This morning your father told me that I had to write an essay for him" (Dreyer, interview).

In March 2002 Monro developed pneumonia and began to drift in and out of consciousness. On Sunday, 24 March, Phil and Janet were called and told he would probably not survive the night. They rushed to his side and found him breathing with difficulty and barely conscious. He lingered for four more days. Janet recalls a final stroke of grace that occurred on 28 March, the eighteenth anniversary of Dottie's death: "It was the most amazing connection I had ever had with him. He just lay there, and I was sitting next to him and holding his hand and he just looked at me. He made eye contact with me that did not falter. He was barely blinking. He lay there and looked at me for at least an hour, and it was penetrating. I just kept talking to him, even though he was very hard of hearing. Finally I said, 'Dad, I think you should just try to go to sleep'" (interview). He held on until just past midnight and died in the early morning of 29 March.

Obituaries appeared in newspapers across the country, in academic journals, and in the several publications of the College Board, Phillips, Harvard, Miles, and Tougaloo. At the University of South Carolina, where she was working as coordinator of Library Instruction, Rose Davis—now Rose Parkman Marshall—added five hundred dollars to the Dottie Monro Memorial Fund and changed its name to the John and Dottie Monro Memorial Fund. Until her retirement in 2010 she continued to dip into it whenever a student needed help paying for a graduate school application or a tank of gas (Marshall, interview).

At Phillips, Barbara Landis Chase sent a memo to the trustees, wrote condolence letters to both Ann and Janet, and offered the use of Cochran Chapel for a memorial service (5 Apr. 2002, PAAA). In the end there were two services, one at the United Church of Christ in South Freeport on 13 August and one at Harvard's Memorial Church on 6 October. The eulogists at the Harvard service were a living catalog of the causes Monro had championed: student diversity (Hubert Sapp), administrative diversity (Archie Epps), educational opportunities for veterans and other nontraditional students (Fred Glimp), needs-based financial aid (George Hanford), educational outreach into impoverished areas (Sapp again), and the abiding value of black colleges (Richard Arrington). In their eulogy Phil and Janet addressed other topics, including Monro's military career, his reading habits, and his tender care for all things neglected, from spindly plants to the stray cats stalking Tougaloo's campus.

Peter Gomes, who presided at the service and hosted a reception at his home, recalled Monro's deanship and the period when the two of them were directing freshman programs at black colleges in Alabama. Reflecting on Monro's refusal to be stereotyped or constrained by his official position, Gomes said: "A dean has a difficult job to do, and when it is done, he is expected to slink back into the obscurity from whence he came. It is not often that a dean rises to the level of a hero."

Though the voice is quiet, the spirit echoes still.

—ANONYMOUS

EPILOGUE

Like his father and brothers before him, Monro was cremated, but figuratively speaking, his remains are widely dispersed. Every year, as college application deadlines loom, countless high school seniors feel his influence as they fill out financial aid forms modeled on the formulas he developed. As he had hoped, the College Board has grown from a small coterie of selective colleges to an organization with fifty-nine hundred members.

Monro's recruiting trips to unearth hidden talent are imitated in the most selective colleges, as admissions officers crisscross the country searching for bright students whose test scores may not tell the whole story. In line with his belief that scholarships should go to students who would not otherwise be able to afford college, most Ivy League scholarships are now needs based, a trend that encourages economic diversity as well as equal opportunity. At Harvard, where tuition, room, and board are waived for any student whose family earns less than sixty-five thousand dollars a year, 20 percent of the students in the class of 2013 qualified for the waiver (Jan).

Miles College, which was struggling for survival when Monro arrived, is now one of the fastest-growing members of the United Negro College Fund, and its student body, which once consisted almost entirely of local high school graduates, draws students from thirty-two states. The Freshman Studies Program that Monro helped design is still in existence, and in order to graduate, students must pass the kind of in-house, customized writing proficiency exam he fought for.

Monro's paper trail forms a cross-country web, reaching from Claremont, California, where Phil and Janet hold his personal papers; to a multitude of archives, including those at Brown, Camp Abnaki, the College Board, Harvard,

Miles, Phillips, Tougaloo, and UAB. The contents of the messy office that he never succeeded in tidying are now part of the Tougaloo College Civil Rights Collection and are housed in the Mississippi State Archives, under the steward-ship of his former colleague and friend Clarence Hunter.

At Tougaloo students still come to the John Monro Writing Parlor for help with their writing, and the senior research guide that was Monro's brainchild is updated every year. Now, however, the manual contains only guidelines and a recommended schedule; the abstracts and sample papers that Monro spent his summers preparing have been discontinued because, as English Department Chair Candace Love Jackson explained, "Nobody could duplicate the work that he did" (personal interview, 28 Mar. 2010).

Finally, his spirit survives in the thousands of students he taught: timid Helen Foster, learning to swim; young Sutton, boning up for his Latin exam; the men of the *Enterprise* crew, mastering the life-and-death business of damage control; the undergraduate and extension students at Harvard, Miles, and Tougaloo; the Miles summer workshop participants, struggling to master the skills they would need in college; the Tougaloo seniors preparing their research assignments with the assistance of the guide he created; the writers whose work he scrutinized so carefully and thoughtfully in the Writing Center; and the countless people whose values were shaped by their encounters with him or with the life he chose to lead.

MONRO PORTRAITS

Two portraits of Monro bracket his life and are visible reminders of his legacy. One is a handsome oil painting, part of a series sponsored by the Harvard Foun-dation for Intercultural Relations, "to reflect the diversity of individuals who have served Harvard University for at least twenty-five years with distinction" (Ireland). Monro is one of only two Caucasians to be included in the series, which numbered fourteen in 2011. Each portrait is hung in a spot closely associ-ated with the individual; Monro's is mounted in Phillips Brooks House, whose fourteen hundred volunteers confirm his belief that college should widen stu-dents' horizons rather than swaddling them in privilege.

In the portrait, artist Stephen Coit, class of 1971, has depicted Monro in his middle-aged prime, nattily dressed in a sport jacket, button-down shirt, and plaid tie.[1] He stands in the doorway of an amphitheater-style classroom, where students of both genders and many ethnicities and skin tones wait for him to enter. Neither the diverse student body nor the Science Lecture Hall, on which Coit modeled the background, existed in Monro's day, but Coit explains, "I have placed Monro in the dream [of diversity] he had for Harvard, but never experienced himself" (e-mail, 2 Aug. 2011).

The other portrait, in acrylic, is the work of artist Johnnie M. Maberry Gilbert, and it hangs in the Writing Center at Tougaloo, where Gilbert is chair of the Fine Arts Department. Unlike the Harvard portrait, which places Monro at a decorous distance from the viewer, the Tougaloo portrait thrusts his body up against the picture plane in a tight close-up, giving him an air of urgency. His hair is white, wild, and askew, and he wears a casual pullover jersey, with the edge of his T-shirt showing. Behind dark-framed glasses his eyes appear unnaturally large, giving him, as Ken Autrey once observed, "an owlish, wide-eyed look, as though by seeing more acutely he could compensate for his deafness." When I first saw the portrait, its ferocious intensity reminded me of both Samuel Beckett and John Brown.

Perhaps the most significant difference between the two portraits is that the oil painting situates Monro firmly in a Harvard context—albeit one on which Coit had worked some time-traveler wizardry—whereas the background of the acrylic is abstract and undefined. As the juxtaposed portraits dramatically illustrate, Monro's quest took him far from his New England roots, in search of a community knit together by a common goal rather than by background, geography, class, ethnicity, or race.

He fondly described Tougaloo, his final professional posting, as "my home in all the world, a home I spent many years in finding." Throughout his life John Monro's restless pursuit of social justice compelled him to pull up stakes whenever he saw a greater opportunity elsewhere, making each new destination home. Yet in the end he was content to conclude his career in a quiet corner where, in spite of his diminishing powers, he could continue to make a difference, one student at a time.

Notes

Chapter One

1. John's middle name, Usher, made him Hezekiah's namesake, and he was saved from the onus of *Hezekiah* only because his grandfather went by his middle name, signing himself "H. Usher Monro."

2. Hezekiah's annual starting salary at St. Paul's was one thousand dollars, the equivalent of about twenty-one thousand dollars in today's currency.

3. Granddaughter Mary grew up to be a strong-minded woman with little time for chaperoning. After a brief marriage to musician and composer Leland S. Ramsdell, she became one of the first two female state troopers in Massachusetts (Foley 1).

4. Fifty-five years later Monro returned to Phillips to receive the Claude Moore Fuess Award for "distinguished contribution to public service." The medal bore a quote from Fuess that by that time could equally be applied to Monro: "Give me a robust non-conformist who has the strength of his convictions" ("Fuess Award").

Chapter Two

1. All family letters referred to in this chapter are in the Dreyer Papers.

2. When *Harvard Crimson* president Morison got two Ds and an E on his midterm exams, Hanford treated him very differently than he had treated Monro. "That's all right, son," Morison recalls Hanford saying. "We knew you had *The Journal* to contend with. We decided not to do anything about [the failing grades] right now. Just get them all up to Bs by the end of the year" (personal interview, 24 May 2005).

3. Incredibly, the *Crimson* did not write a news story about the Hanfstaengl controversy until 5 May 1934, although it had been brewing since 29 March, when a story about it appeared in the *New York Times*.

4. Kahn failed in his bid to join the *Crimson*, but he wrote brilliantly and prolifically for the *New Yorker*—including a lengthy profile of Monro published in 1971—until his death in 1999 in an automobile accident.

5. Today the *Crimson* frequently scoops the Boston dailies on news with a Harvard connection, offers the wide-ranging coverage Monro was constantly goading it toward, and is a model of gender equality: in 2003–4, when I began researching this book, it boasted an all-female leadership team (Lauren Schuker, personal interview, 29 Aug. 2005).

Chapter Three

1. After this foray into purple prose, Monro returned to his usual concise, journalistic style and never departed from it again. He encouraged the same style in his students, and he praised writers such as Robert Frost, George Orwell, and John Steinbeck, whom he considered its master practitioners. According to Craig Comstock, one of Monro's section men at Harvard, "He liked spare writers who turned out honest, workmanlike prose and who got beyond one social class" (e-mail, 3 Nov. 2005).

2. Alcoholics Anonymous founders Bill Wilson and Bob Smith, who met while members of the Oxford Movement, added six preliminary steps of their own to come up with their famous twelve-step program.

3. The measure automatically expired when the city council term ended, but the campaign finally bore fruit in 1942, when Washington Elms, a 324-unit affordable housing project built with federal assistance, was completed (Charles M. Sullivan, e-mail, 25 Nov. 2006).

4. When I visited the cottage in South Freeport, I saw for myself how thin Monro had become. Hanging in a closet was his uniform, an unusual olive drab color, unlined—probably in deference to the muggy Pacific climate—and cut so narrowly that it looked like the garment for a paper doll.

5. Truman ordered the military desegregated in 1948, and the first black midshipman graduated from Annapolis in 1949 (Negri).

6. He also drew on naval and military figures of speech in some very unlikely contexts: showing Phil how to scythe the grass in South Freeport, Monro explained that they were giving the grass a Spruance haircut, after Admiral Raymond Spruance and his thorough destruction of ground cover in preparation for marine attacks (Dreyer, interview, 3 Aug. 2005).

7. The *Enterprise* legacy lives on, despite the younger generation's tendency to confuse it with *Star Trek's Enterprise*. The USS *Yorktown*, the surviving aircraft carrier that most closely resembles the *Enterprise*, includes a room dedicated to the exploits of the "Big E," and when I toured the carrier with Charlie Russert, a former member of Monro's damage control crew, many visitors noticed his *Enterprise* cap and stopped to shake his hand and thank him for his service.

Chapter Four

1. All four seniors ended up at Harvard. I was able to locate two of the three surviving members of the group, and neither remembers the dungaree incident, although it's not clear whether Monro was invoking poetic license or the seniors were invoking selective memory.

2. Such convenience did not last long. Shortly after the office opened, the family moved to suburban Winchester.

3. Although the organization's legal name is still the College Entrance Examination Board, it is now referred to as the "College Board," even in its official materials (Hanford, *Life* 161).

4. The apparently sexist language here and elsewhere is often due to the fact that Harvard, Phillips, and other institutions were still all male.

5. Today half the students at Phillips are drawn from public schools, and a wide variety of outreach programs connect the campus to the community and the world at large (Phillips Academy website).

Chapter Five

1. In 1964 the seminar program shed its experimental status and was absorbed into the curriculum, where it remains today. In 1960–61, when Monro taught his final seminar, there were 27 on offer; in 2010–11 there were close to 130.

2. Monro was also accurate in pinpointing isolation as a serious morale problem. In January 1962 Murray Frank, who frequently served as the only connector among far-flung volunteers, created a monthly newsletter, the *Tilley Lamp*. It was stuffed with gossip, news, progress reports, recipes, book reviews, and personal notes, such as the one Dave Hibbard wrote in February 1962: "I have a big Shell map of Nigeria on my wall, with a tack in for everyone. It does me good to realize that I'm not alone in what seems sometimes to be a thankless and hopeless job. I get a psychological boost from viewing our work here as the sum of the efforts of all of us, and this can be extended to the international level."

Chapter Six

1. Monro adopted the "over the top" analogy, using it to describe the difficulties blacks faced in a white-dominated culture; he also likened the task to shouldering a heavy sack of rocks.

2. King's realization that the potential for tragedy was a valuable source of publicity further distinguished him from the cautious leaders of the earlier boycott. News editors ordered reporters: "Go where the Mahatma goes. He might get killed" (McWhorter 308).

3. Shores, an attorney, was a popular target, since he defended many of the blacks jailed for their involvement in demonstrations as well as for various trumped-up charges; this was the second time his house had been bombed (McWhorter 499).

4. The 1963–64 skirmish in the parietals battle ended in a draw: the policy remained unchanged, and there was no noticeable increase in enforcement. By 1970 parietals had been abolished completely (Bliss).

5. Epps dedicated his book, *The Speeches of Malcolm X,* to Monro and became dean of students in 1971. He held that position until 1999, when he retired after double bypass surgery and a kidney transplant. He looked alarmingly frail at Monro's memorial service in October 2002, and he died the following year, at the age of sixty-six (Flint).

6. Potential Head Start hosts in metropolitan Birmingham, with the exception of the local Unitarian church, backed down when they learned that the program would be integrated (LaMonte, interview, 23 July 2003).

Chapter Seven

1. The bungalow had been built by Willie "Cat" Mays Sr., Willie's father, in the early 1940s, and when Cat moved to Detroit to take a lucrative job, Willie and his two aunts moved in. He loved watching the Miles football games from the top of a nearby tree, but his aunt put a stop to the practice after he dozed off and fell thirty feet, breaking his throwing arm in the process (Hirsh 25–26).

2. Pitts needed much more than an assistant to whittle his job down to a manageable size. In the absence of a financial aid officer, a registrar, a director of admissions, a dean of students, and an administrative vice president, the college revolved almost wholly around one powerful but overtaxed man (Burke).

3. Barney Frank served as U.S. representative from the Fourth Congressional District of Massachusetts for sixteen consecutive terms, from 1981 to 2013. He was chair of the House Committee on Financial Services from January 2007 to January 2011 and was its ranking member during the following term.

4. Identifying with the Harvard students became increasingly difficult as Monro learned about the Miles students and their complicated lives. By the time George Cook was elected president of his junior class, for example, he was a pastor with his own church, a married man with a family, and a night shift worker at a funeral parlor (Townsend, "Teaching" 14).

5. Monro would have been gratified by the comparison to Thoreau, one of his favorite authors, whose style he likened to an acorn: "compact, polished, and with surprising potential" (Craig Comstock email, 3 Nov. 2005).

6. A projection of only ten more active years might appear pessimistic for a man whose grandfather had survived into his eighties, but both Monro's and Dottie's fathers had died in their fifties, one of cancer and one of a heart attack.

Chapter Eight

1. Don Nickerson, one of Monro's section men at Harvard, observed that Monro taught writing "as a craft that could be learned through patience, practice and hard work. . . . Sometimes he almost seemed to be teaching carpentry; the joining together of words and sentences as carefully as a great cabinetmaker" (e-mail, 12 Jan. 2010).

2. In 1986 Woolfolk joined the task force planning the Birmingham Civil Rights Institute. She served as president of the institute's board until 1998, when she was made president emeritus. Today a gallery at the institute bears her name (Kemp).

3. Gates, who converted to the Baha'i faith shortly after Monro's arrival, left Miles in 1982 and moved to Liberia with her sister, Henrietta, who was also a teacher and a Baha'i convert. Betty died there on 8 May 1990 (Robert Dahl, e-mail, 15 Apr. 2008).

4. While she was still studying at Wellesley, Deptula discovered that she had Parkinson's disease, but she continued to work for another fifteen years, eventually becoming administrative officer of Harvard's East Asian Research Center, Council on East Asian Studies, and Edwin O. Reischauer Institute of Japanese Studies. Like Monro, she retired very reluctantly and only after her illness made

it unsafe for her to ride her bike to work. She succumbed to cancer and Parkinson's on 6 Feb. 2002, predeceasing him by less than two months.

5. Shane completed her nursing studies at UMass Amherst and worked as a nurse for thirteen years before returning to her art. Today she gives workshops for fellow artists and exhibits her work in galleries in Andover and Lawrence as well as in Maine.

6. Townsend is now professor emeritus of English at Amherst and is writing a study of John William Ward, Amherst's president from 1972 to 1979.

7. Apparently, these tactile experiences were extremely potent. Phillips Brooks House member Jack Fitzgerald described a similar moment with a grade school child during a field trip, and Richard Parker, an exchange student from Dartmouth who became romantically involved with a black student, recalls "being struck by the feel of the girl's hair, its wiriness when I ran my fingers through it, and marveling—sometimes with a sense of disembodiedness—as I looked close up at the color of our skin pressed against each other" (e-mail, 19 Oct. 2007).

8. Later that summer Williams replaced Dale with his own choice for dean, Alandus C. Johnson.

9. On 25 Feb. 1974, less than three years into his presidency at Paine, Pitts died, felled by the final heart attack his friends and family had been dreading for years ("Lucius Pitts").

Chapter Nine

1. Although Bundy and Monro had worked smoothly together at Harvard, they had not been especially close. Monro characterized Bundy as "a perfect subordinate, because he had few firm convictions of his own but was articulate enough to justify absolutely any position" (Autrey, e-mail, 6 Aug. 2010), and Bundy once prevented Monro from speaking up at a meeting, stating, "That's okay, John, we all know what you're going to say" (Shinagel, interview).

2. Commencement took place at Hill Auditorium (Rachel Dreyer, e-mail, 13 Oct. 2008), a short distance from the Michigan Union, where presidential candidate John F. Kennedy had first proposed the concept that eventually became the Peace Corps.

3. By designating World War II as the end of an era, Monro could continue to take pride in his military career while criticizing the Vietnam War.

4. In addition to his athletic achievements, Mays was recognized by his teammates as a peacemaker on and off the diamond. On one occasion he broke up a fistfight between two players, and on another he headed off violence when a reporter bridled at a manager's racially insensitive remark. In 1968 he lent his star quality to Miles, heading a $2.5 million national fund-raising campaign to pay for a badly needed athletic center ("Willie Mays to Head Fund Drive").

5. In 1980 Clemon became Alabama's first black federal judge; he served as chief judge of the Northern District of Alabama until 2006 (Fair).

6. Fancher graduated from Miles Law School in 1983 and has been a Jefferson County district court judge since 1997 (telephone interview, 24 Apr. 2008.).

7. At the end of his career Monro still had fond feelings for UAB, telling interviewer Jessica Brooks that if he had been offered a position at UAB, he would have accepted it (Brooks).

8. Neither Royster nor Rutledge replied to letters and phone calls asking about the column, so I

was unable to learn whether Royster's statement had been written or spoken elsewhere or whether she prepared it specifically for Rutledge's column.

Chapter Ten

1. The probability that Beittel's failing health necessitated his resignation is highly unlikely, since he lived to be almost one hundred and at the age of ninety-nine participated cogently in an oral history interview at his home in Marin County, California (Johnson, Clifton).

2. The person he talked to was Hotchkiss, executive secretary of the organization, who wrote Beittel an angry letter contradicting his version of their encounter and accusing him of endangering the partnership with Brown.

3. In spite of his frugal personal habits, Monro was openhanded with friends and family. In 1934, when he knew he would have to come up with an additional semester of tuition at Harvard, he lent two hundred dollars to his friend John Spencer, who had still not repaid it two years later (Spencer letter). He lent the same amount to Tom O'Connor so that he could pursue a writing career in glamorous Los Angeles, while Monro postponed his own ambitions and remained in Cambridge. In addition to cosigning a loan for Betty Gates, he loaned money to several colleagues at Miles and Tougaloo, and he helped Phil and Janet with the down payment on a farm near the South Freeport cottage (Dreyer, interview, 3 Aug. 2005).

4. All sources in this section are from the Tougaloo College Archives.

Chapter Eleven

1. Ward is currently professor of English and African World Studies at Dillard University and recently coedited, with Maryemma Graham, *The Cambridge History of African American Literature*.

2. Clearly, Monro missed the now-defunct Basic Studies policy of giving a nonpunitive NG—for "no grade"—to a student who had not succeeded in meeting the course criteria, instead of putting a failing grade on his or her record.

3. One welcome addition to the group was Peter Gomes, who had returned from Tuskegee in 1970 and served as chaplain since 1974.

4. Monro meticulously revised the interview transcription, reserving the right to check and/or edit any passages directly quoted for publication. Because it is no longer possible to honor this request, I have paraphrased when possible and quoted only from the version he revised.

5. Small wonder Monro liked the direction the Extension School was taking, since Shinagel had resolved to become "an activist dean" in the Monro mold. Under his watch the program has become more accessible and comprehensive than ever: there are more scholarships and graduate programs available; the Tuition Assistance Plan (TAP) provides study and degree opportunities to Harvard staff (Shinagel 122); and custom-designed courses address specific local needs, such as Advanced Placement equivalency courses for students whose cash-strapped high schools have had to discontinue their own AP courses (interview).

6. Today Harvard's leadership team boasts an impressive number of minority members in ad-

dition to Poussaint; they include Henry Louis Gates Jr., director of the W.E.B. Du Bois Institute for African and African American Research; Evelynn Hammonds, who holds Monro's former position as dean of the college; Professor Emeritus of Government Martin Kilson; and Professor Emeritus of Music Rulan Pian, the college's first minority housemaster; Archaeology Professor Emeritus Stanley Tambiah; Divinity School Professor Emeritus Preston Williams; and Education Professor Emeritus Charles V. Willie ("Harvard Foundation Unveils Portraits" 13). Sadly, Peter Gomes, minister and Plummer Professor of Christian morals, arguably Harvard's best-known black leader, died on 28 February 2011 of complications from a stroke.

7. Monro confided to Rose Davis that he regretted depriving Dottie of the friends she had made in Birmingham (Marshall, interview, 8 Mar. 2009), and he wrote to John Merrifield, "I put my wife and children through a lot then [during the war], and again in the move to Birmingham, and again (1978) in the move to Mississippi" (1992). Ed LaMonte believes that the rewards Monro found at Miles came at Dottie's expense (interview, 22 July 2003), and Mike Shinagel, who admired Monro's accomplishments, sympathized with his family, pointing out, "It's not easy to be Mrs. Gandhi" (interview, 26 Oct. 2004).

Chapter Twelve

1. Monro was an avid patron of secondhand bookstores, telling a reporter that with the exception of colleges, they were the best institutions in the country ("Teachers in Action").

2. As the contents of his library show, Monro's reading tastes were highly eclectic, despite his professed preference for a concise, direct style. Of the four books he claimed to reread in constant rotation—*Don Quixote, The Grapes of Wrath, Moby-Dick,* and *War and Peace*—only the Steinbeck could be considered concise or direct, and one of his favorite black writers, W.E.B. Du Bois, wrote in a highly wrought, complex style (Hoehler).

3. Monro was an enthusiastic if amateur pianist for most of his life. Even before he took to blowing off steam at the Smith House piano as a Harvard freshman, he played well enough to criticize a mediocre performance he heard during his first trip to South Freeport, noting sarcastically that the pianist could play between the keys as well as on them (Journal). He was always eager to explain the Circle of Fifths, a circular-shaped visual demonstration of chord patterns that he said he had picked up either in a Chicago jazz club or from a shipmate on the *Enterprise* (Dreyer eulogy). After he learned that Claxton's wife, Vicki, also played the piano, he joined her at the keyboard for wild jazz duets, and for the Dreyers' first Christmas in California he sent a check so that they could buy a secondhand piano.

Epilogue

1. Although Coit was careful to use the correct clan plaid for Monro's tie, nitpickers point out that the portrait shows him wearing a white shirt, whereas he wore blue shirts so habitually that friends accused him of owning only one shirt.

Bibliography

E-mails, unless otherwise indicated, are to the author from the person mentioned in the source. Personal and telephone interviews, unless otherwise indicated, are between the author and the person mentioned in the source.

Academic Preparation for College: What Students Need to Know and Be Able to Do. New York: College Board, 1983.

ACS Minutes. 4 Apr. 1988. MSA, box 8.

"An Act of Involvement." *Time,* 17 Mar. 1967, 60.

Afro-American Materials Center. Miles College, n.d. MCA.

Albert, Frank. *From the Prairies of Chicago: USS* Enterprise *(CV-6): The Most Decorated Ship of World War II.* Chicago: Frank Albert: 1995.

Allis, F. S. *Youth from Every Quarter: A Bicentennial History of Phillips Academy, Andover.* Hanover, NH: Phillips Academy, 1979.

Andover City Directory. Andover, MA, 1929.

"Andover Man Tells How Seabees Saved Carrier." *Lawrence Evening Tribune,* 24 Jan. 1945. PAA.

Ashabranner, Brent. *A Moment in History: The First Ten Years of the Peace Corps.* New York: Doubleday, 1971.

Aubry, John. "Oral History Interview with John Monro." Transcription, with handwritten revisions by Monro. Jackson, MS, 26 July 1989. College Entrance Examination Board, NY.

Autrey, Ken. "John Monro and the Tougaloo College Writing Center." Paper presented at the Conference on College Composition and Communication. San Francisco, 17 Mar. 2005.

"Award Honorary Scholarships to 109 Students in First Group of Rank List." *HC,* 14 Dec. 1932, 4.

"Awards Honor 'Turning Moral Conviction into Positive Action.'" *Harvard Foundation Newsletter* (Spring 1993): 2–4.

"Awards and Contributions." *Miles College Vanguard* (Sept. 1974): 1. MCA.

Bailey, Sarah Loring. *Historical Sketches of Andover (Comprising the Present Towns of North Andover and Andover).* 1880. Reprint. Andover: Andover Historical Society, 1990.

Baker, Russell. "Observer: The Prodigal Generation." *NYT,* 14 Feb. 1965, E8.

Ballard, Frederic L., Jr. "Dean Stresses Large Role of Peace Corps." *HC,* 2 Oct. 1961, 1.

———. "Monro Avoids Prediction on Peace Corps." *HC,* 17 Oct. 1961, 1.

"Band, Red Carpet Welcome Dr. Pitts Home." *Birmingham News,* 5 Dec. 1969. UAB Archives.

Banks, A. R. "A Cruise to Remember." *USS* Enterprise *CV-6 Bulletin* (Spring 2004): 10–11.

Barter, J. Malcolm. "'Handyman' Opens Harvard Center for Needy Students." *Boston Globe,* 1 Mar. 1950, 1+.

Barry, William David, and Bruce Kennett. "The World According to Foster." *Down East* (Mar. 1989): 50–53.

"Behind the Harvard Ivy—Sex." *Boston Herald Tribune,* 1 Nov. 1963, 1+.

"Big 'E' Carrier Wins Fightingest Title." *NYT,* 28 Aug. 1945, 4.

"'Big E' Docks at Boston to Be Converted." *Christian Science Monitor,* 1 Nov. 1945, 1.

Blake, Herman. Memo to Blake, 18 Feb. 1985. MSA, box 3.

Bliss, Katherine E. "The Harvard Sex Scandal That Shook the Nation." *HC,* 5 June 1989, B3.

"The Boat Rockers." *Newsweek,* 22 May 1967. Reprint. MCA.

Bok, Derek. Letter to Richard Johnson, 25 July 1988. TCA.

Bramson, Leon. Report on Training—First Phase, Harvard-Nigeria Peace Corps Program. HUA: UAV, 609.

Brelis, Dean. "Ex-Student Monro Lands New Job." *Boston Globe,* 12 Jan. 1959, 10.

———. "Monro Loaned Millions to Needy Students." *Boston Globe,* 11 Jan. 1959, 44.

Brock-Shedd, Virgia. "Special Collections Area in Coleman Library." *Tougaloo News* (Feb. 1980). TCA.

Brooks, Jessica. Interview with John Monro, 22 and 24 June 1993. Jessica Brooks Papers, MS-1ZUT-1, BUA.

Brown, Hamish M. *Hamish's Mountain Walk: The First Traverse of All the Scottish Munros in One Journey.* London: Victor Gollancz, 1978.

Brown-Tougaloo Exchange Website, www.stg.brown.edu/projects/FreedomNow.

Bunting, Chuck. *Collected Thoughts on Teaching Freshman English at Miles—Sometimes Collected from Others.* Report. Miles College, 22 Aug. 1966. TCA.

Burke, Dustin. Letter to Lucius Pitts, 23 Feb. 1966. Provided to the author by Burke.

"Calendar." *Miles Alumni Bulletin* (May 1964): 3.

"Camp Abnaki." *Vermont Association Notes.* State Committee of YMCAs of Vermont, various dates.

Campbell, Clarice T., and Oscar Allen Rogers. *Mississippi: The View from Tougaloo.* Jackson: University of Mississippi Press, 2002.

"Cecil J. Roberts, 76, Alabama Arts Patron." *NYT,* 30 May 1990, B20.

"CEP May Make Change in First-Year Program." *HC,* 18 Apr. 1959, 1.

Chisum, James. "At Miles College, a Mere Lack of Knowledge Is No Bar." *Southern Education Report* (May 1967): 14–19.

"Church Union Commission Assembles at Miles." *Miles College Vanguard* (Sept. 1974): n.p. MCA.

Clan Munro Website, www.clanmunro.org.uk.

Clark, Blair. Letter to John U. Monro, 1 Sept. 1939. DP.

———. Letter to John U. Monro, 9 Apr. 1927. DP.

Class Album: 1934. Cambridge, MA: Harvard University, 1934. HUA: HUD334 04 RR.

Class of 1906: 20th Anniversary Report. Cambridge, MA: Harvard University, 1926. HUA: HUD306 20B RR.

Class of 1906: 30th Anniversary Report. Cambridge, MA: Harvard University, 1936. HUA: HUD306 20B RR.

Class of 1906: Secretary's Second Report. Cambridge, MA: Harvard University, 1912. HUA: HUD306 10B RR.

Class of 1906: Secretary's Third Report. Cambridge, MA: Harvard University, 1916. HUA: HUD306 10B RR.

Class of 1934: 25th Anniversary Report. Cambridge, MA: Harvard University, 1959. HUA: HUD334 25B RR.

Cobb, Charles E., Jr. "Trail Blazes with Symbols of Struggle." *Boston Globe,* 1 June 2008, M1+.

"College Receives $100,000 Anonymous Gift to Establish Philosophy, Religion Chair." *Tougaloo News* (Feb. 1967): 1. TCA.

College Scholarship Service: Celebrating Fifty Years of Excellence, 1954–2004. New York: College Board, 2004.

Conley, B. M. "Paine 'Golden Decade' Looms." *Augusta Chronicle* (Apr. 1973): 1C+. PCCCLA.

Cooper, Donald E. "Alliance for Opportunity." *Encore* (Nov. 1973): n.p.

"Councilors and Tutors." *Time,* 14 Dec. 1936, www.time.com.

Counter, Allen S. "In Memoriam: John U. Monro '35." *Harvard Foundation Newsletter* (Spring 2002): 34.

Crabtree, Shane. Diary, 1970–71.

———. Personal interview. 8 July 2003.

"Crossroads Head Tells Anecdotes." *HC,* 16 Nov. 1961, 1.

"The Crucible Handout." Miles College, 1966–67. Provided by Prill Ellis.

Cunnigen, Donald. "The Legacy of Ernst Borinski." *Teaching Sociology* 31 (2003): 397–411.

Currivan, Gene. "Colleges' Social Bias Bars Able Entrants, Panel Says." *NYT,* 26 June 1960, 1.

Darlington, Elizabeth. Letters to John U. Monro, 7 June and 27 Aug. 1980. MSA, box 2.

"David Roberts III '36." *Princeton Alumni Weekly,* 27 Sept. 2006. MCA.

"Dean Brelis, 82: Foreign Correspondent Also Wrote Nonfiction, Novels." *Los Angeles Times,* 22 Nov. 2006.

"Dean Monro." *HC,* 10 Mar. 1967, 2.

"Dean Monro: Position Doesn't Mean Anything." *Boston Globe,* 10 Mar. 1967, 21.

"Dean Monro's Enormous Reward." *Nation,* 27 Mar. 1967, 389.

Death Register of the Town of Andover. Claxton Monro, Item no. 57, 14 May 1936, 13.

Delaney, Paul. "Private Black Colleges in Fight to Survive." *NYT,* 4 Dec. 1971, 20.

DeVoto, Bernard. Handwritten comments on undated class assignment. DP.

Dickerson, Joseph. Oral history. Civil Rights Institute, Birmingham, AL.

Dittmer, John. *Local People: The Struggle for Civil Rights in Mississippi.* Urbana: University of Illinois Press, 1994.

"Doing Something Relevant." *Newsweek,* 19 Feb. 1968, 86.

Donovan, Robert J. "From Harvard to Alabama; Back 50 Years in Time." *San Francisco Examiner and Chronicle,* 9 Jan 1972. Reprint. MCA.

"Draft Sets Dates of Student Tests." *NYT,* 26 Feb. 1966, 1.

Dreyer, Philip. *The American Woolen Company: A Case Study in New England Economic History.* Cambridge, MA: Harvard University, 29 Mar. 1963. HUA: HU02 63.336.

Dreyer, Philip, and Janet Dreyer. "Eulogy for John Usher Monro." Memorial Church, Cambridge, MA, 6 Oct. 2002.

———. "Eulogy for John Usher Monro." South Freeport Church, 13 Aug. 2002.

"Dr. Alandus Johnson Named Dean at Miles." *Birmingham Post-Herald,* 26 Nov. 1971. MCA.

"Dr. B. H. Royster Returns to Miles with PhD." *Birmingham Post-Herald,* 1976. MCA.

"Dr. Ben Bailey: 27 Years of Service at Tougaloo College." *Tougaloo News* (Spring 1992): 3.

"Dr. John Monro." *What's New at Miles* (June 1975): 1. MCA.

"Dr. Wayman Shiver Jr. to Direct Miles College Services to Enhance Education Potential." Miles College News Release. News Releases, 1969–70. MCA.

"Drug Case Is Stated." *New Hampshire Sentinel,* 8 Aug. 1967.

Dreyfuss, Joel. "Ethnic Studies: A Springboard, Not a Trap." *Change* (Oct. 1979): 13–15.

Dukes, Frank. Oral History. Civil Rights Institute, Birmingham, AL.

Durgin, Larry. "Oaks, Eagles, the Good Shepherd and the Challenge Today." Tougaloo College, 12 Oct. 1980. TCA, Office of the President Records.

"Education: End of an Era." *Time,* 6 Aug. 1956. Reprint. MCA.

Egerton, John. "Lucius H. Pitts and U. W. Clemon." *A Mind to Stay Here,* 107–27. New York: Macmillan, 1970.

Ellis, Priscilla. Letter to Ed LaMonte, 16 Sept. 1965.

Epps, Archie. "Comments." Memorial Service for John U. Monro. Harvard Memorial Church, 6 Oct. 2002.

Eskew, Glenn T. *But for Birmingham: The Local and National Movements in the Civil Rights Struggle.* Chapel Hill: University of North Carolina Press, 1997.

Esters, Stephanie D. "Hello Beautiful." *Harmabee,* 6 Apr. 1984, 6. TCA.

"Eutaw College Still without Students, Still Draws Track Money." *Birmingham News,* 12 Aug. 1991, 1B+.

Ewing, Steve. *USS* Enterprise *(CV-6): The Most Decorated Ship of World War II: A Pictorial History.* Missoula, MT: Pictorial Histories Publishing Co., 1987.

Executive Session Minutes, Tougaloo Board of Trustees. 16 Jan. and 24 Apr. 1964. TCA.

External Evaluation Report. Tougaloo College, 1987. MSA, box 2.

Fair, Bryan K. "U. W. Clemon." *Encyclopedia of Alabama* Website, www.encyclopediaofala bama.org/face/Article.jsp?id=h-1633, 11 Aug. 2008.

Fenton, John H. "Harvard Drops Peace Corps Task." *NYT,* 30 Oct. 1962, 6.

———. "Harvard Men Send McNamara Apology." *NYT,* 11 Nov. 1966, 1+.

———. "Marijuana Users Disturb Harvard." *NYT,* 11 Feb. 1965, 31.

———. "Ousted Educator Rebuts Harvard." *NYT,* 29 May 1962, 13.

———. "Students Set Up Weekly in South." *NYT,* 2 May 1965, 54.

Ferede, Martha. "Moving into the Semi-Colon: Influences and Contributions of Financial Aid Pioneer John Usher Monro." Final paper. Harvard University, 19 May 2009.

Ferrell, John D. "The Birmingham Experiment." *AFL-CIO American Federationist* (Nov. 1964): n.p.

First Congregational Church Group. Interview with Rev. Rodney Franklin, June and J. Mason Davis, Corrine Moseley Coleman, and Helen M. Lewis, 20 June 2003.

"First Faculty Meeting Focuses on Afro-American Studies Program at Miles." *Miles Ahead,* 14 Oct. 1968, 1–3. MCA.

Fitzgerald, Jack. *Some Thoughts after a Summer at Miles College, Birmingham, Alabama.* HUA: UAV688.5.13.

Flint, Anthony. "Harvard's Archie Epps Is Dead at 66." *Boston Globe,* 23 Aug. 2003, 1+.

Foley, Michael. "Mary Ramsdell, Pioneer among Woman, Dies." *Lawrence Eagle-Tribune,* 16 Aug. 1986, 1+.

"Former Official Removed by Death." *Andover Townsman,* 15 May 1936, 1.

Foster, William Harnden. *New England Grouse Shooting.* New York: Scribners, 1942.

Fouquet, Douglas M. "College Moves to Integrate Machinery for Financial Aid." *Harvard Crimson,* 24 Feb. 1950.

"Frances Monro." *Andover Townsman,* 19 Feb. 1976, 19.

Frank, Murray. "Murray Frank Remembers." *Friends of Nigeria Newsletter* (Fall 1999): n.p.

Franklin, Jimmie Lewis. *Back to Birmingham: Richard Arrington Jr. and His Times.* Tuscaloosa: University of Alabama Press, 1989.

French, Robert W. Letter to Promode Patnaik, 6 June 1977. UABA, Collection 1.3.2, folder 8.34.

———. Memos to S. Richardson Hill, 31 Jan. 1972 and 11 and 19 Feb. 1977. UABA. Collection 1.3.2, folder 23.30

Friedman, Neil. "1968: Why I Left the South." *Kindred Spirits: Essays in Race, Politics, and Psychology, 1960–2002*, 151–66. N.p.: Xlibris, 2002.

———. "The Miles College Freshman Social Science Program: Educational Innovation in a Negro College." *Journal of Negro Education* 4 (1969): 361–69.

Friedman, Thomas. "Farewell to Geronimo." *NYT*, 4 May 2011, A23.

Frost, George B. "In Memoriam." *Andover Townsman*, 6 Apr. 1939, 3.

Fuchs, Gil. "The Dean of Harvard Goes South." *Boston Globe Parade*, 30 Nov. 1969, 20–22.

"Fuess Award to Monro, Watts." *Andover Bulletin* (July 1982): 1+.

Fuess, Claude M., ed. *The Story of Essex County.* 4 vols. New York: American Historical Society, 1935.

Galbraith, John Kenneth. Letter to the Editor. *HC*, 2 Nov. 1963, 3.

Gewertz, Ken. "Champion of Disadvantaged, Monro, Dies at 89." *Harvard Gazette*, 11 Apr. 2002, 14.

Glassman, James K. "Deans Attempt to Discourage Drug Use; Doctor Reveals More LSD Side-Effects." *HC*, 30 Mar. 1967, 1.

———. "Use of Drugs in Yard Is Increasing; Administration, UHS Show Concern." *HC*, 29 Mar. 1967, 1.

Gomes, Peter. "Remarks." Memorial Service for John U. Monro. Harvard Memorial Church, 6 Oct. 2002.

Goodwin, Doris Kearns. *No Ordinary Time: Franklin and Eleanor Roosevelt: The Home Front in World War II.* New York: Simon and Schuster, 1994.

Gordon, Ronnie. "Teacher Helps Students Find Their Inner Voices." *Springfield Union News*, 6 Dec. 2002, E3–4.

Gove, Ruth Voutselas. "The Value of Telling John Usher Monro's Story." MS, 15 Mar. 2010.

"Great Revolutionary Effort Needed to Save Nation." *Stanford Observer Commencement Issue* (June 1973): 1+.

Greenhouse, Linda. "The Reincarnation of John Monro." *New York Times Magazine*, 15 Mar. 1970, 53+.

Grunsfeld, Mary Jane, and Jack L. Ellison. "The Sarah Greenebaum Distinguished Visitors." In *Between Home and Community: Chronicle of the Francis W. Parker School, 1901–1976*. Ed. Marie Kirchner Stone, 290–303. Chicago: Francis W. Parker School, 1976.

Hamlin, Arthur Tenney. *John Usher Monro as a Harvard Undergraduate.* 28 Dec. 1964. HUA: HUG 4575.36.

Hanford, George H. "Comments." Memorial Service for John U. Monro. Harvard Memorial Church, 6 Oct. 2002.

———. *Life with the SAT: Assessing Our Young People and Our Times.* New York: CEEB, 1991.

———. *Minority Programs and Activities of the College Board: An Updated Report.* New York: College Entrance Examination Board, 1982.

"Harvard Apology Sent to McNamara in Student Protest." *NYT*, 9 Nov. 1966, 3.

Harvard Crimson Comment Book, News Board, 1934–35. HUA: HUD3304 714.

The Harvard Crimson: *Seventy-Fifth Anniversary, 1873–1948.* Cambridge: Harvard Crimson, 1948.

Harvard Journal. 1934. HUA: HUK 468FB.

"*Harvard Crimson* Faces Opposition." *Boston Globe*, 29 Mar. 1934, 25.

"Harvard Dean Clarifies Student Deferment Stand." *NYT*, 19 Mar. 1966, 25.

"Harvard Foundation Unveils Portraits." *Harvard University Gazette*, 12 May 2005, 13–14.

Harvard Foundation Website, www.harvardfoundation.fas.harvard.edu.

"Harvard Hired Men on Vermont Farms Test New Theory of U.S. Youth Camps." *Boston Evening Transcript*, 23 Nov. 1939, 1+.

Harvard Journal, 9 Apr.–4 June 1930. HUA:HUK468F A.

Harvard/Radcliffe Class Day, 1991. Videocassette.

"Harvard Square 'Riot' Fizzles Out." *Boston Herald*, 14 May 1964, 36.

Harvard Student Agencies Website, www.hsa.net.

"Harvard Students: It Ain't So!" *Boston Herald Tribune*, 2 Nov. 1963. Reprint. DP

"Harvard Taps 14 for Honors." *Boston Globe* (Evening ed.), 15 June 1967, 1+.

Hechinger, Fred M. "Dean Quits Harvard to Aid Negro College." *NYT*, 10 Mar. 1967, 1+.

———. "Drug Issue." *NYT*, 28 Feb. 1965, E7.

———. "On the Ailing Negro College." *NYT*, 19 Mar. 1967, E9.

———. "'Should I Throw in the Towel?'" *NYT*, 20 June 1971, E9.

———. "Use of 'Mind-Distorting' Drugs Rising at Harvard, Dean Says." *NYT*, 11 Dec. 1962, 1+.

Hicks, Nancy. "Miles College President to Return to Alma Mater." *NYT*, 24 Dec. 1970, 41.

Hirsh, James S. *Willie Mays: The Life, the Legend.* New York: Scribners, 2010.

Hogan, Ben. "Dean John Monro of Miles College Sees New Trend in Race Relations." *Birmingham News*, 4 Feb. 1968. Reprint. MCA.

Hood, Gilbert. Letter to John Monro, 26 Dec. 1978. MSA, box 3.

Illuminator. Miles College (Dec. 1969). MCA.

"Inauguration of President Owens." *Tougaloo News* (Apr. 1966): 5.

"In the Right Direction." *Christian Science Monitor* 13 Mar. 1967. DSCTCWL.

Ireland, Corey. "Portrait of Former Dean of the College Fred L. Jewett Is Unveiled." *Harvard University Gazette*, 1–7 Feb. 2007, 15–16.

Iseman, Joseph. *Journal of the Crimson Schism, 6 Apr. 1934.*

Jackson, Emory O. "Ms. Rutledge, Alabama Born Poet, Making Good." *Birmingham World*, 28 Dec. 1974. MCA.

Jan, Tracy. "He's Redefining Acceptance at Harvard." *Boston Globe*, 1 Dec. 2009, A1+.

Jencks, Christopher, and David Riesman. "The American Negro College." *Harvard Educational Review* 37 (1967): 3–60.

John Howland Society Website, www.pilgrimjohnhowlandsociety.org.

Johnson, Clifton H. Interview of A. D. Beittel. Marin County, CA, 1987. Amistad Research Center.

Johnson, Richard. Letter to Adib Shakir, 6 Apr.1988. TCA.

Jones, Boisfeuillet, Jr. "Goldberg to Face 'Panel,' SDS Asserts." *HC,* 9 Feb. 1967, 1+.

———. "Miles College: Non-Accredited School Struggling for Pride, Respectability." *HC,* 10 Mar. 1967, 1+.

———. "Monro to Resign July 1 as Dean of College; Glimp Will Be Recommended as Successor." *Harvard Crimson,* 10 Mar. 1967, 1+.

Kahn, E. J., Jr. "A Whale of a Difference." *New Yorker,* 10 Apr. 1971, 43+.

Karabel, Jerome. *The Chosen: The Hidden History of Admission and Exclusion at Harvard, Yale, and Princeton.* New York: Houghton Mifflin, 2005.

Katagiri, Yasuhiro. *The Mississippi State Sovereignty Commission: Civil Rights and States' Rights.* Jackson: University Press of Mississippi, 2001.

Keeney, Barnaby. Letter to John U. Monro, 4 June 1964. BUA.

Keller, Morton, and Phyllis Keller. *Making Harvard Modern: The Rise of America's University.* New York: Oxford University Press, 2001.

Kemp, Kathy. "Celebrating Odessa." *Birmingham News,* 14 Nov. 1999, E1.

Kemper, John. Letter to Boys Club, 15 Dec. 1960. PAA.

King, Martin Luther, Jr. *Why We Can't Wait.* New York: Signet, 1964.

King, Richard G. "The Educational Function of Financial Aid." *College Board Review* (Spring 1955): 9–13.

"Lady Encore." *Encore* (Nov. 1973): n.p. TCA.

LaMonte, Edward S. *Report on the Seminars in American History Held during the Summer of 1964.* HUA: UAV688.5.13.

Lawless, Greg, ed. *The Harvard Crimson: An Anthology: 100 Years at Harvard.* Boston: Houghton Mifflin 1980.

Lawrence, William. Letter to George E. Kunhardt, 26 Sept. 1919.

Learning and Teaching Website, www.learningandteaching.info/learning/piaget.htm.

"Leary and Alpert Attack Monro Stand on Drugs." *HC,* 11 Dec. 1962, 1.

A Light in the Shadows. Fairfield, AL: Miles College, 1966.

"Lila Sutton Scoville" *NYT,* 7 May 1945, 17.

Locke, Alan. "Girls' Visits to Continue at Harvard." *Boston Herald,* 31 Oct. 1963, 1+.

Long, Tom. "John Monro; Ideals Led Dean from Harvard to Alabama Classroom." *Boston Globe,* 4 Apr. 2001, B9.

Lottman, Michael S. "Dean Monro Reports on Progress of Arrangements for Peace Corps. *HC,* 20 Apr. 1961, 1.

Lowe, Maria R. "An Unseen Hand: The Role of Sociology Professor Ernst Borinski in Mississippi's Struggle for Racial Integration in the 1950s and 1960s." *Leadership* (Feb. 2008): 27–47.

"Lucius Pitts, Educator, Is Dead; President of Paine College, 59." *NYT*, 27 Feb. 1974, 42.

MacGregor, Mary (Monro). *A Brief History of the Rev. Claxton Monro.* 1 Apr. 2006.

Maeroff, Gene I. "Ex-Harvard Dean Quits Black College Post." 7 May 1978, 26.

Mahoney, Frank. "Dean Doubts 25% Use 'Pot' at Harvard." *Boston Globe*, 29 Mar. 1967, 16.

"The Man from Harvard." *Newsweek*, 24 Sept. 1973, 88.

Martin, Douglas. "Archie Epps, 66, Unusual Dean and Administrator at Harvard." *NYT*, 23 Aug. 2003, B16.

Martin, Jim. Letter to Arnie and Peg Olson, n.d.

Matejyzyk, Anthony. "Police Dogs Fuel Harvard Melee." *Boston Herald*, 8 May 1964, 1+.

McCabe, Aloysius, "Faculty Profile." *HC*, 8 Mar. 1949, 2.

McCahill, Barbara K. "A Note from the Parish Historian." *Apostle* (May 2006).

———. "St. Paul's Church, North Andover." In *The Episcopal Diocese of Massachusetts, 1784–1984: A Mission to Remember, Proclaim and Fulfill.* Ed. M. J. Duffy, 498–501. Boston: Episcopal Diocese of Massachusetts, 1984.

McClung, Merle. "Miles College: A Chance for Birmingham's Black Student?" *American Oxonian* 2 (1970): 349–54.

McDonald, Sheila, "Mission Involvement Offers Range of Educational Experiences." *Harambee* 4 May 1990, 1. TCA.

McDougall, Harold A. "AAAAS: Negro Students Test Liberalism." *HC*, 16 June 1967, 10.

McLaughlin, Loretta, and Harold Banks. "Harvard Dean Reveals 'Shocking' Dorm Parties." *Boston Record American*, 1 Nov. 1963, 3+.

"McNamara Replies to Dean." *NYT*, 11 Nov. 1966, 8.

McVeigh, Linda G., and Richard Blumenthal. "McNamara Sees Lottery as a Way to End Present Draft Injustices." *HC*, 19 Nov. 1966, 1.

McWhorter, Diane. *Carry Me Home: Birmingham, Alabama: The Climactic Battle of the Civil Rights Revolution.* New York: Simon and Schuster, 2001.

McWilliams, Tennan S. *New Lights in the Valley: The Emergence of UAB.* Tuscaloosa: University of Alabama Press, 2007.

Memorial Resolution for Sutton Monro. Lehigh University, 1 May 1995.

Merrifield, John. Letter to John Monro, 25 May 1992.

"Miles Alumnus to Serve as Dean, '70–'71." *Mirror* July 1970. MCA.

Miles Chapel Center Report. HUA: UAV688.5.13.

"Miles College-Eutaw Project." *What's New at Miles* 7 Mar. 1975. MCA.

"Miles College Opens Law School." *Miles College Alumni Bulletin* (Fall–Winter 1974): n.p. MCA.

Miles College–Phillips Brooks House Association Volunteer Teaching Project. HUA: UAV688.5.13.

Miles College: The First Hundred Years. Charleston, SC: Arcadia, 2005.

"Miles College Undergoing Major Reorganization." *Miles College Alumni Bulletin* (Fall 1976): n.p. MCA.

"Miles Eutaw Makes Impact in Black Belt." *Milean* Oct. 1978, 1+. MCA.

"Miles's Mileage." *Time,* 8 Nov. 1963, www.time.com/time/magazine/article/0,9171,
897040,00.html.

"Miles Receives $75,000 from Danforth Foundation." News Release Booklet, 3 May 1973.
MCA.

Mississippi Secondary School Mathematics Summer Institute 1990 Materials. Provided
by Sharon Streeter.

Monro, Claxton. Letters to John U. Monro, various dates. DP.

"Monro Deplores Narrow Coverage, Omission of Community Interests." *HC,* 30 Jan.
1948, 4M.

Monro, Edith. Letter to the Editor. *Bristol Phoenix,* 14 Apr. 1967. DP.

Monro, Frances. Letters to John U. Monro, various dates. DP.

"Monro-Foster." *Andover Townsman,* 24 July 1936, 2.

Monro, John U. "Albert Sloan Inauguration Speech." Birmingham, AL, 28 Mar. 1992. DP.

———. "The Black College Dilemma." University of Michigan Commencement Address,
19 Dec. 1971, BHLUM.

———. "The Case for Special Attention to Black Student Needs in Higher Education."
College Board Seminar. Denver, CO, 29 Apr. 1977 DP.

———. "The College as Agent for Social Change." In *New Directions for Higher Education:
Planning the Future of the Undergraduate College.* Ed. Donald G. Trites, 51–63. San
Francisco: Jossey-Bass, 1975.

———. "Comments on a Paper by W. Todd Furniss." American Council on Education
52nd Annual Meeting. Washington, DC, 9 Oct. 1969.

———. "Cranbrook Commencement Address." Bloomfield Hills, MI, 20 June 1962. Cranbrook Archives.

———. "Current and Emerging Roles of Black Colleges and Universities." N.d. DP.

———. "Escape from the Dark Cave." *Nation,* 27 Oct. 1969, 434–38.

———. Foreword. Monro, *Search for Talent,* v–viii.

———. "Francis W. Parker School Dedication Speech." Chicago, 20 May 1962. FWPSA.

———. "Francis W. Parker School 75th Anniversary Speech." Chicago, 23 Oct. 1976.
FWPSA.

———. "Gentlemen of 1970." *HC,* 19 Apr. 1967, 1.

———. "Grand Lodge Masters Speech." Boston, 11 Aug. 1960. DP.

———. "Harvard Official Says Drug Estimate Errs." *NYT,* 15 Mar. 1965, 30.

———. "Helping Him Pay His Way." *Harvard Alumni Bulletin,* 11 Feb. 1960, 378–81.

———. "Helping the Student Help Himself." *College Board Review,* May 1953, 351–57.

———. "How to Live with Paradox." *Harvard Alumni Bulletin,* 15 Oct. 1966, 13–14.

———. "Inauguration of Albert Sloan Speech. Birmingham, AL, 28 Mar. 1992. MCA,
box 4.

———. "Introduction to School Assembly." Miles College, 31 Aug. 1988. MSA, box 9.

———. Journal (unpublished). Summer 1930. DP.

———. "Journal to Open Competitions to '35, '36, '37 Today." *Harvard Journal*, 9 Apr. 1934, 1. HUA: HUK 468FB.

———. "Leighton Speech." Cambridge, MA, 1 Dec. 1958. HUA: John Monro, Speeches 1958–59.

———. Letters to Barbara Landis Chase, 26 Sept. 1994 and 26 Feb. 1997. PAA.

———. Letter to Barnaby Keeney, 31 Mar. 1964. BUA.

———. Letter to Ben Bailey, 25 Feb. 1991. MSA, box 8.

———. Letter to Edward S. LaMonte, 6 Jan. 1969. UABA: Record Group 3.3: Urban Studies Center.

———. Letter to Elizabeth Darlington, 1980. MSA, box 2.

———. Letters to George Owens, 17 June 1980 and 22 Apr. 1981. MSA, box 2.

———. Letter to Grant Miller, 12 Oct. 1991. MSA, box 9.

———. Letter to John Kemper, 14 Oct. 1967. PAA.

———. Letters to John Merrifield, 24 August 1967 and 18 July 1992. DP.

———. Letter to John William Ward, 8 Feb. 1973. ACA, J. W. Ward Presidential Papers.

———. Letters to Ken Autrey, 22 Sept. 1984 and 7 June 1985. Provided by Autrey.

———. Letter to Kim Townsend, 25 May 1979.

———. Letter to Louis Dale, 4 May 1971.

———. Letter to Leon Bramson, 25 Oct. 1961. HUA: UAV609.5.

———. Letter to McGeorge Bundy, 26 Apr. 1971. DP.

———. Letter to Robert Wilder, 18 May 1964. UABA.

———. Letter to Sharon Streeter, 14 Oct. 1991. DP.

———. Letter to Mrs. Wyffels, 15 Jan. 1943. Enterprise CV6 Association Public Affairs Files.

———. "Literacy in College: Problems and Solutions." Orthopsychiatric Association. Chicago, 11 Apr. 1986. Provided by Jerry Ward.

———. "Look Hard at History." Ramsay High School, Birmingham, AL, 14 Feb. 1973.

———. Memorandum. *Miles College in Pursuit of a Goal* (1967): 1.

———. "Men's Fraternal League Speech." Vermont, n.d. DP.

———. "Miles College Assembly Speech." Fairfield, AL, 28 Oct. 1987. DP.

———. "Moral Values in Education Speech." Harvard Club, New York, 16. Jan. 1964.

———. News Release, n.d. HUA: UAV605.438.

———. Nwachukwu Writing Center Log, TCA.

———. "The Negro and Education in America." The New School, New York, 27 Feb. 1968. DP.

———. "Negro Colleges—Their Outlook." *U.S. News and World Report*, 3 June 1968, 74–78.

———. "Old Lessons for a Deadly New Age." *Andover Bulletin* (July 1982): 12.

———. "Responsibility of the Colleges to Help Find Submerged Talent." College Scholarship Service Annual Meeting. New York, 25 Oct. 1960.

———. "ROTC Conference Paper," June 1960. DP.

———. "Saint Bonaventure Commencement Speech," 15 May 1981. MSA, box 8.

———. "Second Commuters' Dinner Speech, 1952. Cambridge, MA. 8 Apr. 1952 DP.

———. *Senior Research Paper Handbook*. Tougaloo, MS, 1993.

———. "Seventy-Fifth Anniversary Speech." Francis W. Parker School, 23 Oct. 1976. Francis W. Parker School Archives.

———. "Southeastern Massachusetts Institute Speech." North Dartmouth, MA, 9 June 1966, DP.

———. "Stanford Commencement Address." Stanford, CA, 17 June 1973. Provided by Richard Arrington.

———. "A Summer English Program in Birmingham." In *Speaking about Teaching: Papers from the 1965 Summer Session of the Commission on English*, 78–88. New York: College Entrance Examination Board, 1967.

———. "Teaching and Learning English." In Willie and Edmonds, *Black Colleges in America*, 235–60.

———. "The Tougaloo Experience in Developing Basic Study Skills and Its National Implications." Meeting of Brown-Tougaloo Trustees. New York, 21 Mar. 1980, BUA.

———. "The University of Alabama in Birmingham and the Black College." UAB Summer Commencement Address, Birmingham, AL, 27 Aug. 1972. DP.

———. "Urban Gateways Speech." Chicago, 3 May 1974. MSA, box 8.

———. "Words of Farewell to the Class of 1967." *Harvard Alumni Bulletin* 68 (July 1967): 20.

———. "You Can Always Tell a Commuter." *Harvard Alumni Bulletin* 54, 26 Jan. 1952, 329.

———, ed. *The Search for Talent*. New York: College Entrance Examination Board, 1960.

Monro, Peter. "The Monros." MS, 2002.

"Monro Says 'Job to Do' at Negro College." *Boston Herald*, 10 Mar. 1967, 23.

"Monro Suggests Theses, Tutorial for Freshmen." *HC*, 11 Apr. 1959, 1.

"Montage." *Miles College in Pursuit of a Goal*. Pamphlet, 1967, n.p.

Moore, Geraldine. "Miles Prexy Seeks $2 million for Major Expansion." *Birmingham News*, 28 Aug. 1971.

Moore, Patricia. "Chicagoans Stage 'Fly-In.'" *Chicago Daily News*, 17 Apr. 1970, 15+. MCA.

"More than $22,000 for Charity." *Boston Evening Transcript*, 31 May 1895, 3.

Morgan, Bruce. "Up from Mississippi." *Tufts Medicine* (Spring 2003): 17–25.

"Mrs. D. Leaves Dining Hall Post." *HC*, 5 June 1967, 1.

"Mrs. Frances F. Monro." *Morning Call* (Coopersburg, PA), 13 Feb. 1976.

Munroe, Richard S. *History and Genealogy of the Lexington, Massachusetts Munroes*. Holyoke, MA: Mansir Press, 1966.

Negri, Gloria, "Arthur L Collins, 79; Electrical Engineer Was Star Athlete, Navy Veteran." *Boston Globe*, 23 Sept. 2006, A13.

"Negro Colleges: Their Outlook." *U.S. News and World Report*, 3 June 1968, 74–78.

"New Dental Clinic at Miles." *Miles Alumni Bulletin* (Feb. 1971): n.p. MCA.

"Newly Founded Miles Law School Answers Need for Black Lawyers." *Southern Poverty Law Report* (Feb. 1974): n.p. MCA.

"New Members Named to Tougaloo Board of Trustees." *Tougaloo News* (Apr. 1981): 2. TCA.

"News Office Streamlined over Summer." *HC*, 25 Sept. 1941, 3.

"No Argument." *HC*, 8 Dec. 1966, 2.

Norberg, W. W. Letter to the author, 24 May 2005.

"North Andover." *Andover Townsman*, 23 June 1911, 7.

O'Connor, Thomas. Letter to John Monro, 7 Oct. 1935. DP.

Olson, Arnold. Letter to Janet Dreyer, 11 Apr. 2005. DP.

Osborne, George R. "Boycott in Birmingham." *Nation*, 5 May 1962, 397–401.

"Owens to Retire in 1984." *Harambee* (Sept. 1983): 1. TCA.

The PACE Program, 1967–68. HUA: HUE25.567.68.

Paine College Reports 1.1. Augusta, GA, 1973. PCCCLA.

Paisner, Bruce C. "Deans Will Study Parietal Rules, May Propose Reduction in Hours." *HC*, 24 Sept. 1963, 1.

Parish Record Book, 1888–1937. St. Paul's Episcopal Church, North Andover, MA.

Parker Smith, Betty. Letter to John U. Monro. 11 July 1988. TCA.

Pasternack, Alexander L. "Black Education Pioneer Munro [*Sic*] Dies." *HC*, 8 Apr. 2002, 1+.

"PBH Teachers in South Will Not Demonstrate." *HC*, 11 Apr. 1964, 1.

"Pediatric Service Saves Veterans Cash." *HC*, 4 Oct. 1947, 3.

Phillips Academy Andover. Website, www.andover.edu.

Phillips Andover Yearbook 1930. Andover, MA.

Phillips Brooks House Association. Website, www.pbha.org.

Piel, Gerald. Letter to Robert Jones, 9 Feb. 1981. MSA, box 3.

Pitts, Lucius H. "A Black College President Asks for Advice." *Soundings* (Spring 1971). PCCCLA.

———. "Memorandum: From the President's Desk." *Miles College in Pursuit of a Goal*. Pamphlet, 1967: n.p. MCA.

———. "Presidential Comments." *Miles Alumni Bulletin* (Jan. 1964): 5. MCA.

"Planes of Enterprise in Air 174 Hours at Iwo." *NYT*, 21 Oct. 1945, 3.

Polgreen, Lydia. "African Universities Overworked, Falling Apart." *Boston Sunday Globe*, 20 May 2007, A10.

"Position Doesn't Mean Anything." *Boston Globe* 10 Mar. 1967, 21.

Posner, Bruce G. "Joining the Mainstream: Tougaloo Debates Its Course." *Change* 7.10

(Dec.–Jan. 1975–76). Reprint. TCA.

"Precedent, Deans' Opinion Indicate Dim Chances for Parietals Change." *HC*, 10 Feb. 1961, 1.

Preiss, Jack J. *Camp William James.* Norwich, VT: Argo Books, 1978.

Pressley, Samuel W. "Educator Backs Black Universities." *Philadelphia Evening Bulletin,* 24 Apr. 1976.

"'Project Tanganyika' Departs." *HC*, 21 June 1961, 1.

"A Proper Sequel to John Monro's Story." *South Freeport Times Record,* 16 Mar. 1967. DP.

Proposal for Mission: Involvement. 24 May 1988. MSA, box 2.

Punchard High School Class Book. Andover, MA, 1930.

Records of St. Paul's Vestry, 1901–25. North Andover, MA.

Records of the Dean of Harvard College: An Inventory. Harvard University Archives, http:// oasis.lib.harvard.edu/oasis/deliver/~hua04000.

"Report on Freshman Seminar." *NYT*, 25 Sept. 1960, E11.

"Rev. H. Usher Monro." *Andover Townsman,* 6 Apr. 1939, 5.

"Richard G. King, Researcher, Education Administrator, at 67." *Boston Globe,* 5 Apr. 1990. Williams College Alumni Office Association.

"Rift on Peace Corps Healing in Nigeria." *NYT*, 7 Nov. 1961, 7.

Robinson, Larry. "Student Life." *Encore* (Nov. 1973): n.p. TCA.

Rosenbaum, Beth. Letter to the Editor. *Boston Herald* 9 Mar. 1967.

Routh, Donald. "Award Presentation." College Scholarship Service 30th Anniversary Celebration. New York, 29 Oct. 1984. DP.

"Ruby Justified, Says the Judge." *Boston Globe,* 12 June 1906, 8.

Russakoff, Dale. "Lessons of Might and Right: How Segregation and an Indomitable Family Shaped National Security Adviser Condoleezza Rice." *Washington Post,* 9 Sept. 2009, W23.

———. "Miles from Harvard: The Black College." *HC*, 7 Feb. 1973, 7.

———. "Remembering Birmingham: We Were All Prisoners." *Washington Post,* 21 May 2000, B4.

Russin, Joseph M. "Monro, Farnsworth Warn Students about Drug Use." *HC*, 27 Nov. 1962, 1.

Rutledge, Doris. "The Myth behind Ex-Harvard Dean's Expertise," *Birmingham World,* 15 July 1978. MCA.

Saint Paul's Parish Record Book, 1888–1937.

Salisbury, Harrison E. "Fear and Hatred Grip Birmingham." *New York Times,* 12 Apr. 1960, 1+.

Samuelson, Robert J. "Draft Debate Results Go to Government Study Committee." *HC*, 15 Oct. 1966, 2.

———. "Faculty Shelves Draft Resolution after Debating for Hour and a Half." *HC*, 11 Jan. 1967, 1+.

———. "Mill Street: Chronicle of a Confrontation." *HC*, 15 Nov. 1966, 1+.

———. "Monro Moves to Assure Faculty Debate on Ranking." *HC*, 16 Dec. 1966, 1.

———. "Monro Speaks to SDS Members; Dinner Date Set for Next Week." *HC*, 17 Nov. 1966, 1.

———. "Monro's Altruistic Instinct Influenced Career Change." *HC*, 10 Mar. 1967, 3–6.

Sapp, Hubert. Proposal for a Program in African-American Studies for Miles College. Miles College, 1969. MCA.

Saxon, Wolfgang. "Gerard Piel, 89, Who Revived Scientific American Magazine, Dies." *NYT*, 7 Sept. 2004, C11.

Scheidecker, Ruth. Personal interview with Peter Monro, 27 Dec. 2004.

"Scholarship Funds Must Increase by $200,000 Annually, Council Hears." *HC*, 3 May 1949, 1+.

Schuker, Lauren. Personal interview. Cambridge, MA, 10 Aug. 2005.

Schwartz, John, and Barbara Burgower. "School with a Mission." *Newsweek on Campus* (Nov. 1985). Reprint. TCA.

Scott, Barbara. *Final Report: Simpson Village Center*. HUA: UAV688.5.13.

Seeley, David. *Interim Report—Ibadan Phase, Harvard-UCI Peace Corps*. 6 Feb. 1962. HUA: UAV 609.5.

Seventy-Five Years at Camp Abnaki: Helping the Other Fellow. 1975. Camp Abnaki Archives.

Shapley, Deborah. *Promise and Power: The Life and Times of Robert McNamara*. Boston: Little Brown, 1993.

Sharpe, Lynn. "Tougaloo College: Emphasis on Growing." *Encore* (Nov. 1973): n.p. TCA.

Shinagel, Michael. *"The Gates Unbarred": A History of University Extension at Harvard, 1910–2009*. Hollis, NH: Puritan Press, 2009.

Shore, Debra. "Brown and Tougaloo." *Brown Alumni Magazine* (Mar. 1981): 18–27.

Shores, Elizabeth. "The 13th Grade Push." *Change* (Oct. 1979): 30–32.

"Six Negro Colleges Pool Efforts to Resolve Financial Problems." *NYT*, 9 Feb. 1969, 51.

"Skeet Shooting." *The Hunter's Encyclopedia*, 639–42. Andover: Andover Historical Society Archives, William H. Foster file.

Smith, Robert E. "Psychologists Disagree on Psilocybin Research." *HC*, 15 Mar. 1962, 1.

Snow, Bert. "Abnaki: A Camp and a Legend." MS.

Spencer, John. Letter to John U. Monro, 20 Aug. 1936. DP.

Spergel, Howard. "Profile: Monro Believed Early." *Southern Education Report* (May 1967): 20–21.

Stafford, Edward P. *The Big E: The Story of the USS* Enterprise. New York: Random House, 1962.

"Story of a Local Boy." *Andover Townsman*, 29 Jan. 1910, 10.

Stossel, Scott. *Sarge: The Life and Times of Sargent Shriver*. Washington, DC: Smithsonian, 2004.

Stott, Fred. "Trustee John U. Monro '30 Retires." *Andover Bulletin* (Feb. 1983): 17.

"Students to Teach at Negro College." *HC*, 14 Feb. 1964, 2.

"Students to Tutor Birmingham Youth." *Cambridge Chronicle* (1964). PBHAA.

"Teachers in Action-10." *Harvard Alumni Bulletin*, 18 Jan. 1958, 302.

Thomas, Barbara. "Studies about Negroes 'In' on Campuses across Country." *Birmingham News*, 19 Oct. 1969. MCA.

Thomas, Barbara, and Carol Nunnelley. "The Real L. H. Pitts: Uncle Tom or Radical?" *Birmingham News*, 2 May 1971, 20+. MCA.

Thorndike, Joseph J. Personal interview, Harwich, MA, 20 Aug. 2003.

"Took Stafford for a Burglar." *Boston Globe*, 11 June 1906, 6.

"Tougaloo College Honors Outstanding Leaders." *Tougaloo News* (Spring 1993): 6–7. TCA.

Tougaloo College Senior Research Paper Handbook, 1993–1994. Tougaloo, MS: Tougaloo College, 1993. Provided by Richard Johnson.

"Tougaloo's Special Programs." *Encore* (Nov. 1973): n.p. TCA.

Townsend, Robert C. Journal, 1970–71. MS.

———. Personal interview. 13 Aug. 2003.

———. "Teaching at a Black College." *Amherst* (Fall 1971): 14–16.

"A Tribute to the Giant That God Allowed to Walk with Us." *Painette*, 1 Mar. 1974, 1–8. PCCCLA.

"Truman Saves Enterprise." *Boston American*, 1 Nov. 1945, 2.

"The Tutoring School Racket." *Harvard Crimson*, 18 Apr. 1939, 1+.

"Two Hundred Ask to Be Porters, Only 60 Jobs Available." *HC*, 17 May 1951, 1.

"Upward Bound, a Continued Success." *Miles Ahead*, 7 Oct. 1968, 1–2. MCA.

Urban Gateways Website, www.urbangateways.org.

"USS *Enterprise*: The Galloping Ghost of the Oahu Coast Launched Here October 3, 1936 (Our Hull No. 360)." *Shipyard Bulletin* (Oct. 1945): 10+.

Vann, Lillian Foscue. "New Miles Chief Worked in Africa, Cuba." *Birmingham Post-Herald*, 31 Mar. 1971. MCA.

———. "Testimonial Dinner Honors Departing Educator, Dr. Pitts." *Birmingham Post-Herald*, 24 Apr. 1971, 1–2. MCA.

Volker, J. F. Letter to Lucius Pitts, 7 Oct. 1970. UABA, ser. 3.3.l, folder 6.20.

Vollers, Maryanne. *Ghosts of Mississippi: The Murder of Medgar Evers, the Trials of Byron de la Beckwith, and the Haunting of the New South*. Boston: Little Brown, 1995.

Watson, Bruce. *Bread and Roses: Mills, Migrants, and the Struggle for the American Dream*. New York: Viking, 2005.

"W. Clyde Williams Named President of Miles College." *Miles Alumni Bulletin* (May 1971). MCA.

"W. H. Foster, Sports Writer and Painter, Dies." *Lawrence Evening Tribune*, 1 Nov. 1941, l.

Whipple, Charles L. "Miles College Captivates Dean Monro." *Boston Globe*, 10 Mar. 1967, 21.

Wilder, Robert. Letter to Barnaby Keeney, 8 Apr. 1964. BUA.

Wilkinson, Rupert. *Aiding Students, Buying Students: Financial Aid in America.* Nashville: Vanderbilt University Press, 2005.

———. Interview with John Monro. Jackson, MI, 14 Nov. 1992.

———. "Some Thoughts about John U. Monro after Leaving Him and before Systematically Rereading My Notes—on Plane!" Personal notes, 14 Nov. 1992.

Williams, Clyde. *Annual Report of the President, 1971–1972.* Miles College, Fairfield, AL. MCA.

———. "The State of Miles and the Nature of the New Design." *Miles Vanguard* (Sept. 1974): n.p. MCA.

Willie, Charles V. "Black Colleges Redefined." *Change* (Oct.–Nov. 1979): 46–49. MCA.

———. Prologue to Willie and Edmonds, *Black Colleges in America,* ix–xii.

Willie, Charles V., and Ronald R. Edmonds, eds. *Black Colleges in America: Challenge, Development, Survival.* New York: Teachers College Press, 1978.

Willie, Charles V., and Marlene Y. MacLeish. "The Priorities of Presidents of Black Colleges." In Willie and Edmonds, *Black Colleges in America,* 132–48.

Willie Mays Website, www.williemays.com.

"Willie Mays Receives Honorary Degree." *Milean* (Nov. 1973): 2. MCA.

"Willie Mays to Head Fund Drive for a Negro College in Alabama." *NYT,* 17 Apr. 1968, 26. MCA.

Wright, Ralph, and Garland Reeves. "BSC to Stay Put in Westside as Sale Called Off." *Birmingham News,* 16 May 1975. MCA.

"The Writing Center Expands." *Harambee,* 8 Dec. 1995, 1. TCA.

Zorn, Jeff. Harvard Graduate School of Education Course Paper. Fall 1971.

———. "Monro at Miles College: The Yankee at Full Stride." Paper delivered at Conference on College Composition and Communication. San Francisco, 17 Mar. 2005.

———. "Monro, a Great Educator, Deserves Remembrance." *Birmingham News,* 18 Apr. 2002, A8.

Index

Harrington, Michael, 183

Harvard Advocate, 30

Harvard Alumni Bulletin, 27, 38

Harvard Center for Research and Personality, 88

Harvard Club, 101, 142

Harvard Club of Boston, 79

Harvard Club of Chicago, 58

Harvard Club of New York, 94, 119

Harvard College: Academic Standing Committee, 167, 207, 210, 214, 216; Advisory Committee on Peace Corps Training, 70; as Birmingham on the Charles, 95; black college conference at, 174–75; Center for International Affairs, 71; Center for Research and Personality, 88; and Chicago recruitment, 55–57; Class Day, 126; Committee on Educational Policy, 67; cram parlor crusade, 34–35; Department of Afro-American Studies, 174; draft deferment, 113–14; drug controversy, 88–90, 109–10, 116–18; financial aid and, 59–63; Freshmen Seminars, 67–68; and growing ties to the south, 96–98; increasing diversity, 95–96; Kennedy Institute of Politics, 114, 126; and McNamara fracas, 114–16; Memorial Church, 232; Monro's announcement to leave, 119–20; Monro's departure from, 125–26; Monro's papers, 233; national scholarships at, 56, 58, 83; Office of Graduate and Career Plans, 79; Overseers' Committee on University Extension, 187; and parietals controversy, 92–95; and Peace Corps, 3, 69–72, 74–75, 83; public reaction to Monro's leaving, 121–25; reflections of Monro, 222–24; Russian Research Center, 146; "Save the Sycamores," 95, 108; Selective Service exam, 113; and Student Employment Office, 60–61; student initiative at, 108–9; subway school, 77–79; University Extension, 75–77, 78, 105, 174, 178, 187; Urban Studies extension program, 78; Veteran's Bureau at, 54–55; Young People's Socialist League, 123

Harvard Financial Aid Office, 28, 59, 67, 79, 122

Harvard Foundation for Intercultural Relations: Lifetime Achievement award for Monro, 222–223; as sponsors of Monro portrait, 234–35

Harvard Graduate School of Education, 70, 71, 123, 136

Harvard Journal: the aftermath, 33–35; professionalism and inclusiveness, 28–33; reporting on the outside world, 33

Harvard Law School, 103, 108, 127

Harvard National Scholarships, 57, 58, 122

Harvard News Office, 36–38, 40, 42, 66

Harvard Policy Committee. *See* HPC (Harvard Policy Committee)

Harvard-Radcliffe group, 103, 104, 110

Harvard Student Agencies. *See* HSA (Harvard Student Agencies)

Head, Marvin, 104

Head Start programs, 99, 190

Hechinger, Fred, 89, 109, 120

Hertzberg, Hendrik, 27

Hibbard, David, 72, 75

Hill, Gladwin, 34

Hill, S. Richardson, 177–79

Hill Crest (Sutton home), 13–15

Hillel Round Table in World Affairs, 74

Holy Cross College, 230

home front during World War II, 50–51

Hood, Gilbert H., 193, 199

Horizon, 34

Hotchkiss, Wesley, 107

Howard University, 104, 110, 175

Howe, Anna, 12

Howe, Mark DeWolfe, 108, 127–28

HPC (Harvard Policy Committee), 108, 122, 126

HSA (Harvard Student Agencies), 60–61

Huckleberry Finn (Twain), 135, 137

Hunter, Clarence, 228, 234

Hunting and Fishing and *National Sportsman,* 37

Illinois Institute of Technology, 196, 207

Ingram, Osborn "Ozzie," 30, 31, 32

Interdenominational Theological Center, Atlanta, GA, 160

Mays, Benjamin, 125
Mays, Willie, 169
McClung, Merle, 128, 143
McGinnis, Richard, 194, 207, 210
McGrath, Earl J., 161
McMillan, Edith Estes, 191
McNamara, Robert S., 3, 114–16, 126
McPherson, Jonathan, 90
McWhorter, Diane, 86
Memorial Church at Harvard College, 232
Memphis State, 212
Men's Fraternal League, 17, 64
Merrifield, John, 57–58, 122
Messer, Ronald, 58–593
Meyers, J. L., 210
Michelmore, Margaret, 72–73, 74
Miles Ahead, 138
Miles College: accreditation of, 85; Afro-Ameri-
can Materials Center Program, 144–45; Afro-
American Studies program at, 144–46; alum-
nus as state senator, 171–72; Brown Hall, 98;
building bridges, 138–39; Center for Urban
Studies, 140; civil rights tradition at, 85–88;
conditions at, in 1967, 2; daring to dream,
130–31; dental clinic at, 141; and department
store boycott of 1961, 86–88; Educational
Program for the Individual Child, (EPIC),
141; Eutaw project, 165, 166–68, 176, 180;
Freshman English program, 132–34, 143–44;
Freshman Studies Program, 175; Freshmen
Social Science program, 134–35; getting
with the program, 131–39; and grade school
tutoring program, 99–101; happy campers,
135–37; Health and Physical Education Building, 127; Interdisciplinary Program in Humanities, 176; *Miles Ahead,* 138; Miles College
Press, 138–39; as "Militant Youth Arm," 86;
Monro moving towards, 1962–1964, 83–105;
Monro's departure from, 180; Monro's fifth-
year anniversary, 162–64; Monro's move to,
118–25; precollege workshops, 105–6; promoting institutional strength, 129–30; reaccreditation at, 148–50; Services to Enhance
Educational Potential program, 161; social

life at, 143–44; summer school, 109–10;
summer tutoring program, 97–101; swim-
ming against the mainstream, 137–38; Tag-
gart Science Laboratory, 127; tension on and
off campus, 128–29; Williams Hall, 98; writ-
ing proficiency exam, 155–58
Miles College Press, 138–39
Millsaps College, 183
Minor, Bill, 195
Minority Achievement Program of the Ameri-
can Association of Colleges, 202
Mission, The (Brelis), 79
Mississippi Council on Human Relations, 183,
186
Mississippi Family Health Care Center, 190
Mississippi Secondary School Mathematics
Summer Institute, 218
Mississippi State Sovereignty Commission, 181
Mitchell, Martha, 149
Moment in History, A (Ashabranner), 70
Monro, Alexander, 7
Monro, Anne, 40, 91, 119, 178
Monro, Clarissa Usher Sanford, 7
Monro, Claxton (John's father), 8, 10–11, 12,
14–15, 25–26, 125; death of, 37–38
Monro, Claxton, Jr. (John's brother), 19, 91;
birth of, 16; change in career, 80–81; death
of, 225–26; graduation from MIT, 39; mar-
riage of, 51
Monro, Dorothy (daughter of Hezekiah), 10
Monro, Dorothy "Dottie" Stevens Foster. *See*
Foster, Dorothy "Dottie" Stevens
Monro, Dr. Thomas (1731–85), 7
Monro, Edith (daughter of Hezekiah), 8, 40,
121
Monro, Frances (Sutton). *See* Sutton, Frances
Monro, George Thomas, 7
Monro, Hezekiah Usher, 2, 7–10, 14, 19, 40
Monro, Janet: birth of, 42; early years, 80; fam-
ily life and career of, 119, 159, 178, 192; and
marriage, 91; and Monro's final illness, 227,
231–32; and wartime memories, 50
Monro, John Usher: aboard the Big E, 43–48;
academic honors earned, 62–63, 180, 199–

200, 206, 211, 213–14, 223; and aftermath of war, 51–53; and Alpert-Leary imbroglio, 88–90; and Alzheimer's disease, 213–14, 227–28; announcement to leave Harvard, 119–20; association with John Garner, 221–22; birth of, 6–7; and "Black College Dilemma," 162; and College Board, 200–201; crime, embarking on a life of, 26–28; death of, 231–32; and death of wife Dottie, 203–4; and departure from Harvard, 125–26; departure from Miles College, 180; and diversity at Harvard College, 55–57, 81; and draft deferment issue, 113–14; drug controversy at Harvard, 88–90, 109–10, 116–18; family background and childhood, 1912–1930, 6–23; "Father of Modern Financial Aid Practices," 62; final postings, 1995–2002, 227–33; and financial aid at Harvard, 59–63; first look at Birmingham, 91–92; fitting in at Miles College, 139–44; and Francis W. Parker School, 56–57, 81, 173; as full-time teacher, 192–94; girl next door and, 21–23; going it alone, 1971–1978, 159–80; guest appearances, 164–66; as Harvard administrator, 1946–1958, 54–65; and Harvard commuters, 64–65; and Harvard Crimson, 28–35; as Harvard dean, 1958–1962, 66–82; as Harvard dean, 1964–1967, 107–26; and Harvard Journal, 28–353; and high school years, 21–23; and the home front, 50–51; honorary degrees earned, 165, 230; and increasing diversity at Harvard, 95–96; interim years and war years, 1935–1945, 36–53; lasting legacy of, 223–35; Lifetime Achievement Award, 222–23; and the lure of Tougaloo, 187–91; and McNamara fracas, 114–16; military awards earned, 47, 48; and the move to Miles, 118–25; moving towards Miles College, 1962–1964, 83–105; and naval duty during WWII, 42–53; new addresses, new schools, 18–21; new homes, new challenges, 1967–1971, 127–58; as newlywed, 15–16, 39–40; papers of, 230; and parietals controversy at Harvard, 92–95; and the Peace Corps, 69–74; and Phillips Academy, 63–64, 146–48;

Pitts rift, 155–58; portraits of, 234–35; positive press, 120–21; and Precollege Workshop, 105–6; problems at Tougaloo, 216–20; public reaction to Monro's leaving Harvard, 121–25; reaccreditation at Miles College, 148–50; reflecting on Harvard, 222–24; reflecting on Tougaloo, 222–24; rehearsal for adulthood, 17–18; relocating to Mississippi, 192–95; retirement from Tougaloo, 228; and rheumatic fever, 16; saying goodbye to Harvard College, 119–20, 125–26; second summer at Miles, 110–13; and student employment, 60–61; student initiative at Harvard, 108–9; and the Subway School, 75–79; and summer tutoring program at Miles, 98–101; as Teacher of the Year, 206, 207, 210; teaching schedule at Tougaloo, 192–94; teaching solo and in tandem, 213–16; at Tougaloo, 192–95, 206–7; and Tougaloo presidency search, 96–98, 107–8; Tougaloo research handbook, 220–21; tributes to, in later life, 210–11; undergraduate years, 1930–1934, 24–35; weathering changes, 1984–1995, 205–26; and World War II, 42–50

Monro, Marion Dorothy Lowd. See Lowd, Marion Dorothy
Monro, Mary, 225
Monro, Phoebe, 8
Monro, Sir Hugh T., 6
Monro, Sue Carlton. See Carlton, Sue
Monro, Sutton, 234; death of, 225–26; at Officers' Training School, 51; school years of, 40; teaching at Lehigh University, 91
Monro, Thomas (1731–1785), 7
Monro, Thomas, Dr. (1794–1821), 7
Monro, Victoria "Vicki" Booth Demarest. See Demarest, Victoria "Vicki" Booth
"Monro Doctrine," 61–63
Monro family background and childhood, 1912–1930, 6–23
Montgomery, Kenneth, 199
Montgomery Bus Boycott, 85, 164, 171
Morehouse College, 110, 125, 211
Morison, John H., 29